The Vedic Origins of Karma

SUNY Series in Hindu Studies
Wendy Doniger, Editor

Sri Garib Dass Oriental Series No. 108

The Vedic Origins of Karma

Cosmos as Man in Ancient Indian Myth and Ritual

HERMAN W. TULL

SRI SATGURU PUBLICATIONS
DELHI - INDIA

Published by :
SRI SATGURU PUBLICATIONS
Indological and Oriental Publishers
40/5, Shakti Nagar,
Delhi - 110007,
INDIA

The Publication of this Book in India is made by permission of State University of New York Press.

FIRST INDIAN EDITION : DELHI – 1990

ISBN - 81-7030-241-2

Library of Congress Cataloging-in-Publication Data

Tull, Hermenn Wayne

The Vedic origins of Karma: cosmos as man in ancient Indian myth and ritual/by
Herman W. Tull

P. cm.
Bibliography; p.
Includes Index -

1. Karma. 2. Vedic Literature – History and criticism. **I. Title**

BL 2015 K3T85 1989 88-37610
294.5'22 – dc19 CIP

10 9 8 7 6 5 4 3 2 1

PRINTED IN INDIA

For Chini and Jasha

Contents

Acknowledgments

This book is a somewhat unexpected by-product of my doctoral dissertation, submitted to the Department of History and Literature of Religions at Northwestern University in 1985. Simply because the completion of a dissertation is an arduous enough task, I did not originally see my work as something that might later be published in the form of a book. An odd coincidence has brought this book back into the hands of Wendy Doniger, who first encouraged me to seek a publisher—though as I now recall it, it was encouragement stated in the imperative mood. Certainly, without her support I would not have so willingly revised it "one more time," nor so readily submitted it to the scrutiny of a publisher. This latter process—due to the efforts of William Eastman of the State University of New York Press—has been a surprisingly agreeable one.

Over the years many people taught me a great deal and along the way became close friends. I now find that many of my questions were their questions; for, those who taught me left an indelible mark—though each one of a different sort—on my way of thinking: what I thought about as well as how I thought about it. They are, at Hobart College, Professors Marvin Bram, Lowell Bloss, Chris Vescey (now at Colgate University), and my classmate John Blodgett; at Northwestern University, Professors George Bond, Edmund Perry, Isshi Yamada, and Robert Cohn (now at Lafayette College); and at the University of Chicago, Professors Edwin Gerow (now at Reed College) and Wendy Doniger, and my colleague David Lawrence. Most recently my colleagues at Rutgers University, Professors Henry Bowden, Alberto Green, James Jones, Chun-fang Yu, and Mahlon Smith, and, at Princeton University, Professor John Kelly, have by their examples challenged me to explore further in my own field.

I am especially indebted to Wendy Doniger, who gave unstintingly of her time to nurture this project, as she shared with me her ideas, her library, and the invaluable stray references that textualists tend to collect over the years. The remarkable enthusiasm with

Introduction

J. C. Heesterman has recently observed that the Vedic sacrificial texts propose "a separate self-contained world ruled exclusively by the comprehensive and exhaustive order of the ritual."[1] The closed world of the Vedic sacrifice recalls the larger closure of the Hindu universe, depicted from an early period as an egg "whose total contents can never increase but can only be redistributed."[2] As Wendy O'Flaherty has noted within the world egg "the Hindu cosmos is a series of receding frames, circles within circles."[3] This image of circles within circles leads back to the world of the Vedic sacrifice, which itself consisted of a series of concentric circles;[4] and so articulates again the close resemblance between the world of the ritual and the larger cosmos.

The world of the sacrifice is intentionally made to resemble the larger cosmos. The Vedic ritualists sought, in their own sacrificial activity, to recreate the primordial events which shaped the cosmos. An often-quoted passage that appears in the Śatapatha Brāhmaṇa thus declares: "This [ritual act] done now is that which the gods did then [in the beginning]."[5] What the gods did then was to create the world, an event that the late Vedic texts often depict as having occurred through the sacrifice of an anthropomorphic being, whose dismembered body was formed into the ordered cosmos.

However, the death and destruction implicit in the primordial event created an untenable situation for the sacrificer; in particular, the reenactment of the cosmogony would seem to have required the sacrificer to give up his own life.[6] The Vedic ritualists attempted to circumvent this actuality by employing various substitutes (ranging from grain and animals to a gold effigy) for the sacrificer's own person. Moreover, the closed world of the ritual, with its carefully delimited boundaries, seems to have been constructed to keep out the reality of death;[7] for, just as the sacrificial arena itself represented a symbolic cosmos, so, too, the death that occurred in the ritual was only symbolically that of the sacrificer. There was one situation, however, in which the body of the sacrificer was used as the material of the offering; namely, the funeral rite, which is appropriately called the *final sacrifice* (*antyeṣṭi*). This final sacrifice, in which the death of the sacrificer is a real death, moves the sacrificer from the world of the ritual to the larger cosmos.

This transition forms the subject of what is considered to be the earliest statement of the karma doctrine, a statement that appears in the Bṛhadāraṇyaka Upaniṣad. After discussing how the deceased enters into the various planes of the cosmos, a process that replicates the dismemberment of the primordial man, the famed Brāhmaṇic sage Yājñavalkya is asked: "What then becomes of this person?" Yājñavalkya then enunciates the doctrine of action (*karman*): "Indeed one becomes good by good action, bad by bad [action]."[8] In the context of Vedic ritual thought good and bad apparently refer to a valuation of action based on ritual exactitude; good being equated with the correct performance of the rite, bad with the incorrect performance. And, since the funeral sacrifice is not performed by the sacrificer who is about to attain either a good or a bad state, Yājñavalkya is apparently referring not to the funeral sacrifice but to the actions of a lifetime of sacrificial performances. The nature of that activity, which had been contained in the closed world of the ritual, now determines the conditions of the sacrificer's afterlife within the larger cosmos.

This interpretation of the karma doctrine differs from the doctrine's apparent meaning in later texts, which propose that an individual attains a specific state in the afterlife, or is reborn, according to the moral quality of all sorts of actions performed prior to death. If the context in which Yājñavalkya enunciates his doctrine of action is presumed not to be that of the Vedic ritual, then this general meaning can easily be seen in Yājñavalkya's statement, "one becomes good by good action, bad by bad [action]." And, in fact, this was precisely how nineteenth and early twentieth century Indologists tended to view this and other presentations of the karma doctrine in the Upaniṣads. These scholars remained curiously silent about the doctrine's attachment here to the paradigmatic event of the Vedic ritual, the sacrifice of the cosmic man, and focused instead on how, in isolation, the phrase "one becomes good by good action, bad by bad [action]" seemed to express a principle of morality extending to all sorts of actions.[9]

How and why scholars of an earlier generation adopted this view of the karma doctrine is discussed in the first chapter of this book. At the simplest level, this viewpoint owes much to a larger tendency among these scholars to disparage "priestcraft," a perspective rooted in the philosophy of the Enlightenment.[10] In its application to the ancient Indian context this tendency led scholars to separate the Brāhmaṇas, ritual texts par excellence and the exclusive possession of the Vedic sacerdotalists, from the Upaniṣads, discursive texts that seek to express the nature of reality. Accordingly, the karma doctrine, which is first articulated in the Upaniṣads, was seen as addressing itself to issues not germane to the Vedic ritual tradition. There is strong textual evidence, however, suggesting the continuity of the Brāhmaṇas and the Upaniṣads: their physical contiguity; their use of a similar "idiom";[11] their claims of a shared authorship. In the early Upaniṣads, the Bṛhadāraṇyaka and the Chāndogya in particular, the Vedic rites represent the starting point for the disquisition into the nature of what is real: beneath increasingly greater levels of abstraction lies the concrete event of the sacrifice.

It is this ritual substratum that scholars of an earlier generation failed, or were simply unwilling, to recognize in their examination of Upaniṣadic thought. Such lack of recognition, I believe, was at the base of these scholars' inability to understand generally the origin of the karma doctrine,[12] for at least certain aspects of the doctrine are clearly rooted in the conceptual context of the Vedic ritual milieu.[13] Certainly, the notion that particular actions lead an individual after death to the attainment of a particular state ("becoming good by good action, bad by bad") reflects precisely the sort of effective action that, albeit in the closed world of the ritual, was believed to result from the sacrifice. In examining this ritual substratum I shall draw out some of the difficulties inherent to the sacrifice; in particular, those that resulted from the relationship of the officiants, who performed the ritual, to the sacrificer (*yajamāna*), who was supposed to benefit from the rite. How this relationship affected notions of the attainments of the afterlife—that is, the transition from the world of the ritual to an existence in the larger cosmos—is clearly articulated in the formulation of the Upaniṣadic karma doctrine.

In moving from the world of the ritual to the larger cosmos the sacrificer becomes *saloka*, "one together with the world(s)." The ability to attain this state implies that the sacrificer's own existence is in some sense correlative to that of the cosmos—though perhaps this relationship could not be realized in the sacrificer's ordinary experience. The late Vedic cosmology expresses this idea of a correlation between man and cosmos in the ideology of the cosmic man (Puruṣa in the Ṛgveda, Prajāpati in the Brāhmaṇas). The investigation of this ideology—as the notion that the cosmos arose from the sacrifice of a primordial anthropomorphic being expresses it—is the subject of Chapter 2, "The Cosmos as Man: The Image of the Cosmos in Vedic Thought." This myth's implicit notion that the cosmos has the shape of a man reflects the belief that man might potentially integrate himself with the cosmos. Here, the correlation between body and cosmos, senses and natural phenomena, that the Vedic cosmogony proposes, seems to facilitate—at least theoretically—this integration.

However, as noted earlier, the application of this cosmogonic theory would seem to have required the dismemberment and death of the individual who attempted to re-create the primordial activity of the cosmic man. Although the sacrificer may have been able to meet this requirement in the funeral rites, the "final sacrifice," the event of the sacrificer's death in the ordinary (i.e., nonfuneral) rituals creates an untenable situation. Death would keep the sacrificer from meeting a myriad of ritual obligations, obligations which could be fulfilled only through a lifetime of sacrificial performances. One particular response to this problem is seen in the Brāhmaṇic myth of Prajāpati, which modifies certain elements of the established Vedic mythology of the cosmic man. This myth, which is the subject of the second half of Chapter 2, replaces the act of a cosmogonic dismemberment with a combination of creative activities: heating, desire, and in particular, sexual generation. Whereas in each instance the body of the cosmic man shapes the cosmos, the emphasis shifts from a disjunctive to a conjunctive model of creation: Puruṣa establishes the various cosmic spheres with his own dismembered body parts (he is said literally to be "divided up," *vi-/dhā*); Prajāpati puts himself into the cosmos by a process of "uniting [with it] as a pair" (*mithunaṃ sam-/bhū*). The Brāhmaṇic myth thereby proposes a model that, in its application, would seem to alleviate man of the need to die in the ritual performance.

To meet the demands of the ritual theory—that is, the notion that the sacrificer reenacts the cosmic man's primordial activity—these modifications required a complex ceremonial. The ritual of constructing the fire altar (*agnicayana*), as it is presented in the Śatapatha Brāhmaṇa, is considered to be the greatest practical expression of this modified cosmogony.[14] The complexity of the Agnicayana, like the complexity of the Prajāpati mythology, derives from its attempt to circumvent the problem of death. The Vedic sacrifice, accurately described by J. C. Heesterman as "a controlled act of death and destruction,"[15] by its nature would seem to oppose this attempt. How the Agnicayana ritualists responded to the problem of death in the sacrifice and how their response allowed the human sacrificer to replicate the events of the cosmogony forms the subject of Chapter 3, "The Fire Altar as Man and Cosmos."

Chapter 4 returns to the nature of the sacrificer's transition, through his death, from the self-contained world of the ritual to the larger cosmos. How the ritual event prepares the sacrificer for the afterlife, and how it facilitates his transition into the larger cosmos on the event of his funeral forms the particular subject of this chapter. The relationship between the Agnicayana and the funeral rite for one who in life performed the Agnicayana, exemplifies this relationship. For, the funeral rite for one who in life performed the Agnicayana replicates the Agnicayana, with the apparent intention of ensuring that the same attainments experienced in the ritual event are attained again in the sacrificer's transition into the larger cosmos. Along with this specific relationship between rites performed in life and the funeral rite there are certain general ritual theories that express how the sacrificial oblation—which, at the funeral rite, was the sacrificer—moved from this world to the other planes of the cosmos. One prevalent theory explains this event through the model of a cycle of generation and regeneration; thus, the smoke from the sacrifice forms clouds in the other world, which then return to this world in the form of rain, which nourishes the plants and creatures, which again form the objects of the sacrifice.[16] These theories lead us back to the karma doctrine, as they represent an essential aspect of the theory of rebirth as it appears in the earliest expressions of this doctrine.

The Vedic Origins of the Karma Doctrine

Recent studies suggest a consensus regarding the origins of the karma doctrine, a subject that really is "shrouded in the mists of time." On the one hand, the karma doctrine seems to contain an agricultural component, specifically one that reflects the cultivation of rice: as O'Flaherty notes, "rice is planted twice, first the seed and then the seedling that is replanted; rice is also harvested over and over in a year, rather than at a single harvest season; hence it is a natural symbol for rebirth."[17] And, because rice cultivation was not a feature of the Indus Valley, where Vedic culture arose, these notions support a "tribal" origin for the karma doctrine. However, the supposition of a tribal origin in a certain sense evades the issue of karma's origins, for, citing O'Flaherty once again: "To postulate a . . . 'tribal origin' is to some extent a way of passing the buck away from the major religions which must be explained; it is a scholarly way of saying 'somewhere else.' "[18]

Throughout India's history, there has been a constant exchange of ideas and practices between tribal (non-textual, local) and textual traditions. The osmotic nature of the Indian tradition is evident from what has been a tired and fruitless attempt to delineate Vedic from non-Vedic (an enterprise rooted in the nineteenth century desire to separate racially ancient India's Aryan and non-Aryan populations)[19] in the development of the ancient Indian tradition. Quite simply, once an idea or practice, whatever its origins, was incorporated in the Vedic tradition, the nature of which can be understood through the evidence of a substantial textual record, it must be considered Vedic—that such ideas and practices may have been antithetical to the established Vedic tradition bears no relevance here. For example, the Brāhmaṇas contain a notion of the sacrificial oblation that seems based in agriculture (though perhaps not in rice culture per se); that is, the notion that the oblation went from the smoke of the sacrifice to become the clouds, rain, plants or food, semen, and again creatures, which form the oblation.[20] Although this notion may have originated outside the Vedic sphere, its association with the sacrifice means that, at least by the time these texts were composed, this notion was Vedic. In choosing to discuss karma's *Vedic* origins, I have in mind this inclusive view of what is Vedic.

At the most basic level, the Vedic tradition employed the term *karman*, from the Sanskrit root /*kṛ* ("to do"), to describe the "doing" of the sacrificial ritual. However, over the many centuries during which it represented India's "culturally hegemonous" system of belief and practice,[21] the Vedic sacrifice developed into an entity of astounding complexity, and the "doing" of the sacrifice became more than a matter of simple action.

Karma, as a "doctrine," emerges from these complex structures; the textual point of this emergence is the early Upaniṣads. This textual epoch represents a "privileged" point in the history of the Indian tradition; for these texts represent at once the furthest edge of Vedic sacrificial thought and the first stage in the rise of classical Hindu thought. And at this point certain notions, such as karma, attain the stature of "doctrines"; that is, they are articulated in ways quite similar to their later existence as the presuppositions for nearly all (post-Vedic) Hindu thought.

The aim of this book is to examine and delineate the Vedic structures leading to this emergence, for, I believe, the earliest statements of karma in the Upaniṣads look back to structures, patterns, and paradigms already contained—in both ideology and practice—in the Vedic rite. And, though not all these structures may have been "originally" Vedic, before the karma doctrine emerges in the Upaniṣads, its antecedents were already entrenched within the sphere of the established Vedic tradition.

A Note on Texts, Method, Terms, and Translations

The Vedic texts—Saṃhitās, Brāhmaṇas, Upaniṣads and Vedāngas ("limbs" of the Veda)—with their many recensions, constitute a vast corpus. Although a number of the texts in this corpus have been used in this study, it has not been my intention to present a comprehensive view of the Vedic textual tradition. For the most part, the texts cited in this study are from the late Vedic period (ca. 800–600 B.C.E.), when the latest of the Brāhmaṇas and the earliest of the Upaniṣads were composed. One Brāhmaṇa in particular, the Śatapatha Brāhmaṇa, reflects this transition in textual epochs, as it contains within its final book the Bṛhadāraṇyaka Upaniṣad, a text with which it has much in common.[22] This Brāhmaṇa, said to occupy "the most significant and important position of all the Brāhmaṇas"[23] and described as "one of the highest achievements in the whole range of Vedic literature,"[24] has been used as the chief source for the views expressed in this book.

Despite this praise the Śatapatha Brāhmaṇa has not escaped the general disdain Western scholars have expressed for the Brāhmaṇas. In 1860, more than a decade before critical editions of a significant number of Brāhmaṇas became available to scholars in the West,[25] Max Müller declared that: "The general character of these works is marked by shallow and insipid grandiloquence, by priestly conceit, and antiquarian pedantry."[26] If this warning did not sufficiently discourage scholars from investigating the Brāhmaṇa texts, Müller went on to note a few years later that: "No person who is not acquainted beforehand with the place which the Brāhmaṇas fill in the history of the Indian mind, could read more than ten pages without being disgusted."[27] For Müller, only a trained Sanskritist—much in the same fashion as the physician alone is able to bear the raving of madmen—possessed the intestinal fortitude to face these texts "which no circulating library would touch"[28] and study them "as the physician studies the twaddle of idiots."[29]

From the mid-nineteenth century through the first decades of the twentieth century, Indologists repeatedly expressed these same sentiments.[30] Müller's legacy is clearly seen in Julius Eggeling's translation of the Śatapatha Brāhmaṇa. Eggeling spent twenty years on this task. Yet, he introduces his translation with a warning to his readers about the vapidity of thought they were about to encounter:

> The translator of the Śatapatha Brāhmaṇa can be under no illusion as to the reception his production is likely to meet with at the hand of the general reader. In the whole range of literature few works are probably less calculated to excite the interest to any outside the very limited number of specialists, than the ancient theological writings of the Hindus, known by the names of Brāhmaṇas. For wearisome prolixity of exposition, characterized by dogmatic assertion and a flimsy symbolism, rather than by serious reasoning, these works are perhaps not equalled anywhere; unless indeed, it be by the speculative vapourings of the Gnostics, than which, in the opinion of the learned translators of Iranaeus, "nothing more absurd has probably ever been imagined by rational beings."[31]

In view of Eggeling's remarks it is not surprising that the Śatapatha Brāhmaṇa, despite its accessibility as part of the Sacred Books of the East series, has remained the nearly exclusive domain of a few specialists.

Before I read Eggeling's warning I read his translation of the Śatapatha Brāhmaṇa, and then read it a second and a third time. Having by this time gained a general idea of the structure and peculiarities of the text I proceeded to make my own translations of all the parts that I found particularly interesting. This procedure has been my "method of interpretation." For the most part the passages on which I focused contained some sort of incongruity: one sage contradicting another sage, one myth overlayed on another myth, a certain ritual procedure juxtaposed on another procedure. I read and reread, translated and retranslated these passages until I thought I had some idea of what the conflict was about, and then looked for other patterns in the text and in contemporary texts to which the conflict seemed related. Although this method of interpretation largely ignores the historical factors that may underlie some of these conflicts, it does concern itself with understanding the larger structures into which these conflicts were resolved. As Wendy O'Flaherty has stated of this method: "for the question to ask is not where the disparate elements originated, but why they were put together, and why kept together."[32]

By asking these questions of the Brāhmaṇas, texts that to Müller were "simply twaddle, and what is worse theological twaddle,"[33] the outlines of a coherent system of thought begin to emerge. The Brāhmaṇa period represents a crucial period in the development of the Indian tradition; many of the patterns that later dominate both the ritual and philosophical spheres were established in this epoch. Certainly, the conceptual paradigms first articulated in the Brāhmaṇas dominate the Upaniṣads, the watershed texts of the Indian speculative tradition. To the modern reader the Brāhmaṇic thinkers seem to have expressed themselves in a style that is at best idiosyncratic, at worst incomprehensible. During the long period, more than a hundred years by the most conservative estimates, in which these texts were composed, the Brāhmaṇic thinkers seem to have encountered a number of disparate ritual and philosophical elements, which challenged and thus needed to be assimilated into the existing Vedic tradition. Yet, although the process of assimilation seems to have led to changes in how established rites were performed and in how they were understood, the several authors of the Brāhmaṇas did not concern themselves with eradicating obsolete views (an enterprise that in an oral tradition such as the Brāhmaṇas would have destroyed the "text") but rather tended to juxtapose one set of views over another.

It is undeniable that the authors of the Brāhmaṇas often resorted to what Eggeling called a "flimsy symbolism." Yet, in view of the peculiar circumstances in which these texts were composed, this "flimsy symbolism" represents the means by which the Brāhmaṇic authors could, and did, bind together any number of seemingly disparate elements into what is in fact an elaborately conceived system of thought and practice. Within this system many of the presuppositions of later Indian thought, such as the doctrine of karma and rebirth, were first articulated. And thus, consigning the Brāhmaṇas to a shadow existence as the aberrations of a cultural epoch leaves an unassailable gap in our understanding of the Indian tradition.

The system of transliteration used follows the now well-established conventions for the Sanskrit language. These conventions, however, have not been imposed on quotations from other authors, particularly those who wrote in the last century. The style of transliteration preferred then is most noticeable for using *ri* for the vocalic ṛ (for example, *Rig* instead of *Ṛg*), and *sh* for the lingual ṣ (for example, *Upanishad* instead of *Upaniṣad*).[34]

One convention adopted for this study is the use of the term *Brāhmaṇic* to indicate the milieu of the *Brāhmaṇa* texts and not to refer simply to the priestly caste, the Brahmans, who were chiefly responsible for these texts. The distinction here may seem insignificant; the Brāhmaṇas were the nearly exclusive domain of the priestly caste, thus their content is in some sense "priestly." What I seek to avoid, however, is the implication of a simple equation between *Brāhmaṇic*, which reflects a vast textual epoch, and *priestly*; for, in the works of an earlier generation of Indologists where this equation was implied, *Brāhmaṇic* bears a distinctly pejorative sense. Throughout this book *Brāhmaṇic* is used in precisely the same manner as the term *Upaniṣadic* has long been employed; that is, to refer to a textual milieu and not to reflect the character of the authors.

Unless otherwise noted, translations from the Vedic texts are my own. In the case of the Śatapatha Brāhmaṇa, Julius Eggeling's translation—though its style is cumbersome—has been a constant guide.[35] (And, in view of its accessibility, quotations from the Śatapatha Brāhmaṇa have been kept to a minimum.) My debt to Eggeling, though large, represents one part of a much larger debt to the Indologists of the last century and their remarkable legacy—a vast body of critical editions, translations, and analyses of the Vedic texts. Certainly, the nineteenth century was a privileged period in the history of Indology; for it seems the best minds in the West turned their attention to the Vedic texts.[36]

The prodigious ability of these scholars, however, did not make them immune to a certain narrowness of perspective, a narrowness that reflected the ethnocentrism of nineteenth century scholarship in general. Nonetheless, because these scholars possessed a breadth of knowledge of the Vedic texts that has been achieved only sporadically in recent decades (e.g., in the work of Renou and of Gonda), their works yet remain for the modern researcher the point of entry into the Vedic world. However, while the works of this earlier generation of Indologists allowed me to find my way through the maze of Vedic literature, I did not allow their interpretations of Vedic thought and practice to define the limits of my own views. I often found that although these scholars knew where things were, their understanding of why they were there was inadequate; accordingly, in the case of karma these scholars rightly identified the early manifestations of the doctrine but, because they believed the Upaniṣadic thinkers sought only to denigrate and dispense with the thought of the preceding Brāhmaṇic period, failed to discern karma's roots in the Vedic sacrifice. If my treatment of the views held by this earlier generation of scholars at times appears unkind, it reflects, I believe, a process endemic to scholarship; as Max Müller himself observed in his pioneering work, *A History of Ancient Sanskrit Literature*: "Our own studies may seemingly refer to matters that are but secondary and preparatory, to the clearance, so to say, of the rubbish which passing ages have left on the monuments of the human mind. But we shall never mistake that rubbish for the monuments which it covers."[37]

1.

The Problem of Karma and the Textual Sources

The doctrine of karma and rebirth was well known to Western Indologists long before the Indian textual tradition had been fully investigated. In one of the earliest knowledgeable accounts of Hindu beliefs and practices, Abbé J. A. Dubois noted the "doctrine is, as is generally known, one of the fundamental principles of the Hindu religion" and cited a popular religious text that accurately represented the main tenets of the karma doctrine,[1] while he depicted with wild inaccuracy the Indian philosophical schools, grossly misrepresenting their doctrines as well as those found in other orthodox Hindu texts.[2] This is not at all surprising; although the doctrine is found as a presupposition in almost all Indian philosophical thought,[3] it is perhaps most widely disseminated on the level of popular culture. As the anthropologist Ursula Sharma has noted: "In practice the individual receives the concept of karma as a part of a living folk tradition."[4]

However, that the doctrine imbues virtually every level of Indian thought seems to hinder the task of arriving at an explicit def-[illegible] karma.[5] Because the general parameters of the doctrine are so well known, the doctrine is often defined by default—as one eminent Indologist remarked: "The doctrine is so well known that it seems hardly necessary to define karma."[6] This approach assumes the meaning of karma is fundamentally the same regardless of its context. Yet, not all its several elements—causality, rebirth, ethicization[7]—are implied in each instance the doctrine occurs. To understand what karma means first requires an assessment of its context.[8]

The failure to assess properly the doctrine's context has been an enduring problem in efforts to understand the nature of karma in its earliest appearances. Scholars have generally agreed that the earliest formulation of the karma doctrine occurs in the Upaniṣads.[9] However, the doctrine's pre-Upaniṣadic history represents, as the great nineteenth century Sanskritist W. D. Whitney noted, "one of the most difficult questions in the religious history of India, how that doctrine arose, out of what it developed, to what feature of the ancient faith it attached itself."[10] The problem of ascertaining the karma doctrine's pre-Upaniṣadic history may be attributed to the view that nineteenth and early twentieth century Indologists held regarding the relationship of the Upaniṣads to the preceding Brāhmaṇic period; namely, that the Upaniṣads rejected entirely the viewpoints expressed in the Brāhmaṇas and so expressed views unprecedented in ancient Indian thought. As a result of this view scholars often failed to acknowledge—or simply ignored—that the Upaniṣadic contexts in which the doctrine first appears exhibit themes clearly drawn from the Brāhmaṇas. And, because the meaning of the karma doctrine is inextricably linked to the circumstances of its presentation, these scholars often incorrectly assessed the import of the karma doctrine in its earliest appearances.

In particular, there was a marked tendency in these scholars' interpretations to emphasize that, similar to its later occurrences, the Upaniṣadic karma doctrine was characterized by a concern with a broad range of ethical behavior and its consequences. The supposed range of the Upaniṣadic karma doctrine's ethical concern contrasts sharply with the limited sphere of Brāhmaṇic ethics, which values behavior in terms of ritual performance. Yet, rather than turn to the Brāhmaṇas' ritual orientation, which is an obvious aspect of the early Upaniṣadic karma doctrine, scholars preferred to interpret this doctrine through imposing upon it a broad notion of ethics. This approach resulted not only in the estrangement of the karma doctrine from its original context but, in an odd circular argument, in the estrangement of the thought of the Upaniṣads from that of the Brāhmaṇas. For, if karma in its earliest appearances in the Upaniṣads was indeed broadly ethical in scope, then the doctrine itself evinced a gulf between Brāhmaṇic and Upaniṣadic thought.

Although many of the views expressed by scholars of the nineteenth and early twentieth centuries regarding the relationship of Upaniṣadic and Brāhmaṇic thought, and the role of the karma doctrine in that relationship, are no longer considered to be authoritative, the work of these scholars represents the foundation of modern Indological studies (and also a large part of the foundation of the modern study of history of religions). Accordingly, these views, which led scholars to discount the role of Brāhmaṇic thought in the formulation of the karma doctrine, underlie the confusion that still reigns regarding the doctrine's early history.[11] The attempt to discern the Vedic origins of karma thus requires a reexamination, of how and why an earlier generation of scholars arrived at their peculiar view of the relationship of the Brāhmaṇas and the Upaniṣads, to see where scholarship made a wrong turn and so obfuscated karma's early history.

Following this examination, I shall turn to a detailed study of the karma doctrine's earliest appearances in the Upaniṣads. I do not intend here to formulate an explicit definition of the karma doctrine; rather, my intention is to ascertain its meaning within the larger context of Brāhmaṇic thought, where I believe the origins of the Upaniṣadic karma doctrine lie. Here, it appears the doctrine represents the natural outgrowth and culmination of certain developments in the performance of the Vedic ritual—in particular, those concerning the role of the individual sacrificer and the nature of the results of the ritual performance in both this world and the next.

The Brāhmaṇas and Upaniṣads in the View of Nineteenth Century Indology

Although a realistic depiction of the Vedic texts appeared in 1805, it was not until the second half of the nineteenth century that Western scholars were able to undertake a systematic investigation of the whole of the Vedic literature.[12] Significant for the later course of Vedic studies was the availability during this interval of a Latin translation of the Upaniṣads, Anquetil-Duperron's *Oupnek'hat*,[13] and its introduction into Western academic circles by scholars such as Arthur Schopenhauer and Friedrich Schelling, who embraced the philosophy of these texts.[14] These scholars esteemed what they perceived to be the timeless spirit of these texts; Schopenhauer, in fact, anticipated that the influence of the Upaniṣads "will not be less profound than the revival of Greek in the fourteenth century."[15] However, as Edward Said has recently noted of early Oriental studies: "almost without exception such overesteem was followed by a counterresponse: the Orient appeared lamentably underhumanized, antidemocratic, barbaric, and so forth."[16] In the early history of Vedic studies, the obvious overvaluation of Upaniṣadic thought inevitably led to an undervaluation of other aspects of the Vedic literature. Even before the Vedic literature had been thoroughly investigated, Schopenhauer thus expressed the opinion that "the Upaniṣads were the only portion of the Veda which deserved our study, and that all the rest was priestly rubbish (*Priesterwirtschaft*)."[17]

When scholars did turn their attention to the early Vedic texts, they found this preconceived notion of "priestly rubbish" disproved by the tenor of the earliest of these texts, the Ṛgveda. In this text scholars believed they glimpsed the Vedic religion before the rise of Indian sacerdotalism. Writing soon after Western scholars began studying the Ṛgveda, W. D. Whitney noted:

> To characterize the Vedic religion in general terms is not difficult . . . it is not one which has been nursed into its present form by the fostering care of a caste or priesthood; it is one which has arisen in the whole body of the people, and is the true expression of the collective view which a simple minded, but highly gifted nation, inclined to religious veneration, took of the wonders of creation and the powers to which it conceived them ascribable.[18]

However, this exalted view of the religion of the Ṛgveda, like the previous estimation of the Upaniṣads, seems to have been established at the expense of nearly all other aspects of Hinduism. With the exception of Upaniṣadic thought, the history of Hinduism following the Ṛgvedic period appeared to be one of complete degeneration. Rudolph von Roth, exemplified this view when in 1853 he wrote of the Ṛgveda:

> The charm of primitiveness which surrounds these ancient hymns in a yet higher degree than the immortal poems of Homer, is united with a nobility of diction, a pure and fresh earnestness of thought, which are no longer to be met with in the later literary productions of India. . . . [One] finds the high spiritual endowments which belong of right to the Indo-European family of nations, and which have placed it foremost in the world's history, still fresh and vigourous in

> the most eastern branch of that family, and not yet disfigured by the manifold excrescences of the later Indian people, that, were it not for their language, the European would scarcely recognize them for his own kindred.[19]

According to von Roth and other nineteenth century Indologists the initial stages of this decline occurred within the Vedic period itself; being clearly visible in the texts that immediately followed the hymns, the Brāhmaṇas. In von Roth's estimation, the displacement of the Vedic hymns by the Brāhmaṇas resulted in the degeneration of all Hinduism in the post-Vedic period, a condition empirically verified by the British colonial experience.[20] As von Roth noted: "[India] has, indeed, carefully treasured up and at all times regarded as sacred, the productions of its earliest period [i.e., the Ṛgveda]; but it has attached the main importance to a worthless supplement [i.e., the Brāhmaṇas], and lost from sight and from knowledge the truly valuable portion."[21]

Although the composition of the Upaniṣads immediately followed that of the Brāhmaṇas, scholars tended to posit a line of development that aligned Upaniṣadic thought with that of the Ṛgveda, milieus they perceived to be in opposition to the intervening Brāhmaṇic period.[22] Nowhere is this more apparent than in the view scholars took of the Upaniṣadic doctrine of karma and rebirth, particularly in regard to this doctrine's problematic origin. In contrast to the corrupt trends that pervaded the Brāhmaṇas, the Upaniṣadic karma doctrine—with its wholesome ethical tenor—seemed to signify a return to the healthy atmosphere of the Ṛgveda. The notion that the Upaniṣadic karma doctrine arose in concert with the intent of much earlier Ṛgvedic beliefs, while it opposed that of the Brāhmaṇas was partly due to what scholars perceived to be a general pattern in the evolution of a religious tradition. Referring to such an evolutionary model, W. D. Whitney thus noted of the doctrine's origin that: "Its introduction later is equally in accordance with the general course of religious history; it is a part of the prevailing shift from the basis of nature to that of morality."[23] In the case of the karma doctrine, this pattern of evolution was given added support by what was perceived to be the degenerate state of the religion of the Brāhmaṇas. The shift to morality found in the Upaniṣadic karma doctrine, was interpreted as being "antisacrificial," to oppose the "corrupt" sacerdotalism systematically promoted in the Brāhmaṇas.

The tendency to separate the Ṛgveda and the Upaniṣads from the Brāhmaṇas, and to position them in opposition, may be attributed to the general view that nineteenth century Indologists held of the role of priestcraft in the decline of a religious tradition.[24] The Brāhmaṇas, which were compiled over several centuries (ca. 900–600 B.C.E.), record the growth of the sacrificial (*śrauta*) ritual and its subsequent dominance in ancient Indian religion. The growth of the sacrifice (in both complexity and stature) during this period naturally coincided with the growth of a specialized sacerdotal class. In the view of many nineteenth century Indologists, the religion of the early Veda became devitalized at the hands of these sacerdotalists. As one scholar remarked: "the priests had lost the inspiration that came from action; they now made no new hymns; they only formulated new rules of sacrifice. They became intellectually debauched and altogether weakened in character."[25] Every aspect of the Brāhmaṇic ritual was interpreted in light of this supposed debauchery. More than one scholar asserted that the priests maintained their interest in the sacrifice because it provided them with a pretense to sanctity and thus an exalted position in society: "the age is overcast, not only with a thick cloud of ritualism, but also with an unpleasant mask of phariseeism."[26]

The task of interpreting the Brāhmaṇas, with their bulk and esoteric subject matter, was a formidable one to the Western scholar uninitiated in the intricacies of the Vedic sacrifice.[27] The authors of the Brāhmaṇas created unique sacrificial events by correlating basic ritual techniques with a complex theoretical base. The focus of this theory was the mythical event of the cosmic man's (Prajāpati's) primordial sacrificial activity, which, replicated in the individual sacrificer's own ritual performances, established the symbolic identity of the sacrificer and the cosmos.[28] The authors of the Brāhmaṇas employed their peculiar theory of the sacrifice to conjoin what apparently were already existing rituals and ritual techniques into unique sacrificial events. However, whereas the developed Brāhmaṇic sacrifices often combined several different rites, the connections between them were established not on the level of physical performance but through a series of metaphysical propositions. Consequently, the discussions that appear in the

Brāhmaṇas are often abstruse and esoteric; the authors apparently "supposed their audience to be well acquainted with the course of the ritual, its terminology and technicalities,"[29] and therefore could (and did) limit their discussions to the higher significance of the rite.

For example, the Brāhmaṇic rite of the piling of the fire altar (*agnicayana*) incorporated several distinct ritual events, among them an initiation (*dīkṣā*), an animal sacrifice (*paśubandha*), an offering to Rudra (*śatarudriya homa*), and a Soma sacrifice.[30] Because these several ceremonies probably were well known in themselves, the descriptions of the Agnicayana that appear in the various Brāhmaṇas do not present a detailed conspectus of the physical performance of this sacrifice. The Brāhmaṇic narrative instead concerns itself with the metaphysical implications of virtually every detail of the rite and, in this way, transforms the several elements of this sacrifice into a singular event. In the Agnicayana rite, this transformation is brought about through the symbolic identification of the ritual event with the primordial sacrifice of the cosmic man, Prajāpati, which itself brought the cosmos into being. This identification is made to extend through each discrete ritual act (initiation, construction of the altar, soma sacrifice, etc.), despite the lack of connection of these acts to the Prajāpati mythos in earlier Vedic contexts. While the Agnicayana comprises a multiplicity of ritual performances, the integrity of the sacrifice is maintained as the sacrificer replicates one or another aspect of the cosmic man's primordial activity in each separate ritual event. The discrete elements of the rite are thus subsumed to the ritualist's larger metaphysical vision.

It is this specialized knowledge of the ritual that brought the sacrificial rite under the dominion of the sacerdotal class. Nineteenth century scholars, however, with their deprecatory view of sacerdotalism, had little patience for the intricacies of Brāhmaṇic thought. Maurice Bloomfield, for example, remarked of the Brāhmaṇas that: "Both the performances and their explanations are treated in such a way, and spun out to such lengths, as to render these works on the whole monuments of tediousness and intrinsic stupidity."[31] Hence, scholars agreed that these texts did not even merit the most cursory examination: "Even a resume of one comparatively short ceremony would be so long and tedious that the explication of the intricate formalities would scarcely be a sufficient reward."[32] (Though, at least as an exercise in philology, these same scholars produced critical Sanskrit editions of nearly all the extant Brāhmaṇas, translating several into European languages.)

Scholars vindicated their reluctance to examine thoroughly these texts—that is, beyond producing critical editions of them—by appealing to their peculiar view of the development of the Vedic religion. Their assertion that the Upaniṣads represented a renascence of the high spiritual achievements of the Ṛgveda meant that the intervening Brāhmaṇic period represented a dark age. In fact, if the Brāhmaṇas were studied at all, it was only to emphasize this characterization.[33] On the one hand, the Brāhmaṇas represented the utter degeneration of the high spiritual attainments of the early Vedic religion, exhibiting what Max Müller called "a most important phase in the growth of the human mind in its passage from health to disease."[34] Accordingly, Müller noted that "every page of the Brāhmaṇas contains the clearest proof that the spirit of the ancient Vedic poetry, and the purport of the original Vedic sacrifices, were both beyond the comprehension of the authors of the Brāhmaṇas."[35] On the other hand, however, the diseased thought of the Brāhmaṇas represented the necessary foundation from which a healthier period might arise. This revival in Vedic thought was seen in the advent of the Upaniṣads; as Charles Lanman noted: "[In the Upaniṣads] the Hindu character has been transformed almost beyond recognition. The change is wonderful. It would also be incomprehensible, but for the literature of the Brāhmaṇas . . . they are puerile, arid, inane."[36] For these scholars the Brāhmaṇic domination of the religious sphere impelled this transformation: "The Indian mind was by no means dead, although sacerdotalism was drunk with supremacy and in its folly and arrogance was hastening the day of revolt."[37] This "revolt" manifested itself in what was believed to be the antisacrificial attitude that appeared first in the Upaniṣads, and afterwards in the heterodox sects, especially Buddhism.[38]

With such a view in mind, Max Müller made the broad claim that the object of the Upaniṣads was "to show the utter uselessness, nay the mischievousness of all ritual performances; to condemn every sacrificial act which has for its motive a desire or hope of reward."[39] To prove this assertion scholars cited repeatedly certain

Upaniṣadic passages that they believed derided the sacrifice.[40] One such passage appears in the Bṛhadāraṇyaka Upaniṣad:

> who knows thus, "I am Brahman," he becomes this all. The gods do not control his attaining [this state]; indeed he becomes their self (*ātman*). Now the one who worships to another god, thinking "I am one, he is another," he does not know. He is like a [sacrificial or domestic] animal (*paśu*) for the gods. Now as many animals are useful to men, each man serves the gods. When even one animal is taken away, there is unhappiness. What about many? Therefore it is not pleasing to the gods when men know this.[41]

The apparent opposition here between the performers of the sacrifice (those who serve the gods) and those "who know" was viewed by scholars such as Deussen as evidence that the Upaniṣads are "radically opposed to the entire Vedic sacrificial cult."[42] This view, however, assumes that the activity, which is not specified in this particular passage, of those "who know" is not sacrificial, or is perhaps even antisacrificial in nature. A passage that occurs in the Śatapatha Brāhmaṇa clarifies the nature of the activity of those "who know":

> They say: "[Who] is better, the one who sacrifices for the self (*ātmayājin*), or the one who sacrifices for the gods (*devayājin*)?" Indeed he should say, "The one who offers for the self." Indeed the self offerer is the one who knows that by this [ritual] the body is formed for me; by this ritual that body is placed near to me . . . so he arises in the heavenly world.
>
> Now the god offerer is the one who knows, "I indeed offer to the gods; I honor the gods." He is [the same] as the inferior who brings tribute to the superior. . . . Indeed he does not win a world of the same extent as the other [i.e., the self offerer].[43]

This passage indicates the Brāhmaṇic thinkers recognized two paradigms for sacrificial activity: the self offerer, who attains the results of the sacrifice directly, and the god offerer, who attains the results of the sacrifice through the intercession of the gods. Furthermore, the Brāhmaṇa passage clarifies what is left unsaid in the Bṛhadāraṇyaka Upaniṣad; namely, that the one "who knows thus," (the self offerer in the Brāhmaṇa passage) is yet a sacrificer, albeit one who couples his ritual activity with a certain type of knowledge, and thereby minimizes the role of the gods (an unhappy circumstance, according to the Upaniṣad passage, for the gods). And, although this pattern of sacrifice is represented in the Brāhmaṇa as being "better" than offering to the gods, neither this text nor the Upaniṣad negates this latter pattern.[44] Most important, the similarity between these passages from the Bṛhadāranyaka Upaniṣad and the Śatapatha Brāhmaṇa, indicates that, contrary to the views of nineteenth century Indologists, the Upaniṣadic thinkers continued to acknowledge and to draw upon the patterns for sacrificial action already established in the Brāhmaṇas.

The similarity between these passages from the Bṛhadāraṇyaka Upaniṣad and the Śatapatha Brāhmaṇa, and the continuity in thought they express, reflects the proximity of the Brāhmaṇas and Upaniṣads—the latter are appended to the former—in the Vedic textual tradition. Though scholars were aware of the practical relationship between these texts, their notion of how the religion of ancient India evolved—from the healthy (and simplistic) tenor of the Ṛgvedic worship of nature, through a period of disease in Brāhmaṇic ritualism, to a revitalization in the Upaniṣads—led them to emphasize an underlying dissension in the growth of the Vedic tradition. To establish the opposition of Upaniṣadic thought to the preceding Brāhmaṇic period required scholars to vitiate both the textual evidence of physical contiguity and the contextual evidence, which strongly suggested the ideological continuity of the Brāhmaṇas and Upaniṣads. This process is clearly visible in these scholars' treatment of the karma doctrine, the result of which was to detach karma from whatever roots it possessed in the thought of the Brāhmaṇas.

The Upaniṣads and the Vedic Origins of the Karma Doctrine

In the Vedic textual tradition, the older Upaniṣads are contiguous with their corresponding Brāhmaṇas.[45] These Upaniṣads, together with an intermediary portion of the text referred to as an Āraṇyaka, were physically inseparable from their Brāhmaṇas; in manuscripts, the texts were appended to one another, and often could not be differentiated easily.[46] The continuity of these texts is seen not only through their physical contiguity but also through their contextual similarity. Even Deussen, who vigorously supported the separation of the Brāhmaṇas and Upaniṣads on theoretical grounds,[47] admitted that "the separation of the material is by no means strictly carried out, but in all three classes, Brāhmaṇas, Āraṇyakas, and Upanishads, there are found occasional digressions of a ritual as well as of an allegorical or philosophical nature."[48] The conjoint nature of these texts is reflected in their titles: the Āraṇyaka and Upaniṣad portions are often referred to as *brāhmaṇa-upaniṣad, upaniṣad-brāhmaṇa,* and *āraṇyaka-upaniṣad.*[49]

Furthermore, the compilers of the Upaniṣads employed several "literary" devices to indicate the continuity of these texts with the Brāhmaṇas. Perhaps chief among these is the use of recognizable Brāhmaṇic motifs to present their teachings. For example, the authors of the Bṛhadāraṇyaka Upaniṣad place their teaching regarding the distinct natures of the gods, asuras, and men in a frame story that recounts how these three classes of beings approached Prajāpati to be instructed:

> The threefold offspring, the gods, men, and asuras, dwelt as students, unmarried, with Prajāpati, [their] father. The gods, having dwelt as students, spoke: "Instruct us, sir!" To them he uttered the syllable "da," and said: "Do you understand?" They said: "We understand. You said to us: You must control yourselves (*dāmyata*)." "Indeed," he said, "You have understood."[50]

Subsequently, Prajāpati tells the men and asuras who approach him to practice respectively giving and compassion.[51]

The frame story here is clearly drawn from the Śatapatha Brāhmaṇa, the Brāhmaṇa to which the Bṛhadāraṇyaka is appended: "Living beings once approached Prajāpati. These living beings, [his] offspring, spoke: 'Give us a manner of living!' Thereupon the gods, having been properly invested for the sacrifice, came [to him] on their knees. He spoke to them: 'The sacrifice is your food; immortality your strength; and the sun your light.' "[52] Subsequently, Prajāpati bestows a distinct manner of living on the fathers (they eat monthly, their light is the moon), men (their eating is daily, their light is the fire), creatures (they eat all things), and asuras (their lot is darkness and illusion) who approach him.[53]

While the specific doctrines presented in these two texts differ, the texts follow a remarkably similar format; both present Prajāpati as the father of the various classes of beings who inhabit the cosmos, both depict these beings as having completed their studentship (making them eligible to sacrifice), and both express, through Prajāpati's teachings, the distinct natures of these beings.

Related to this use of similar motifs is the employment throughout the Brāhmaṇas and Upaniṣads of a set of terms, suggesting the existence of an idiom specific to these texts, to describe the cosmos.[54] These descriptions focus on the interrelations, often through a process of homologization, of the breaths (*prāṇa*), the sense organs (eye, ear, speech, taste, mind), the divinities (Agni, Vāyu, Rudra, Āditya, Candramas), and the spheres of the cosmos (a category that includes the earth, sun, moon, and quarters of the heavens, as well as units of time—the year, months, fortnights).[55] At the very least, the existence of such an idiom indicates the discussions of the nature of the cosmos, discussions that typify the Upaniṣads, were built on patterns already established in Brāhmaṇić thought.

Another device employed by the compilers of the Upaniṣads was the attribution of many of their teachings to the same sages that appear in the Brāhmaṇas or to sages whose lineages are traced to Brāhmaṇic teachers.[56] Best known among these sages is Yājñavalkya, who is cited as a doctrinal authority in both the Śatapatha Brāhmaṇa and the Bṛhadāraṇyaka Upaniṣad. Although the Bṛhadāraṇyaka indicates that it is the same Yājñavalkya who appears in both the Upaniṣad and the Brāhmaṇa,[57] this is clearly not intended to represent a historical fact; for, even by the most conservative estimates, at least a century separates the composition of these two texts.[58] Rather, the figure of Yājñavalkya seems to have been employed in the Bṛhadāraṇyaka Upaniṣad to establish a sense of continuity between the Upaniṣad and its Brāhmaṇa.

In their interpretations of the Upaniṣads, Western scholars tended to minimize the importance of such devices. Robert Hume, for example, dismissed the idea that the textual evidence implied an integral relationship between the Brāhmaṇas and Upaniṣads, as he noted that the material drawn from the Brāhmaṇas, such as "explanations of the sacrificial ritual, legends, dialogues, etymologizings . . . and so forth are, in the main, merely mechanically juxtaposed [in the Upaniṣads]."[59] Macdonell and Keith, following the view of Oldenberg, noted that "no importance can be attached to the mention of Yājñavalkya [in the Bṛhadāraṇyaka Upaniṣad]."[60] That scholars failed to attribute any importance to these points reflects an assumption that the chief doctrines of Upaniṣadic thought originated outside the bounds of the Brāhmaṇic ritual cult. The view that epitomizes this assumption is that of Deussen, who asserted that the doctrines of the Upaniṣads had originally been "fostered primarily among the Kshatriyas and not within Brahman circles, engrossed as these were with the ritual."[61] Although few scholars fully endorsed Deussen's assertion,[62] the premise upon which it was established represents an important presupposition of early Vedic studies; that is, that the Upaniṣads are "radically opposed to the entire Vedic sacrificial cult, and the older they are the more markedly does this opposition declare itself."[63]

Rather than consider the possibility that the Brāhmaṇic motifs that appear in the early Upaniṣads was the result of an orthogenetic process, scholars attributed their appearance in the Upaniṣads to a later textual appropriation by the Brahman ritualists. According to Deussen:

> Soon also the Brahmans laid claim to the new teaching as their exclusive privilege. They were able to point to princes and leaders, as Janaka, Jānaśruti, etc., who were said to have gone for instruction to Brahmans. Authorities on the ritual like Śāṇḍilya and Yājñavalkya were transformed into originators and upholders of the ideas of the Upanishads.[64]

The Brahmans' appropriation of the Upaniṣads was a natural corollary of the notion that, in an earlier age, the Brahmans had appropriated all aspects of the Vedic ritual to attain their dominant position in the religious sphere. Moreover, such an appropriation, which would have allowed the Brahmans to maintain their religious hegemony in spite of the depreciation of the sacrificial rite by groups (Kṣatriya or Brahman) disaffected with the sacrifice, was in accord with the perverse motives that scholars had attributed to the priesthood; as A. B. Keith noted: "the process is one of steady accommodation to the popular view, which was at the same time the profitable view to the priests."[65] Thus, with their preconceived notions of the debilitating effect of priestcraft, scholars vitiated the textual evidence that seemed to indicate the continuity of the Brāhmaṇic and Upaniṣadic traditions. Furthermore, it was apparent that if the Brāhmaṇic concerns that appeared in the Upaniṣads were merely a priestly fabrication then no substantial link existed between the thought of the Upaniṣads and that of the Brāhmaṇas. Accordingly, although scholars such as Max Müller reflected that "the sacrificial technicalities, and their philosophical interpretations with which the Upaṇishads abound, may *perhaps in time* assume a clearer meaning, when we shall have fully mastered the intricacies of the Vedic ceremonial"[66] (italics mine), they were confident that such an element—or, as Müller referred to it, "such utter rubbish"—was largely inconsequential to an understanding of the import of the Upaniṣads.[67]

The tendency to separate the thought of the Brāhmaṇas from that of the Upaniṣads is especially apparent in these scholars' interpretation of the origins of the doctrine of karma and rebirth. In general, the doctrine was believed to be unprecedented in Brāhmaṇic thought.[68] In fact, scholars were so firmly convinced of karma's absence in the Brāhmaṇas, they viewed its acceptance in the Upaniṣads as the point of bifurcation between the Brāhmaṇas and Upaniṣads. According to Keith: "The distinction corresponds, we may fairly say, in the main to a change of time and still more to a change of view. The Upanishads hold in some degree at least the doctrine of transmigration . . . the Brāhmaṇas, which, taken all in all, know not transmigration."[69]

Nonetheless, certain afterlife beliefs that appeared first in the Ṛgveda and then in the Brāhmaṇas were widely accepted as suggesting transmigration.[70] In the Ṛgveda these beliefs occur in a passage addressed to the individual after death: "May your eye go to the sun, your life's breath to the wind. Go to the sky or to earth, as is your nature; or go to the waters if that is your fate. Take root in the plants with your limbs."[71] Whereas scholars correctly identified this passage as containing incipient elements of the later karma doctrine—in particular, the doctrine's idea that the rebirth process entails the individual's integration into the constituents of the cosmos—they did so for what now appears to be the wrong reason. Although it represents an obvious reversal of the central Brāhmaṇic mythology of the cosmic man (Puruṣa, Prajāpati), according to which the cosmos arose from the body of a primeval anthropomorphic being, scholars tended to discuss this passage as a reflection of animistic beliefs.[72] According to these scholars, in such animistic beliefs "there is a first rude idea of the theory of metempsychosis."[73]

Animism, which either came from "contact with the rude aboriginal inhabitants of the Indian peninsula" or "had maintained its hold upon the lower strata of the Aryan people themselves from savage times,"[74] represented a level of belief that was clearly antithetical to that which, according to nineteenth century scholars, pervaded the Ṛgveda. According to one scholar: "This notion [animism] seems to belong to religious beliefs of a lower type, which this collection [the Ṛgveda] despises."[75] In other words, this level of belief was viewed as an aberration, and therefore was not considered to be of any consequence in the evolution of Vedic thought.[76] The Ṛgvedic passage just cited seemed to exemplify this level of aberrant belief; as A. B. Keith commented, the "view once found in the Rigveda, which sends the eye of the dead to the sun, the breath to the wind, bids him go to the heaven and the earth, or if he prefers to the waters, and to dwell among the plants with his members, cannot be treated as more than a mere deviation of no great consequence for the general view of Vedic religion."[77] Yet, as a reflection of the cosmic man mythology, this view that homologizes the body of the deceased with the spheres of the cosmos is found throughout the Brāhmaṇas.[78] Nonetheless, by suggesting that underlying this text was nothing more than an aberrant, though decidedly popular, belief in animism scholars discounted the role of this mythology in the formation of the karma doctrine. In its place they emphasized the ethical dimensions of the Upaniṣadic karma doctrine. A. B. Keith, in his monumental study *The Religion and Philosophy of the Veda and Upanishads* (perhaps the summation of nineteenth century Vedic studies in the West), thus remarked:

> What is necessary is to point out that, while the ideas thus recorded are of some value as showing the presence in Indian religion of the belief of the incorporation of the souls of the dead now and

> then in animals or plants—of the latter there is even a hint in the Rigveda itself—*the importance of transmigration lies precisely in the fact that the doctrine is an ethical system, and . . . is thereby referred for its real origin to something quite other than popular belief.*[79] (italics mine)

By "popular belief" Keith refers not only to animism but to a range of beliefs that nineteenth century scholars believed led to the formation of Brāhmaṇic thought (itself an aberration in the evolution of Vedic religion). In their discussions of karma's earliest appearances in the Upaniṣads, scholars quickly disposed of these elements that might lead them back to the Brāhmaṇas. Deussen, for example, referred to the Brāhmaṇic afterlife beliefs that encompass an early presentation of the doctrine in the Upaniṣads as being "evidently primitive," and remarked that: "We must therefore look for the original doctrine where it appears by itself."[80] Keith commented of the Brāhmaṇic motifs[81] that occur along with the doctrine's first appearance in the Chāndogya Upaniṣad that: "The mythical character of the whole is obvious, and reminds us that the new doctrine of action as determining the future life was decidedly disadvantageous to the sacrificial priest, and that it was natural to reserve it as a holy mystery."[82] Here, Keith minimizes the interpretive value of the context in which the doctrine occurs by appealing to the notion that the priesthood was largely motivated by the most perverse concerns: since the doctrine constituted a threat to their stature, the Brahman compilers (or, in the view of many nineteenth century Indologists, the Brahman usurpers) of the Upaniṣads attempted to conceal its intent by drawing on the esoteric symbolism (Keith's "holy mystery") employed in the Brāhmaṇas.

It was precisely this sort of ethical vacuum that scholars believed Upaniṣadic thought in general, and the karma doctrine in particular, filled. Accordingly, the karma doctrine, with its origins in "something quite other than popular belief," was not organically related to the Brāhmaṇic mythology that, in its earliest appearances in the Upaniṣads surrounded it, but arose from ethical concerns that were foreign—perhaps even antithetical—to the Brāhmaṇas' ritual orientation. In this sense, the interpretation of the karma doctrine echoed the larger view that scholars held regarding the relationship of the Brāhmaṇas and the Upaniṣads.

The Earliest Notice of the Doctrine of Karma and Rebirth in the Bṛhadāraṇyaka and Chāndogya Upaniṣads

Scholars have generally agreed that the earliest formulation of the karma doctrine occurs in the Bṛhadāraṇyaka Upaniṣad,[83] a text composed ca. 600–500 B.C.E., and considered to be the earliest of the Upaniṣads.[84] The doctrine occurs here in the context of a discussion of the fate of the individual after death.[85] After stating the Vedic doctrine of the dissolution of the dead person on the funeral pyre (the breath into the air, the eye into the sun, the mind into the moon, the hearing into the quarters, etc.),[86] the sage Yājñavalkya is asked by his colleague Ārtabhāga, "What then becomes of this person?" Yājñavalkya replies, "My dear Ārtabhāga, take my hand. We two alone shall know of this, this is not for us two to speak of amongst [other] people."[87] The text then continues in the third person: "Having gone aside, they engaged in a consultation. That which they spoke about was karma and that which they praised was action (*karman*): one indeed becomes good by good action (*karman*), bad by bad [action]."[88]

Western scholars have considered this passage to present the fundamental premise of the karma doctrine; that is, an individual attains a state after death that is a direct result of the moral quality of his activities before death.[89] The supposed moral aspect of the doctrine presented here was especially emphasized; according to Deussen, in this passage: "the motive which lies at the basis of transmigration is clearly expressed. It is the great moral difference of character . . . which the philosopher explains in our passage on the hypothesis that a man has already existed once before his birth, and that his inborn character is the fruit and consequence of his previous action."[90] That scholars understood this to be the intent of this passage, which is drawn from the earliest strata of the Upaniṣads, is a point of fundamental importance; for, the "great moral difference of character" of the karma doctrine distinguishes this doctrine from the limited, or nonexistent, ethics of the Brāhmaṇas.

According to A. B. Keith, who, among early Indologists, presented the most detailed discussion of the ethics of the Brāhmaṇas,[91] "the question of the nature of right action does not seem ever to have in any degree influenced the speculations of the curious spirits [who composed the Brāhmaṇas]."[92] To exemplify the Brāhmaṇas' "most unedifying indifference to morality," Keith noted that: "The Jaiminīya Brāhmaṇa actually records, without disapproval apparently, a rite, the Gosava, in which the performer pays the ox the compliment of imitating its mode of existence, including incest with mother, sister, and female relative."[93]

In view of the Brāhmaṇas' overwhelming concern with the performance and meaning of the Vedic rituals, this apparent indifference to ethical behavior is not surprising. Nonetheless, within the context of the ritual performance, the Brāhmaṇas do distinguish between good and bad (ritual) acts, and as in other ethical systems, this valuation is based on the consequences of actions.[94] For example, a typical Brāhmaṇic passage declares: "When the Agnihotra is being offered, what he does mistakenly, either by word or deed, that cuts off his vigor, his own self, or his children."[95] Although the idea expressed here that the valuation of actions rests upon results—rather than on the acts themselves—may not reflect morality in a general sense, within the limits of a well-defined system it yet expresses a notion of ethics. J. L. Mackie has discussed this distinction between a general and a narrow morality:

> A morality in the broad sense would be a general, all inclusive theory of conduct: the morality to which someone subscribed would be whatever body of principles he allowed ultimately to guide his choices of conduct. In the narrow sense, a morality is a system of a particular sense of restraints on conduct—ones whose central task is to protect the interests of persons other than the agent and which present themselves as checks on his natural inclinations or tendencies to act.[96]

To fulfill the requisites of a narrowly defined ethical system may require the abandonment of the general norms of conduct. The disregarding of one's "natural inclinations or tendencies to act" in the pursuit for ritual correctness, which is the narrow ethic of the ritual system, is apparent in one Brāhmaṇic passage, which implies that the performance of a certain ritual act might lead the sacrificer's wife to separate from her husband and so, perhaps to become an adulteress. Yājñavalkya, who is cited as a final authority throughout the Brāhmaṇas and Upaniṣads, responds to this conflict by disregarding the ethical constraints of ordinary action; he is thus quoted: "Let it be as directed for the wife; indeed who cares if the wife should be apart from her husband (*paraḥ puṃsā*)?"[97] However, though this act of separation, which seems implicitly to condone adultery, like Keith's example of the Gosava rite's requisite act of bestiality (which the actor impossibly performs as an act of incest), is reprehensible in any ordinary circumstances, this does not mean an indifference on the part of the Brāhmaṇas' authors to morality. Within the narrowly defined ethic of the ritual system—which seeks exactitude in the performance of the rite—such acts, insofar as they fulfill the demands of the ritual, are morally good; as Sylvain Lévi observed, "le bien est l'exactitude rituelle."[98]

Scholars failed to consider this valuation of action in the Brāhmaṇas as the basis of an ethical system; as Keith noted of the Brāhmaṇas: "But though terminology shows a certain advance in view, it remains the case that nothing architectonic arises in the way of conception of good and evil."[99] Consequently, the earliest formulation of the karma doctrine, the statement "one becomes good by good action, bad by bad [action]" suggested a sudden flowering of a broadly based moral concern; as one scholar noted, it indicated a "moral advance on earlier ideas; for it gave all conduct a moral meaning."[100] Yet, it is not entirely certain that the expression "one becomes good by good action, bad by bad [action]" refers to a broad spectrum of conduct. The context in which this phrase occurs, and certain aspects of the phrase itself, suggest that it refers only to the activity of the sacrifice. The context, namely the notion that upon cremation "the speech of this dead person enters into the fire, the breath into air, the eye into the sun, the mind into the moon . . . ,"[101] clearly recalls the symbolism of the Brāhmaṇic ritual. Underlying this symbolism was the theory that, "every great sacrifice is a repetition of the archetypal sacrifice in which Prajāpati . . . while being dismembered, was transformed into the universe."[102] As Jan Gonda has observed, in its application, the purpose of this ritual theory was to "bring about a transformation, new birth and higher existence of the sacrificer who in and through this ritual is identified with Prajāpati."[103] The obvious similarity between the fate of the deceased described here and the fate of the dismembered Prajāpati—as they are both transformed into the various elements of the cosmos—signifies that the

Upaṇiṣadic karma doctrine was theoretically commensurate with the Brāhmaṇic sacrifice.

Moreover, the notion that "one becomes good by good action, bad by bad [action]" appears to be a reflex of the Brāhmaṇic idea of the merit resulting from the well-done (*sukṛta*) sacrifice and, its opposite, the demerit resulting from the poorly done (*duṣkṛta*) sacrifice, that awaits the sacrificer in the next world. According to Jan Gonda, these terms—*sukṛta, sādhu kṛta, puṇyakṛta, puṇya karman* (the term used in the Bṛhadāraṇyaka Upaniṣad to denote "good action")—and their opposites—*duṣkṛta, pāpa karman* ("bad action" in the Bṛhadāraṇyaka Upaniṣad)—represent two parallel complexes in the Vedic ritual sphere.[104] *Sukṛta*, on the one hand, expresses "the lasting merit, the effective and positive result of the correct performance of the ritual acts [which] accumulate for the benefit of the performer [in the next world]";[105] its opposite, *duṣkṛta*, refers to "omissions, negligence or reprehensible behaviour in the ritual or religious sphere," resulting in the diminution or destruction of the individual's afterlife realm.[106] In view of the established meanings of these terms in the Vedic ritual sphere, the phrase "one becomes good by good action" in the Bṛhadāraṇyaka Upaniṣad may refer only to the acquisition of, and a consequent state of becoming one with, the merit (the "good") or demerit (the "bad") accumulated through a lifetime of sacrificial activity.[107]

This early presentation of the karma doctrine does not refer to any specific sphere of being (plant, animal, caste) that, in the classical formulation of the doctrine,[108] relates the fact of rebirth to the moral efficacy of an individual's deeds. Another passage in the Bṛhadāraṇyaka Upaniṣad, also attributed to Yājñavalkya, seemed to many scholars to suggest this aspect of the karma doctrine.[109] This passage first describes the different forms (*rupa*) that an individual might attain after death: "Just as a jeweler, having taken an ornament, renders it into another newer and more beautiful shape, so this very self, having thrown away this body, and having dispelled ignorance, makes another newer and more beautiful form, either [that of] a father, or a *gandharva*, or a god, or Prajāpati, or Brahmā, or other beings."[110] This passage is immediately followed by a restatement of the doctrine that Yājñavalkya had previously imparted to Ārtabhāga: "As one does, as one conducts oneself, so one becomes. The one who does good becomes good, the one who does bad becomes bad; one becomes good by good action, bad by bad [action]."[111]

Yet, it is unclear whether the description here of taking on "another newer and more beautiful form, either [that of] a father, or a *gandharva*, or a god . . . " indicates an afterlife existence based on the moral quality of an individual's conduct in general or only on the specific activity of the sacrifice. The notion that an individual might attain a variety of forms (that of a god, a father, etc.) after death again recalls the Brāhmaṇic notion of acquiring, and becoming one with, the merit accumulated through a lifetime of sacrifice. However, in place of an integration into the cosmos or, more precisely, into the cosmic body of Prajāpati, the deceased attain one of the various spheres (*loka*) that, in Brāhmaṇic thought, are associated with one or another of the beings, gods, fathers, and so on, that inhabit the cosmos.[112] This corresponds to the Vedic-Brāhmaṇic notion that: "Ritual techniques enable a sacrificer to become *saloka*—'of one *loka* with' a power, to gain access to lokas characterized by the 'presence' of a particular divine power, to enter into communion with that power, and henceforth to be a 'denizen of heaven.' "[113]

Unlike later formulations of the karma doctrine, according to which evildoers are reborn in an inferior form (animal, insect, etc.) or even, as one text states, "fall down into hell,"[114] this passage discusses only the attainment of "newer and more beautiful forms." The failure to depict a sphere (*loka*) that is exclusively associated with evildoers is in accord with the Brāhmaṇic notion that the poorly done (*duṣkṛta*) sacrifice results in the diminution or destruction of the sacrificer's world of merit (*sukṛta loka*), rather than the attainment of a lower form of life, or of a hell.[115] The most important effect of the poorly done sacrifice thus seems to be the denial of a store of merit in the next world, the benefits of which sustain the sacrificer in his afterlife existence.

Among the early formulations of the karma doctrine in the Upaniṣads exists another passage, more elaborate than the passages cited earlier, that scholars generally identified as the "chief text that sets forth the doctrine of transmigration, on which all subsequent texts are dependent."[116] This passage is found in two recensions, appearing in both the Chāndogya and the Bṛhadāraṇyaka Upaniṣads.[117] The doctrine presented here also occurs in the context of a discussion of the fate of the individual after death, although this discussion refers to somewhat different notions than those found in the earlier presentation of the doctrine. Moreover, this passage is distinguished by its concern with the process of birth, which is represented here as being concomitant with death. The passage is accordingly divided into two parts: the first part, referred to as the five fire doctrine (*pañcāgnividyā*), describes the cycle of human generation and homologizes this process with the elements of the sacrifice;[118] the second part differentiates between the two paths traveled by the deceased, the path of the gods (*devayāna*) and the path of the fathers (*pitṛyāna*).[119] According to this latter part of the passage, those who attain the *devayāna* follow a course that ultimately leads them to the world of Brahmā; those who attain the *pitṛyāna* follow a course that leads them to the moon, from which they return just as they ascended to attain another birth. This process of rebirth is established on the model of the five fire doctrine, which precedes it in the text.

The five fire doctrine, which also occurs in the Śatapatha Brāhmaṇa and Jaiminīya Brāhmaṇa,[120] relates the process of human generation to the continuous activity of a cosmic sacrifice. This doctrine represents five spheres of the cosmos--the heavens, atmosphere, earth, man, and woman[121]—as five sacrificial fires, identifying an element associated with each of these five spheres as an element of the fire—fuel, smoke, flame, coals, and sparks. For example, as a sacrificial fire, the heavens are said to have the sun as its fuel, the rays of the sun as its smoke, the day as its flame, the moon as its coals, and the stars as its sparks; and a woman, as a sacrificial fire, is said to have her lap as fuel, "what invites" as smoke, her vagina as flame, "what she does inside" as coals, and pleasure as sparks.[122] The creative process is set in motion as the five sacrificial fires yield, in turn: *soma* (the primal material of the sacrifice), rain, food, semen, and an embryo.[123] The cycle is completed by a sixth sacrifice, the funeral rite. Significantly, whereas each of the five spheres of the cosmos is only symbolically represented as a sacrificial fire (in the sacrifice of the heavenly sphere, for example, the sun is the fire, the day is the flame, the moon is the coals, etc.), the funeral rite is represented as the only real sacrificial event (the fire is the fire, the flame is the flame, the coals are the coals).[124] This final sacrifice regenerates the individual into the cosmos and, depending on which afterlife path he follows (the *devayāna* or the *pitṛyāna*), possibly leads to reentry into the birth cycle. These two afterlife paths—how they are attained, where they lead the deceased—are described in the second part of this passage in the Upaniṣads.

According to the description of the *devayāna* and the *pitṛyāna* in these Upaniṣadic passages, the attainment of one or the other of these paths results from a distinction in ritual activity; that is, the nature of an individual's ritual activity before death leads the sacrificer to attain one or the other of these two paths after death. The *devayāna*, which ultimately leads to the world of Brahmā, is said to be attained by "those who know this [five fire doctrine], and who worship in the forest thinking 'faith is austerity.' "[125] On the other hand, "those who worship in the forest thinking 'giving [to the priests who perform the sacrifice] is for [the purpose of] storing sacrificial merit in the other world,' "[126] attain the *pitṛyāna* and reenter the birth cycle. The distinction in ritual activity made here is that between a traditional path of worship, one that maintains the relationship between gods, priests, and sacrificers and a path that concentrates on the individual, to the point of actually "interiorizing" the sacrifice.[127] Although this latter path attains its most prominent position in the Upaniṣads, it is consonant with certain developments in Brāhmaṇic sacrificial thought. In particular, these developments seem to have been initiated by problems arising from the fact that the sacrificer (*yajamāna*) did not perform the sacrifice himself but depended upon a number of sacrificial priests (*ṛtvij*) to perform the rite for his benefit. Both the officiants and the sacrificer were supposed to accrue merit through the same sacrificial performance.[128] The authors of the Brāhmaṇas began to question the logic of this system: could both those who performed the sacrifice and those for whom the sacrifice was performed attain the rewards of the same sacrifice?[129] The interiorization of the sacrifice resolves this problem by removing the dichotomy between priest and sacrificer (*yajamāna*). [130]

Those who follow the traditional path of worship attain after death the "path of the fathers" (*pitṛyāna*). This path leads them from the smoke of the cremation fire upward through several of the spheres of the cosmos, to the world of the fathers and finally to the moon, where they remain "only as long as there is the residue [of sacrificial merit]."[131] Following this otherworldly sojourn those who follow this path are said to "return again as they came," a process that ends with reentry into the human birth cycle. The nature of this journey reflects the nature of the traditional ritual performance with its corporate format. Because the sacrificer (*yajamāna*) depended on a number of ritual specialists to perform the sacrifice for his benefit, the sacrificer realized the results of the sacrifice indirectly. According to Brāhmaṇic ritual theory, the sacrificer ransoms the merit of the sacrifice through the giving of sacrificial gifts (*dakṣiṇā*) to the priests who perform the ritual.[132] A passage in the Śatapatha Brāhmaṇa describes how, through the agency of the *dakṣiṇā*, the sacrificer acquires the fruits of his sacrifice: "That sacrifice of his goes to the world of the gods, after that goes the *dakṣiṇā* which he gives [to the officiants], and holding on to the *dakṣiṇā* is the sacrificer."[133] Accordingly, in these Upaniṣadic passages, "sacrificial giving" is said to be the chief characteristic of the traditional path of sacrifice.[134]

The problem of acquiring the merit of the sacrifice that arose from the employment of ritual specialists was compounded by the sacrificer's myriad ritual obligations. For, in the traditional sacrificial format, the sacrificer's ritual efforts were undertaken not only for his own benefit, but also for the benefit of his ancestors.[135] Accordingly, those who follow this path of worship and attain the *pitṛyāna* after death do not seem to be able to take total possession of their heavenly store of merit; the pattern of sacrificing for the benefit of others seems, according to one passage in the Brāhmaṇas, to continue in the conditions of the afterlife: "The fathers and grandfathers, swift as thought, approach him (saying): 'What, dear son, have you brought us?' He should answer them: 'Whatever good I have done that is yours.' "[136] A similar fate seems to be implied in the Bṛhadāraṇyaka Upaniṣad's description of the *pitṛyāna* as the sacrificer, upon reaching the moon, is said to become "food," and there the gods feed on him.[137] Because the deceased must share himself, or his accumulated store of sacrificial merit, he does not attain a full and lasting afterlife existence, but remains there "only as long as there is the residue [of his sacrificial merit]"[138] and reenters the cycle of generation.

On the other hand, those who follow the interiorized path of sacrifice attain a lasting afterlife in the world of Brahmā. The chief characteristic of this path is knowledge—its followers are thus described in these passages as "those who know"[139]—an experience that cannot be shared, for it signifies, in its attainment, the unity of subject and object.[140] The singular nature of this attainment is already apparent in one passage in the Śatapatha Brāhmaṇa that describes the world attained by knowledge as the place where sacrificial gifts (*dakṣiṇā*) do not go;[141] that is, an experience independent of the ritual specialists. In the Upaniṣads this independence continues in the development of an interiorized sacrifice; its unfragmented nature, centering entirely on the individual, is thus mirrored in the conditions of the afterlife.

The attainment of the *devayāna* or the *pitṛyāna* reflects the Brāhmaṇic notion that specific ritual acts lead to the attainment of specific "worlds"; thus, for example, the performer of the infamous Gosava rite, which requires the sacrificer to imitate a bull, is said to "win the world of the bull."[142] Several passages in the early Upaniṣads continue to suggest this principle: the Bṛhadāraṇyaka Upaniṣad describes the Pārikṣitas, known as horse sacrificers, simply as going "to the place where the performers of the horse sacrifice are";[143] and those who meditate on the breaths as "winning complete union with that divinity and residence in the same world with him."[144] Other Upaniṣadic passages, however, extend this principle as they extol ritual performances that lead to the winning of all the worlds; that is, to the attainment of the cosmos as a whole. A passage in the Chāndogya Upaniṣad, thus answers the question, Where is the world of the sacrificer? by describing a series of rites, the performance of which lead the sacrificer to the world of Agni (the earth), to the world of Vāyu (the atmosphere), and finally to the world of the Ādityas (the heavens).[145]

The notion of attaining a series of worlds, of becoming integrated into the cosmos as a whole, seems to be the intent of the several Upaniṣadic passages identified as early formulations of the karma doctrine. The description of the fate of the deceased in the Bṛhadāraṇyaka Upaniṣad—"the speech of this dead person enters into the fire (*agni*); the breath into air (*vāta*); the eye into the sun (*āditya*); the mind into the moon (*candra*); hearing into the quarters (*diś*)"[146]—represents this notion by drawing on the symbolism of the Vedic cosmogony. The sacrificer, after death unites with the various spheres of the cosmos that "in the beginning" arose from the body of a primordial anthropomorphic being (Puruṣa, Prajāpati). Similarly, the notion of attaining progressively "newer and more beautiful forms, either [that of] a father, or a *gandharva*, or a god, or Prajāpati, or Brahmā,"[147] suggests the attainment of a number of spheres leading up to an integration with the cosmos as a whole, a notion represented here by the figures of Prajāpati and Brahmā; for their "worlds" are the cosmos.[148] This same level of attainment seems to be implied in the description of the *devayāna*, according to which the deceased travels through a number of cosmic spheres and arrives finally at the "world" of Brahmā.[149]

The *pitṛyāna*, which also leads the sacrificer to the attainment of a series of worlds, differs from the *devayāna* by leading the sacrificer back to this world; that is, those who attain the *pitṛyāna* do not attain a complete and lasting integration into the cosmos, but instead reenter the cycle of birth and death in this world. The difference between these two paths is prefigured in the Brāhmaṇas in the notion that the cosmos is divided into an immortal realm where the gods dwell and a mortal realm of "these creatures [who] die."[150] This distinction is also seen in the Brāhmaṇic representation of Prajāpati, the upper half of whose (cosmic) body is said to be immortal, the lower half mortal.[151] And, although those who attain the *pitṛyāna* remain within this "lower half," the *pitṛyāna* itself—leading the sacrificer from smoke to the night, to the fom night, to the sun, to the moon—suggests an integration with the cosmos similar to that described in the other Upaniṣadic karma passages; namely, an integration into the several spheres of the cosmos that is, at the same time, the body of the primordial man.

All in all the passages identified as early representations of the karma doctrine base the attainments of the afterlife on the model of the sacrifice. As Jan Gonda has succinctly noted: "every great sacrifice is a repetition of the archetypal sacrifice in which Prajāpati . . . while being dismembered, was transformed into the universe."[152] Does this mean, however, that the type of activity valued in moral terms ("one becomes good by good action, bad by bad") in these passages is implicitly limited to the activity of the sacrifice? This question can be answered only by first looking to the unique view of the sacrifice promulgated in the Upaniṣads; namely, that the activity of the sacrifice is not limited to a specific ritual arena but is commensurate with life itself. This notion differs, for the most part, from the view found in the Brāhmaṇas, that only those activities performed by the sacrificer after his initiation (*dīkṣā*) have an effect on the outcome of the sacrifice.[153] A passage in the Chāndogya Upaniṣad thus describes how a man's life represents the activity of the sacrifice:

> Indeed, a person is a sacrifice. His (first) twenty-four years is the morning libation. The *gāyatrī* has twenty-four syllables, and the morning libation is [offered with] the *gāyatrī*. . . . Next the forty-four years, that is the midday libation. The *triṣṭubh* has forty-four syllables, and the midday libation is [offered with] the *triṣṭubh*. . . . And next the forty-eight years, that is the third libation. The *jagatī* has forty-eight syllables, and the third libation is [offered with] the *jagatī*.[154]

Seen in this way, all actions occur within the limits of the ritual—for the ritual's only limitation is life itself—and, thus, all actions ultimately affect its outcome. These results are then manifested in the attainments of the afterlife, which represent the cumulative effects of a lifetime of (sacrificial) activity.

The notion that an individual's life is commensurate with the sacrifice is consonant with the development in Upaniṣadic thought of the interiorized sacrifice, with its emphasis on knowledge. For knowledge, unlike action, is not readily delimited; that is, the individual does not stop "knowing thus" outside the sacrificial arena. The Upaniṣadic thinkers, however, continued to recognize a traditional sacrificial format, the nature of which was reflected in the limitations of the *pitṛyāna*. Just as this form of sacrifice is confined to a certain arena, limiting the sacrificial performance to one aspect of the many that constitute a person's life, so those who follow this path after death do not attain a complete and lasting integration into the cosmos, but remain within the "mortal" realm that leads to a reentry into the sphere of human birth and death. Nonetheless, the description of the *pitṛyāna* that occurs in the Chāndogya Upaniṣad suggests that similar to the interiorized sacrifice, the attainments of the afterlife of those who follow the traditional sacrificial format are based on actions that extend beyond the sacrificial performance:[155] "For those who have been of pleasant conduct here, the consequence is that they attain a pleasant womb, either the womb of a Brahman, Kṣatriya, or a Vaiśya. But for those whose conduct has been stinking the consequence is that they attain a stinking womb, either the womb of a dog, a hog, or an outcaste (*caṇḍāla*)."[156]

Among the several early Upaniṣadic passages that relate an individual's actions prior to death to the conditions of the afterlife ("one becomes good by good action, bad by bad"), this passage corresponds most closely to the formulation of the karma doctrine in the later Hindu tradition.[157] Unlike the terms employed in the other Upaniṣadic texts to denote good and bad actions, the terms used here—*pleasant conduct* (*ramaṇīya-caraṇa*) and *stinking conduct* (*kapūya-caraṇa*)—do not appear to be rooted strictly in the activity of the sacrifice.[158] In other words, this passage is unique in apparently referring to a moral valuation of action in general. Yet, among the several karma passages, this passage, which is attached to the description of the *pitṛyāna*, refers specifically to the traditional sacrificial format; that is, this passage alone describes a form of worship confined to the ritual arena and not equated with life itself. As such this passage suggests how the doctrine of action in the Upaniṣads was extended from the activity and results of the sacrifice to include all actions and their consequences. At the same time, it suggests how in the early Upaniṣads the karma doctrine brought to closure doctrines already under consideration in Brāhmaṇic thought regarding the affects of the ritual performance in the conditions of the afterlife.

Several discussions that appear in the Brāhmaṇas indicate the Brāhmaṇic thinkers recognized two types of sacrifice: the traditional sacrificial format and a form of sacrifice that emphasizes the individual to the point of excluding the priests and perhaps even the gods.[159] Although the Brāhmaṇic authors still asked: "Which [of these two forms of sacrifice] is better?"[160] at least one discussion in the Śatapatha Brāhmaṇa suggests the traditional ritual format led to distressing results in the afterlife:

> now who performs these [rites] for another, he causes these oceans [the rites] to dry up [for himself]; those dried up, his meters are dried up; after the meters, the world [*loka*]; after the world, the body (*ātman*); after the body, (his) children and cattle. Indeed he becomes poorer (*pāpīyas*) daily, who performs these rites for another. . . . now who does not perform these [rites] for another becomes more pros-

> perous (*śreyas*) daily. Indeed this [rite] is his divine, undying, body (*ātman*); who performs these [rites] for another gives his divine body to another. Only a dried trunk remains.[161]

This passage suggests the Prajāpati model, with its emphasis on the single sacrificer,[162] was viewed by at least some Brāhmaṇic thinkers as the exclusive model for the sacrifice; the notion that "a dried trunk" rewarded those who followed a traditional path of worship (indicated here by the practice of performing for another) effectively represents the denial of this mode of worship.[163] The severity of this view is lessened in the Upaniṣads in the contrast between the respective afterlife attainments of those who attain the *devayāna* and those who attain the *pitṛyāna*. Although these afterlife attainments are based on a distinction in performance similar to that described in the Brāhmaṇa passage cited earlier, unlike this Brāhmaṇa passage, the formulation of the *pitṛyāna* indicates that those who follow the traditional sacrificial format do attain an afterlife existence. Moreover, this afterlife existence resembles to a degree the attainments of the *devayāna*, as the *pitṛyāna*—albeit on a different level from that proposed by the *devayāna*—leads the deceased to an integration with the cosmos, thus reenacting Prajāpati's cosmogonic activity. This relationship suggests that rather than denying the traditional sacrificial format, the Upaniṣadic thinkers were concerned with assimilating it to the Prajāpati model; for, as the normative model in Upaniṣadic thought, promulgated in the form of the "interiorized" sacrifice with its emphasis on knowledge, the assertion of its dominance no longer required the rejection of an earlier form.

The Upaniṣadic attempt to correlate two types of worship within the single paradigm of Prajāpati's sacrifice led, I believe, to the promotion of the idea that even for those who follow the traditional sacrificial format—despite its sharply delimited nature—all actions, not just those associated with the ritual performance, affect the conditions of the afterlife. In other words, the conduct of those worshippers following the traditional ritual format was viewed in the same way as the conduct of those following the "interiorized" sacrifice, which was not limited to a specific arena or to a certain aspect of an individual's life. On the one hand, the nature of the *devayāna*, an abiding integration into the world of Brahmā, reflects the "otherworldly" nature of the activity of those who follow the interiorized path of worship: life itself is the activity of the sacrifice. On the other hand, the nature of the *pitṛyāna*, which leads the sacrificer back to this world, reflects the "this worldly" nature of the activity of those who follow the traditional path of worship: except for those acts contained within the sacrificial arena, actions are mundane. Accordingly, the *pitṛyāna* leads finally to this world and the attainment, "for those who have been of pleasant conduct," to a birth as a Brahman, Kṣatriya, or Vaiśya, or, "for those whose conduct has been stinking," to a birth as an animal or an outcaste.[164]

The point that draws the Upaniṣadic karma doctrine out of the realm of ritual activity is simultaneously the point that leads back to the model of the sacrifice. For, only when the activity of the sacrifice became equated with all activity—that is, with life itself—did the Upaniṣadic thinkers begin to envision a doctrine of the moral efficacy of actions that actually were disconnected to the sacrifice. And, although this notion of the moral efficacy of all actions is itself unprecedented in the Brāhmaṇic texts, its presentation in the Upaniṣads suggests it represents the culmination of views that had emerged in Brāhmaṇic thought regarding the relationship between (sacrificial) acts, those performed by the individual sacrificer and those performed by the ritual specialists, and their effects in the conditions of the afterlife.

Conclusion: The Karma Doctrine in the Context of Brāhmaṇic Thought

In this chapter, I have emphasized the continuity of the Upaniṣadic and the Brāhmaṇic traditions and, in particular, the continuity of the Upaniṣadic karma doctrine with the Brāhmaṇic ritual world view. In part, I have emphasized the continuity of these traditions to counter the pervasive bias against the Brāhmaṇas that stands at the foundation of Western Indology. The result of this bias has been a tendency to remove the Upaniṣadic tradition from its historical and conceptual context. In the case of the karma doctrine this failure to investigate, or even to acknowledge, the Brāhmaṇic structures that continue to assert themselves in the thought of the Upaniṣads has been particularly damaging, for scholars tended to view the karma doctrine from its successors, which measure the moral efficacy of actions in all contexts, rather than from its antecedents, which are concerned with the moral effects of ritual action. By not understanding or by simply misrepresenting this Vedic substratum, scholars of an earlier generation believed the appearance of the karma doctrine in the Upaniṣads meant that the Brāhmaṇic notion of the rewards of the sacrifice was no longer considered to be effective; as Deussen remarked: "strictly speaking the entire [Brāhmaṇic] conception of recompense is destroyed."[165] Viewed in this way the karma doctrine represented to these scholars the point of separation between the thought of the Upaniṣads and the thought of the Brāhmaṇas.

Although in this chapter I have emphasized the continuity of the Brāhmaṇic and Upaniṣadic traditions, it is not accurate to assert that the Upaniṣads are entirely inseparable from the Brāhmaṇic tradition—undeniably, even the earliest Upaniṣads express views that are unprecedented in the Brāhmaṇas—or that the karma doctrine in its earliest appearances in the Upaniṣads has the same meaning as karma in later Upaniṣadic and in later Indian thought. In investigating karma's earliest manifestations in the Upaniṣads I have sought primarily to isolate the Vedic antecedents of karma and, thereby, to show that karma does have a prehistory in Vedic thought, an understanding of which is critical to an understanding of the karma doctrine in its earliest appearances in the Upaniṣads. For, the Upaniṣadic karma doctrine continues to develop the structures underlying Brāhmaṇic ritual thought.

In the following chapters, I shall turn to a detailed examination of what is perhaps the chief structure underlying Brāhmaṇic ritual thought; that is, the notion that the cosmos itself arose from the primordial sacrifice of an anthropomorphic being (Puruṣa-Prajāpati). The ideology of this event seems to have been the point from which the Brāhmaṇic ritualists began to question the nature of the sacrificial format—in particular, focusing on the problem of (ritual) death and how it affected, as well as its effect on, the traditional relationship between the sacrificer and the ritual specialists employed by the sacrificer to perform the rites for his benefit. Although the Brāhmaṇic authors naturally framed their discussions in terms of the sacrifice (in developments in both practice and theory), they nevertheless addressed the fundamental questions of human existence: the nature of life and death and man's relationship to the larger cosmos in which he exists. However, the Brāhmaṇic doctrines that treat these fundamental questions, largely as a result of their being constantly related to a ritual format developed over many centuries, are sometimes ambiguous, at other times inconsistent. The Upaniṣadic karma doctrine, which is not only prefigured in these Brāhmaṇic doctrines but is presented as the textual successor to them, represents an important interpretive tool in clarifying their ambiguities. To utilize the karma doctrine toward this end I have "reintroduced" it into its proper historical and conceptual context of Brāhmaṇic ritual thought.

2.

The Cosmos as Man: The Image of the Cosmos in Vedic Thought

In the preceding chapter the attainments of the afterlife—the various paths and states—that contextualize the Upaniṣadic karma doctrine were shown to be prefigured in the thought of the Brāhmaṇas. In particular, these attainments correspond to the Brāhmaṇic idea of *saloka*, having "a world together with" one or another of the constituents that represent the various planes (*loka*) of the Vedic cosmos.[1] In the Brāhmaṇas, the notion of *saloka* is linked to the activity of the sacrifice; the performance of specific rites leads the sacrificer, apparently even before his death, to a union with certain worlds:

> Who sacrifices the Vaiśvadeva [sacrifice] becomes Agni, then indeed, he attains a world, closely united, together with Agni; who offers the Varuṇa-*praghāsa* becomes Varuṇa, then indeed, he attains a world, closely united, together with Varuna; and who offers the Sākamedha offering becomes Indra, then indeed, he attains a world, closely united, together with Indra.[2]

The role of the sacrifice in leading the individual to the attainment of a world reflects the creative nature of this activity; as Jan Gonda has observed: "each performance of the rite holding out a prospect of divinization or of winning a foundation or a residence in heaven, the rite may be said to promote a new 'rising' of the *loka*."[3] However, ritual activity, which consists of a series of predetermined and precisely ordered events, creates through recreating; as the Brāhmaṇas express it: "This [ritual act] done now is that which the gods did then [in the beginning]."[4] What the gods did then was to create the cosmos, an event that the Vedic texts depict as having occurred through the sacrifice of a primordial anthropomorphic figure. The ritual act that enables the sacrificer to become *saloka* entails the re-creation of this primordial sacrifice;[5] just as the body of the primeval being was transformed into the cosmos, so, too, the individual becomes "one together with the cosmos" through his own ritual activity.

Theoretically, every great (*śrauta*) sacrifice replicates the cosmogonic activity of the primordial man.[6] In practice, however, only a few of the rites in the Vedic corpus exhibit an explicit concern with the re-creation of this event. This situation reflects the peculiar relationship between theory and practice in the development of the Vedic ritual tradition. Although the Indian tradition is notorious for the impenetrability of its history, the establishment of the majority of the Vedic rites appears to have preceded the articulation of the theory that the ritual replicates the event of a primordial anthropomorphic sacrifice. Thus, while many of the basic ritual forms that appear in the Brāhmaṇas are in evidence throughout the Ṛgveda, the notion of a primordial anthropomorphic sacrifice, presented in the Brāhmaṇas as the regnant cosmogony, is first articulated only in the latest stratum of the Ṛgveda.[7] Of course, the absence of this theory in the textual tradition does not preclude its presence in Vedic thought; the idea of a cosmogonic sacrifice apparently persisted from the Vedic people's Indo-European past and seems also to have been an important part of the indigenous Indian beliefs that, throughout much of the Ṛgvedic period, were gradually absorbed into the Vedic religion. However, the Ṛgvedic rituals do not appear to be founded on the theory of a cosmogonic sacrifice (though they do replicate other cosmogonic motifs),[8] and this indicates that the early ritual forms actually preceded the establishment of the ritual theory, with which virtually all the *śrauta* rites were later identified, of the cosmic man's sacrifice.

In the post Ṛgvedic texts, the Brāhmaṇas, the notion of the primordial cosmogonic sacrifice was propounded as the foundation of the entire Vedic ritual corpus. Although the implementation of this theory did lead to the addition of new rituals, the older ritual forms did not fall into disuse. In fact, these older rituals are not only highly visible in the texts of this period but are occasionally called on to exemplify the reenactment of the cosmogonic sacrifice of the primordial man.[9] Furthermore, the older rites were used in various combinations to constitute the new rites, such as the Agnicayana, which appear to have been created for the precise purpose of re-creating the cosmogonic sacrifice of the primeval man.[10] Employing the older rituals in this way—though it often forced the authors of the Brāhmaṇas to assert identifications between entities that had no obvious relationship (a process said to characterize the Brāhmaṇic enterprise in general)[11]—lent the authority of tradition to the notion of the sacrifice of a primordial anthropomorphic being.

Despite its late appearance the notion of a primordial sacrifice of a "cosmic man" (Puruṣa, Prajāpati) was not entirely unheralded in Vedic thought. In particular, the connection between the sacrifice and the sacrificer, which stands at the center of this notion, was, as Julius Eggeling noted, "an essential and intimate one from the beginning of the sacrificial practice."[12] The sacrificial stake (*yūpa*), which was used since the Ṛgvedic period to bind the victim at the ritual,[13] demonstrates this relationship between sacrificer and sacrifice. In the traditional ritual format the sacrificer (*yajamāna*) stood outside the action of the ritual, in part, to minimize the danger to his own person.[14] In his place at the center of the ritual arena an animal or another substitute victim was bound to the *yūpa*. To demonstrate the intimate relationship between the victim bound to the *yūpa* and the sacrificer standing outside the ritual arena, the *yūpa* was made to be a representation of the sacrificer himself; according to one passage in the Taittirīya Saṃhitā, the stake was erected to the same height as the sacrificer, and thus was "as great as the sacrificer."[15] Through his identification with the *yūpa*, the sacrificer—at least, symbolically—thus bound himself to the sacrificial victim.

To extend, from this point, the intimate link between the sacrificer and the sacrifice into the notion of a primordial anthropomorphic sacrifice, a model that truly represents man as the sacrificial victim, requires no great imaginative leap; at the very least, its theoretical base is consonant with trends long established in Vedic ritual thought. The application of this theory, however, placed demands on the ritual that threatened to break its carefully delimited boundaries. In particular, the notion of the primordial sacrifice implies that the sacrificer must give up his own life to re-create the cosmogony. How the Vedic thinkers responded to this challenge represents a decisive point in the development of the Vedic tradition, for this challenge appears to have been instrumental in the shift from the external performance of the sacrificial rite to the "interiorized" sacrifice of the Upaniṣads.

In this chapter, I examine the Vedic notion of the cosmic man: how it represents the cosmos and what this representation means for the sacrificer, whose ritual actions are based on the model of the cosmic man's primordial sacrifice. Because the notion of the cosmic man subsumes earlier depictions of the Vedic cosmos this examination requires a brief exploration of Vedic cosmology. Following this I turn to the image of the cosmic man as it first appears in the Ṛgveda, attending, in particular, to the unique demands on the human sacrificer placed by this image, with its underlying notion of an equation between man and cosmos, a notion that appears to be unprecedented in early Vedic thought. The image and ideology of the cosmic man in the Ṛgveda leads to what is the most elaborate account of the cosmic man myth in the Vedic literature; namely, the creation myth that accompanies the Agnicayana ritual in the Śatapatha Brāhmaṇa. Here I focus on how this myth transforms the Ṛgvedic notion of the cosmic man and what this transformation implies for the late Vedic world view.

The Cosmic Image and Its Vicissitudes in Vedic Thought

The Vedic texts contain several depictions of the shape of the cosmos. The Ṛgveda alone contains two basic images of the cosmos:[16] a bipartite cosmos, consisting of the two spheres of heavens and earth,[17] and a tripartite cosmos, consisting of the three spheres of heavens, atmosphere, and earth.[18] The bipartite cosmic image of heavens and earth (*dyāvā-pṛthivī*), which appears .o be closely related to other Indo-European cosmologies, is generally considered to be the earlier of these two images.[19] The tripartite cosmos, which became the favored image in the Ṛgveda,[20] subsumes the features of the bipartite cosmos—the heavens and the earth—and adds to them an atmospheric region. However, the transformation from the bipartite to the tripartite cosmos does not seem to have been made merely for the sake of astronomic precision. In fact, the creation of the tripartite cosmic image reflects a complex of ideas and associations of which the delineation of a region between the heavens and the earth may be the least important.

The Vedic poet's lack of concern with the precise cosmographic relationship of the atmospheric region to the established cosmic image of the heavens and the earth is apparent from the ambiguous name they assigned to it: the *intermediate space* (*antarikṣa*).[21] The idea of an "intermediate" space may not only imply location but also refer in a general way to the extension of two into three. Thus, the location of the three spheres of the cosmos at times seems less important than its triple nature: there are references to three earths, three atmospheres, and three heavens.[22] And although the "intermediate space" is sometimes found between the heavens and the earth, in some instances this sphere seems to be positioned beneath the earth.[23] These points suggest that the tripartite cosmic image may have its most important antecedents in an aspect of Vedic thought that saw a special significance in triplicity and that it does not represent an advancement in the astronomic sophistication of the Vedic poets.[24]

In the Śatapatha Brāhmaṇa the Ṛgvedic tripartite cosmos yields to the image of a pentadic cosmos.[25] Just as the tripartite cosmos was inclusive of the constituents of the earlier bipartite cosmos, so, too, the pentadic cosmos includes the three spheres of earth, atmosphere, and heavens. And, similar to the earlier transformation from a bipartite to a tripartite cosmos, the constituents of the preceding image serve to orient the later image. Thus, the pentadic cosmos is created through the addition of two intermediate regions—one between the earth and the atmosphere and one between the atmosphere and the heavens—to the tripartite cosmos of earth, atmosphere, and heavens. In the Śatapatha Brāhmaṇa these newly added regions bear the same sort of indistinct appellation seen in the Ṛgveda's naming of the atmospheric region as the "intermediate space;" these two regions are referred to as "what is above the earth and on this side of the atmosphere,"[26] and "what is above the atmosphere and on this side of the heavens."[27] Although these terms imply location, the precise cosmographic relationship of the five spheres is overshadowed by the fact that there are five of them. For example, the authors refer to five regions beneath the sun and five regions above the sun,[28] an image that exceeds ordinary cosmography. These points again indicate that the pentadic cosmic image was not developed as an expression of a sophisticated cosmography (though this pentadic imagery certainly suggests a sophisticated *cosmology*). Rather, in the Śatapatha Brāhmaṇa, the notion of a fivefold cosmos is a reflection of the extraordinary importance assigned to pentadic imagery in the thought of this text.[29]

The varied nature of Vedic cosmography has been a source of discouragement to scholars attempting to explicate Vedic notions of the cosmos.[30] Vedic scholarship has thus rarely risen above the view that Vedic cosmology is most notable for its "comparatively indefinite and unsystematic character."[31] However, variety has been improperly equated with inconsistency here, for each of the various depictions of the cosmos appears to be oriented in terms of an earlier image and each draws on the same basic elements of heavens and earth and adds to them one or more intermediate planes. These intermediate planes appear to have no cosmographic significance and, thus, do not affect the shape of the cosmos as much as they do its meaning. As David Knipe has observed "each of the basic triadic, tetradic and pentadic series makes a unique statement."[32]

Knipe refers here to the triad of heavens, atmosphere and earth; the tetrad of the four quarters or directions (*diś*); and the pentad that combines these images and "is quite simply both at once and therefore the most complete expression of all."[33] The extension of three into four, and four into five, is a result of what Knipe has labeled the principle of "x plus one," according to which the extra number "encompasses, succeeds, and completes" the members to which it is added.[34] Thus, the fourfold cosmos adds the four directions to the threefold cosmos of heavens, earth, and atmosphere. And, because the directions are a characteristic of each of the four planes, this added element is not merely a fourth, but a fourth that encompasses the other three elements. Viewed in this way, the extension of the cosmic image, seen throughout the Vedic texts, appears to be a way of re-presenting, apparently on another level of existence, the already existing members of the cosmos.

By the late Vedic period the most significant expression of the cosmic image is found in the figure of the cosmic man (Puruṣa, Prajāpati). In the Ṛgveda the image of the cosmic man (Puruṣa) extends the tripartite cosmos, which is the most common depiction of the cosmos in this text, into a fourfold cosmos. In the Śatapatha Brāhmaṇa, the image of the cosmic man (Prajāpati) extends the

Ṛgvedic Puruṣa's four regions into five. In both instances, however, the cosmos is depicted as being correlative to the body of the cosmic man, and thus, the shape of the cosmos is implicitly that of a man.

To express the notion of an all-encompassing added member in this anthropomorphic cosmos, the Vedic thinkers turned to the peculiar relationship of the mind and the body that characterizes human existence. Although the mind partakes in all levels of physical experience, it also has the capacity to experience independently things that usually belong to the physical realm. Moreover, the presence of the mind is not limited to any one particular sphere of physical existence but seems to encompass all its aspects. This is perhaps best exemplified in Vedic thought in the role of the Brahman priest; as Wendy O'Flaherty has observed: "This priest, the Brahman, did absolutely nothing; his job was to sit there and to *think* the sacrifice while the others *did* it."[35] The relationship between the Brahman's mental experience and the other priests' physical experience reflects the nature of the mind as the embodiment—albeit on its own unique level of experience—of all physical experience. Accordingly, a passage in the Bṛhadāraṇyaka Upaniṣad declares that the Brahman priest, with his mind alone wins an "unlimited" world, whereas the other priests (*udgātṛ*, *hotṛ*, *adhvaryu*) win by their efforts at the sacrifice only one or another world.[36] Just as the mind encompasses the sum of physical experience, so, too, the cosmos founded on Puruṣa (or, in the Brāhmaṇas, Prajāpati) has an inner or essential aspect that seems to encompass the entire physical universe.

The Vedic mythology of the cosmic man presents this relationship between gross and subtle existence, body and mind, in its depiction of the cosmos in a way that suggests the cosmos itself replicates human existence. Accordingly, this mythology posits an integral relationship between man and world.

Puruṣa and the Creation of the Cosmos

The Puruṣasūkta (Ṛgveda 10.90) represents Puruṣa's creative activity as consisting of two distinct phases. In the first phase, Puruṣa's creative activity is described as a "spreading asunder" (*vi-/kram*): "With three quarters Puruṣa rose upwards; one quarter of him remained here. From that he spread asunder in all directions, to what eats and does not eat."[37] The places to which Puruṣa spreads himself are necessarily indistinct; at this point in the cosmogony the specific spheres of the cosmos—heavens, atmosphere, earth, and so forth—are still uncreated. The idea of the undefined primordial cosmos is expressed in another well-known creation hymn, Ṛgveda 10.129, which states that in the beginning: "There was neither existence nor non-existence then; there was neither the realm of space nor the sky beyond."[38] Puruṣa's initial task thus appears to be to establish a material foundation in this primordial absence. And because "Puruṣa is this all, what has been and what will be,"[39] he accomplishes this task by spreading himself into the unformed cosmos; that is, by establishing himself as the stuff or *materia prima* of creation.

The second phase of Puruṣa's creative activity brings forth the manifest cosmos (the earth, atmosphere, and heavens) and its animate constituents (sun, moon, winds, humankind, and wild and domestic animals). This second phase of creation is accomplished through a sacrifice in which Puruṣa is the sacrificial victim: "That sacrifice, Puruṣa born in the beginning, they consecrated on the sacred grass. With him the gods, Sādhyas, and [those] who [were] seers sacrificed."[40]

The form of this sacrifice is dismemberment.[41] Puruṣa's body represents the whole of the undifferentiated cosmos; to bring forth the manifest cosmos, with its several constituents, this whole must be broken up into distinct parts. The act of breaking apart is, of course, potentially an act of disordering. Here, the order that Puruṣa's anthropomorphic features lend to the unformed cosmos is instrumental in the emergence of an ordered cosmos. The Puruṣasūkta poses a series of questions that point to the importance of these features in the act of creating the cosmos: "When they divided Puruṣa, into how many parts did they apportion him? What [became] of his mouth? What [of his] two arms? What are [his] two thighs, [his] two feet called?"[42]

As this verse indicates, Puruṣa's body is distinguished by four points of reference: his head (represented by his mouth), trunk (represented by his arms), pelvis (represented by his thighs), and lower legs (or feet). In conjunction with the notion, "With three quarters he rose upwards; one quarter of him remained here," expressed in a previous verse, these reference points suggest a specific cosmic orientation to Puruṣa's body. Now this orientation lends itself to the emergence of an ordered cosmos, that is, one in which the spheres of the cosmos are correlative to Puruṣa's body parts: "From his navel the atmosphere arose; from his head the heavens; from his two feet the earth; from his ear the quarters: thus they fashioned the worlds."[43]

The general features of the cosmos that emerges from this act correspond to the features of the tripartite image of earth, atmosphere, and heavens seen throughout the Vedic texts and in the Ṛgveda in particular.[44] The addition of a fourth region, the quarters, which represents the four cardinal points, seems to have been made here not to effect a radical transformation in the basic cosmic image but to effect a shift from the established tripartite cosmic image to an image of a fourfold cosmos, in particular, one based on the notion of the cosmic man's body.[45] That this fourth region mediates between the traditional tripartite cosmic image and Puruṣa's fourfold nature is apparent from the unrestricted nature of the quarters; in the Vedic literature, they are not distinguished from any single cosmic plane but represent a characteristic of the cosmos as a whole.[46] However, although the addition of this fourth region does not radically alter the tripartite cosmic image, the establishment of a definite correlation between Puruṣa's body and the ordered cosmos represents a significant innovation in Vedic cosmological thought. The image of the cosmos this correlation establishes is wholly personal; that is, the cosmos, or its foundation, is imagined here as a man, with the earth founded on his feet, and the heavens on his head.

Along with its depiction of the emergence of the gross planes of the cosmos from Puruṣa's body, the Puruṣasūkta describes the origin, from Puruṣa's head, of several constituents that inhabit the cosmos: "The moon was born from his mind; from his eye the sun was born; from his mouth Indra and Agni; from his breath the winds were born."[47] According to the Puruṣasūkta's description of the emergence of the gross planes of the cosmos, the region of the heavens is correlative to Puruṣa's head. However, among the constituents depicted in this verse as emerging from Puruṣa's head—the moon, the sun, Indra and Agni, and the winds—only the sun clearly belongs to the region of the heavens; in Vedic mythology

Agni (fire) is generally associated with the earth, the winds with the atmosphere, and the moon with the quarters.[48] Clearly, Puruṣa's "head" here must be distinguished from that which founds the region of the heavens. Whereas the head from which the heavens emerge is an aspect of Puruṣa's gross body, the head from which these various elements arise represents the subtle aspect of Puruṣa's existence. The mind, eye, mouth, and ear, which are the loci of sensation, represent the underlying or inner nature of man's material being.

The origination of the various natural phenomena, each of which represents a particular cosmic plane, from Puruṣa's head suggests that the head contains the whole of the cosmos. In fact, their relationship to the specific parts of Puruṣa's head reflects the orientation of the gross cosmos to Puruṣa's body. The relationship of Agni to the mouth below, of the sun to the eyes above, and of the wind to the nose or ears that lie inbetween,[49] thus reflects the hierarchy of earth, atmosphere, and heavens, whereas the relationship of the moon to the mind, which seems to be everywhere at once, reflects the ubiquitous presence of the quarters. These relationships suggest that Puruṣa's head is a microcosm of the manifest cosmos (which is at once his body):

Puruṣa's Body:	Gross Cosmos:	Cosmic Phenomenon:	Puruṣa's Head:
head	heavens	sun	eye
navel	atmosphere	winds	nose/ears
feet	earth	fire	mouth
ear	quarters	moon	mind

The correlation between Puruṣa's "head" and the moon, sun, Agni, and the winds—that is, the natural phenomena that animate the various cosmic regions—and Puruṣa's body and the material planes of earth, atmosphere, and heavens establishes a two-tier cosmic image. This image, which is represented as a man, reflects the dual nature of human existence; that is, the material body and the immaterial spirit or that which animates the material body.[50] As such, it attests to the precise nature of the correlation between man and cosmos.

The Reenactment of the Cosmogony

Mircea Eliade has stated that the "cosmogony is the exemplary model for every creative situation."[51] In late Vedic thought, the Puruṣasūkta clearly represents such a model. However, the Ṛgveda contains several cosmogonies, and in the early Vedic epochs, these myths clearly represented the "exemplary models" for many creative (ritual) situations. For example, the chief cosmogonic myth of the early Ṛgveda is the slaying of Vṛtra by Indra and Indra's subsequent separation of the heavens and the earth through propping up the sky with the cosmic tree or pillar.[52] This event was reenacted by erecting a pole at the New Year's festival,[53] and also seems to have been an important part of the mythical background in the many Vedic rituals that featured some type of agonistic encounter.[54] Although the ascendancy of the Ṛgvedic Puruṣa myth very nearly obliterated these ritual practices and the myths that engendered them,[55] it is nevertheless apparent that this older complex has a different ideological orientation than that implied by the Puruṣa cosmogony. In particular, the Puruṣasūkta's assertion of an equation between man and cosmos seems to be unprecedented in the cosmological thought of the early Vedic period.

Nonetheless, by the period of the Brāhmaṇas, the replication of the creative activity of the primordial man represents a fundamental aspect of the sacrificial theory;[56] according to Gonda: "By identifying oneself with the mythical Puruṣa and by ritually repeating the mythical event and so reactivating its inherent power for the benefit of oneself and with a view to one's own reintegration one believed oneself to achieve one's own 'rebirth.' "[57] The idea that the cosmos arose from the body of a primeval man leads to the belief that man might potentially integrate himself with the cosmos. The correlation the Puruṣa cosmogony establishes between body and cosmos, senses and natural phenomena, clearly facilitates the process of integration. However, with the exception of the funeral ritual—the "final sacrifice" (*antyeṣṭi*)—the complete replication of the cosmic man's activity, and hence man's realization of his cosmic potential, creates an untenable situation. A. B. Keith, following Sylvain Levi, observed that in Brāhmaṇic thought: "The sacrifice is essentially commensurate with man, and the conclusion is not doubtfully drawn that the sacrifice should be the sacrifice of man himself. . . . The conclusion would, therefore, appear to be that the perfect form of sacrifice would be suicide.[58] As Keith points out, however, suicide is never mentioned in the Brāhmaṇas.[59] Though it fulfills the requisites of the sacrificial theory, suicide would prevent the sacrificer from meeting his obligation to the gods and the fathers, whom he sustains through the continued performance of various ritual acts and the production of offspring.[60]

The Brāhmaṇic thinkers clearly recognized that the replication of Puruṣa's creative activity might require the dismemberment and death of the human sacrificer. Thus, in the ritual literature (Śrauta Sūtras) the Puruṣasūkta was often cited in association with the Puruṣamedha, the "sacrifice of man."[61] Many scholars have questioned whether the Puruṣamedha was ever actually performed or whether it was merely intended to be a symbolic event.[62] Nevertheless, the simple fact that it was included in the ritual corpus, "as a reasonable complement to the theory of sacrifice,"[63] clearly expresses the difficulties that the demands of Puruṣa's cosmogonic sacrifice raised for the human sacrificer.

Perhaps because the sacrificer's death was the intention, though not necessarily the outcome, of the Puruṣamedha, this rite appears to exhibit an exclusive concern with the material aspect of existence, for man's gross body forms the material of the offering. Thus, the description of the Puruṣamedha that appears in the Śatapatha Brāhmaṇa homologizes the sacrificer's body with the material cosmos—equating the feet with the earth, the legs with the region above the earth, the waist with the atmosphere, the trunk with the region above the atmosphere, and the head with the heavens—but does not mention the inner, or animate, aspect of human existence.[64] And, although an oblique reference is made to the subtle aspect of the cosmos's existence,[65] the authors do not assert even a vague correlation between it and man's inner nature.

Although the ritual paradigm of the cosmic man's bodily integration into the planes of the cosmos continues to assert itself in the thought of the Upaniṣads, the acceptance of the practice of "ritual interiorization" seems to have circumvented the necessity of the sacrificer's physical death and dismemberment. As Eliade has observed, in this type of ritual activity, "physiological functions take the place of libations and ritual objects."[66] In the

Upaniṣads these functions are correlated to the various spheres of the cosmos. A passage in the Chāndogya Upaniṣad thus homologizes this inner aspect of human existence with the cosmos through an offering to the various "breaths" (*prāṇa, vyāna, apāna, samāna* and *udāna*), which in Vedic thought represent the organs of sense:[67]

> What should first be offered he should offer [saying], "Hail to the *prāṇa*." . . . The *prāṇa* being satisfied, the eye is satisfied. The eye being satisfied, the sun is satisfied. The sun being satisfied, the heavens are satisfied . . .
>
> Then what should be offered second he should offer [saying], "Hail to the *vyāna*." . . . The *vyāna* being satisfied, the ear is satisfied. The ear being satisfied, the moon is satisfied. The moon being satisfied, the quarters are satisfied . . . [68]

The passage continues to relate, in the same manner, the *apāna* breath to speech, fire, and the earth; the *samāna* breath to the mind, lightening, and the rain; the *udāna* breath to the skin, the winds, and the atmosphere.[69] Whereas the cosmos is depicted here in terms of its dual nature—the material (the gross planes of the heavens, the quarters, and so forth) and the inner or animate (the sun, moon, and so forth)—there is no mention here of man's material being; that is, his physical body. This implies that the Upaniṣadic thinkers saw man's "inner" existence as the summation of his entire being and therefore was relatable to both the material and the inner aspects of the cosmos's existence. Although this correlation raises its own unique set of problems—for the achievement of the activity it proposes, unlike that of the traditional sacrificial format, cannot be verified empirically—it does seem to lift the onus of the sacrificer's physical death in the performance of the rite.

Between these two positions, ideologically and perhaps historically, stands the Agnicayana ritual, a rite that the Brāhmaṇic thinkers presented as the culmination of the Vedic rites. This rite takes to the extreme both performance, in the form of what is perhaps the most complex ceremonial in the Vedic ritual corpus, and knowledge, for each aspect of the ceremony bears a specific metaphysical implication, the knowledge of which makes the rite effective. In so doing, the Agnicayana presents a model for man's own integration into the cosmos that provides for both aspects of his being: the gross body and the inner nature. To attain this end, however, the Agnicayana ritualists effected a subtle shift in the Vedic notion of the cosmic man, represented in the Brāhmaṇas in the figure of Prajāpati, thereby allowing the sacrificer to replicate the cosmogony in his own ritual activity.

Prajāpati and the Creation of the Cosmos

The creation of the cosmos and its inhabitants from the body of a primeval anthropomorphic figure is the central cosmogonic myth of the Brāhmaṇas.[70] Scholars have long recognized that the Brāhmaṇic myth closely resembles Ṛgveda 10.90, the Puruṣasūkta, with the important distinction that in the Brāhmaṇas Prajāpati takes the place of Puruṣa.[71] However, the factors that led to Puruṣa's displacement in the Brāhmaṇic myth have not been precisely determined.

Recent studies have looked to the cultural amalgamation that occurred during the late Vedic period, the period in which the Brāhmaṇas were composed, as the likely cause of Prajāpati's appearance in Puruṣa's place in the Brāhmaṇic cosmogony.[72] Jan Gonda has argued that many of Prajāpati's noncosmogonic characteristics, particularly those that associate him with domestic animals (hence, the name Prajāpati, which means "Lord of Creatures"), indicate that he originated in the "popular" sphere.[73] Gonda suggests that Prajāpati's rise to the position of the cosmic man and "supreme deity" occurred when

> the poets and ritualists, prompted by the inclination to associate elements of the religious tradition of the Aryans in general with elements of sacrificial lore and practice, had begun to credit him with new qualities and functions, and to make him an often central figure of more or less etiological myths and mythical narratives adapted or even concocted for definite ritual purposes, as well as a subject for ritualistic, theological, and philosophical speculation.[74]

The important point here is that the process Gonda describes suggests the existence of certain "outside" pressures to which the Brāhmaṇic ritualists would have had to respond. On the one hand, such pressures may have led the Brāhmaṇic ritualists simply to incorporate the new beliefs and practices they encountered; on the other hand, this situation may have served to provide these ritualists with a measure of freedom in transforming—albeit subtly—already existing traditions.

Prajāpati, as cosmic man, attains his greatest prominence in the Śatapatha Brāhmaṇa—in particular, in the mythology of the Agnicayana ritual, which is the subject of approximately one-third of the Śatapatha Brāhmaṇa.[75] The obviously synthetic nature of the Agnicayana ritual,[76] supports Gonda's supposition that Prajāpati's rise to prominence resulted from the recasting of a "popular" deity into the established Vedic mythology of the cosmic man (Puruṣa). In fact, the authors of the Śatapatha Brāhmaṇa specifically refer to Prajāpati's "integrative" nature; as all levels of worship, from the "popular" to the hieratic, are said to be merely different ways of acknowledging the same cosmic man. In a passage that employs the sort of etymological reasoning typical of the Brāhmaṇas, the authors of the Śatapatha Brāhmaṇa state:

> That one [Prajāpati] called "Agni" the Adhvaryus (Yajurvedins) worship (or acknowledge) him as the "Yajus" indeed because he yokes (/*yuj*) this whole universe. The Chandogas (Sāmavedins) [worship him as] "Sāma" because in him this whole universe is uniform (*samāna*). "Uktha" the Bahvṛcas (Ṛgvedins) [worship him because] he causes this whole universe to be brought forth. "Demon" those skilled in sorcery [worship him] because by him this whole universe is governed. The serpents [worship him as] "poison." The snake charmers [worship him as] "snake." The gods [worship him as] "vigor." Men [worship him as] "material possessions." The asuras [worship him as] "magic." The fathers [worship him as] "*svadhā*."[77]

Significantly, scholars have not seen Prajāpati's appearance in the Brāhmaṇas as an indication of a radical alteration in the Vedic notion of the cosmic man, which had been previously represented in the figure of Puruṣa. Since nearly a century ago when Julius Eggeling noted that "it might seem rather strange that the name [Puruṣa] . . . should have been discarded [in the Brāhmaṇic myth]," scholars seem not to have viewed Puruṣa's displacement as an indication of anything more substantial than an incidental process of renaming.[78] In other words, though Prajāpati may have been appropriated from the "popular" level, his assumption of the role of cosmic man is so thorough in the Brāhmaṇas that he can be distinguished from the Ṛgvedic Puruṣa in name only. This view, however, fails to consider both the special value which the Brāhmaṇic authors attributed to the word of the Ṛgveda, which in the Brāhmaṇas is designated as "divine speech,"[79] and the importance attributed to names in Brāhmaṇic thought. As Jan Gonda has noted of this milieu: "the connection between a name and its bearer . . . is so intimate that there is for all practical purposes a question of identity, interchangeability or inherent participation so that the name may reveal to the man who understands it well the nature and essence of the bearer."[80] To displace, or even rename, the Ṛgvedic Puruṣa in their cosmogonic speculations suggests a deep motivation for change on the part of the Brāhmaṇic authors.

The identification of the sacrificer with the primeval man represents the chief means by which the cosmogony is recreated in the ritual performance.[81] In this context *puruṣa*, which simply means "man," appears to be an especially apt name for the primeval man, as it establishes an immediate identification with the human sacrificer.[82] Julius Eggeling, clearly recognizing that in Brāhmaṇic thought a name was a potent means of establishing identity, attempted to account for the change in the Brāhmaṇas to Prajāpati, which means the "Lord of Creatures," by suggesting that the name "Prajāpati was manifestly a singularly convenient one for the identification of the sacrificer with the supreme 'Lord of Creatures'; for doubtless men who could afford to have great and costly sacrifices . . . performed for them . . . would almost invariably be 'Lords of Creatures,' i.e., rulers of men and possessors of cattle."[83]

However, Eggeling's remarks trivialize the distinction between Ṛgveda 10.90 and the Brāhmaṇic cosmogony; that the cosmic man is named Prajāpati, the "Lord of Creatures," clearly signifies a different way of thinking about the relationship of man and cosmos than that implied by referring to the cosmic man as Puruṣa, the "Man." In the creation myth, which in the Śatapatha Brāhmaṇa accompanies the discussion of the Agnicayana ritual, this difference is expressed through depicting Prajāpati's primordial creative activity as a process of sexual generation.[84] To a certain degree, the naming of the cosmic man, Prajāpati, "Lord (*pati*) of [that which is] Procreated (*prajā*)," may be attributed to the nature of this activity;

for, unlike Puruṣa whose creative act takes the form of a dismemberment, Prajāpati creates through "propagating." (The Sanskrit *prajā* is derived from *pra-/jan*, "to be born, to propagate offspring.") How Prajāpati's creative activity affects his relationship to the cosmos and what the peculiarities of this primordial activity imply for the human sacrificer who replicates the cosmogony in his own ritual activity is seen in the Śatapatha Brāhmaṇa's detailed mythology of the cosmogony.

The Agnicayana section of the Śatapatha Brāhmaṇa begins with a lengthy narration of the creation of the cosmos.[85] Although this creation myth includes motifs that are seen in several Ṛgvedic hymns,[86] the central episode of the cosmogony presented here—that is, Prajāpati's creation of the cosmos and its inhabitants—resembles the cosmogony described in Ṛgveda 10.90, the Puruṣasūkta. However, in accordance with a general distinction between the Ṛgveda and the Brāhmaṇas, the Brāhmaṇic version of this myth is considerably more verbose and detailed than the myth that appears in the Ṛgveda.[87] Moreover, unlike the Puruṣasūkta, the myth that occurs in the Śatapatha Brāhmaṇa has an immediate ritual purpose; as a prelude to the performance of the fire altar building ceremony (*agnicayana*) it establishes a paradigm for the sacrificer's own activity—and this purpose visibly affects certain details of the myth.[88]

The Agnicayana creation myth begins by stating that, "In the beginning this [all] was nonexistent,"[89] a thought-provoking notion that occurs with some frequency in the Vedic texts.[90] In the Ṛgveda an entire hymn, Ṛgveda 10.129, the "Creation Hymn," is founded upon the notion of a primeval state of nonexistence. There the motif shapes a cosmogony that is very nearly overwhelmed by its nihility: even the first existent principle is wholly enveloped in the primal emptiness.[91] The paradox of this first principle's emergence—that is, how existence arises out of nonexistence—seems almost to deny the event of the creation.[92] And, though the existent is said to emerge through the power of its heat (*tapas*) and desire (*kāma*), the hymn seems to attribute the fact that creation occurs at all to the Vedic poets' extraordinary powers of perception: "Poets (*kavi*) seeking in their heart with wisdom found the bond of existence in non-existence."[93]

The authors of the Śatapatha Brāhmaṇa draw on several motifs that occur in this Ṛgvedic myth: in particular, those of heat, desire, and the Vedic poets or sages (*rsi*), whose knowledge is instrumental to the creation of the cosmos.[94] However, they do not agonize over the conceptual difficulties presented by the idea of primordial nonexistence; by employing the chief elements of the Ṛgvedic myth, the authors of the Brāhmaṇa perhaps imply that this problem has been resolved elsewhere. Accordingly, they freely (and obscurely) construct their own myth of creation from the nonexistent: "They say, 'What was that non-existent?' The Ṛṣis indeed were the non-existent in the beginning. They say, 'Who were the Ṛṣis?' The Ṛṣis [became] the vital airs (*prāṇa*). Before the universe was existent, desiring this [existent universe], they perished (/*riṣ*) by their exertion (*śrāma*) and their heat (*tapas*). Therefore they are called Ṛṣis."[95]

Although this brief myth draws its formal elements from the Ṛgveda's "Creation Hymn" (10.129), its construction here suggests the ideology of the central Brāhmaṇic creation myth of Prajāpati, which it introduces; the elements of an earlier mythology are thus reshaped by the Agnicayana ritualists to establish their own retelling of the Prajāpati myth within the known Vedic corpus. Accordingly, in this version of the myth the activity of the Ṛṣis, which itself combines several Vedic creation motifs, is described in a way that clearly prefigures Prajāpati's own career, during which he creates through his desire (*kāma*), the power of his heat (*tapas*) and exertion (*śrāma*),[96] and finally "falls apart" (*vi-/śraṃs*).[97] The Ṛṣis' activity, however, represents an order of creation quite different from that established by Prajāpati. Prajāpati's creation is the *existent* cosmos. The Ṛṣis, on the other hand, are said to be identical with the *nonexistent*; their activity does not lead directly to the creation of the cosmos, but rather occurs *in illo tempore*, before Prajāpati and apparently before existence itself are manifest. Nonetheless, as a prelude to the central episode of the cosmogony, the Ṛṣis' activity initiates the conditions necessary for Prajāpati's existence and, hence, to a degree shapes the creation of the cosmos.

Prajāpati, like Puruṣa, creates the cosmos and its inhabitants out of his own self; in the Brāhmaṇic myth the totality of this act is made apparent in the initial reference to the nonexistence of the universe.[98] The cosmos that arises from Prajāpati's primordial creative activity, like that which arises from Puruṣa's dismemberment, is ordered in correlation to Prajāpati's being; that is, relative to both the gross planes of his body and the inner planes of his head (the locus of his senses: sight, hearing, speech, and so forth). The authors of the Agnicayana express this correlation in terms of a heptadic symbolism.[99] This symbolism is established immediately in the Agnicayana creation myth in the figures of the Ṛṣis, who in Brāhmaṇic literature were typified as a group of seven.[100]

The Ṛṣis perish as a result of their exertions, leaving behind them the vital airs (*prāṇa*). In the Vedic literature the vital airs often denote the sense organs or, according to Sāyana, the "orifices of the head."[101] Although they seem to have been variously enumerated,[102] in the Agnicayana myth their relationship to the Ṛṣis establishes them as seven in number. That the vital airs arise as a result of the Ṛṣis' diminishment indicates their subtle nature; though in Brāhmaṇic thought they are identified with the physical sense organs, their locus seems to be the intangible aspect of sensation such as sight, hearing, thought, and so forth.[103]

Following their emergence from the Ṛṣis, the vital airs are "kindled" (*/indh*)—another reference to the creative power of heat in this myth—apparently to gain greater substance, and "being kindled they emitted seven separate persons (*puruṣa*)."[104] The seven persons, however, find that the condition of being separate prohibits them from procreating; consequently, they make themselves into one person (*puruṣa*): "They said 'Surely, being thus we cannot procreate. We must make these seven persons into one person.' They made those seven persons into one person. These two were compressed upwards of the naval; two downwards of the navel; a person [in each wing]; one person became the foot."[105]

The seven "persons" form themselves into the gross planes of the body. The head, however, is formed separately from the body. It is constituted as the "essences" (*rasa*)—that is, the vital breaths—of each of these seven persons are "removed upwards" (*urdhvaṃ sam- ud- /ūh*): "Now what excellence (*śrī*), what essence (*rasa*), there was of those seven persons, that was removed upwards, that became his head."[106] This idea not only establishes the head as the microcosm of the body, but a microcosm that represents the essential nature of the body.

The fully constituted person is identified as Prajāpati: "that samé person (*puruṣa*) became Prajāpati."[107] This statement contains several levels of meaning. Superficially, the term *puruṣa* simply refers to the person who becomes Prajāpati. On another level, however, *puruṣa* refers to Puruṣa, the cosmic man, and the statement thus establishes the identity of Prajāpati with his Ṛgvedic predecessor. And finally, *puruṣa* refers to man—that is, the human sacrificer—who in and through the performance of the Agnicayana ritual "becomes" Prajāpati.

Prajāpati immediately expresses his desire that: "I should be manifold; I should reproduce."[108] In the Agnicayana creation myth, Prajāpati's creative activity appears to extend over two distinct phases. In the first phase Prajāpati creates through a process of exerting (*√śram*), heating himself (*√tap*), and finally "emitting" (*√sṛj*).[109] The purpose of this phase of the creation seems to resemble that which the Ṛgvedic Puruṣa achieved through his "spreading himself" into the unformed cosmos; namely, to establish a foundation out of which the constituents of the cosmos can be created. And, because Prajāpati alone exists during this initial phase of the creation, his actions are necessarily self-contained. The cosmic foundation created as a result of this activity allows Prajāpati to externalize his activity in the next phase of the creation. In this phase, Prajāpati's creative activity is described as a process of "coupling" (*mithunaṃ saṃ- √bhū*). This latter activity accentuates what is implicit in Prajāpati's act of heating during the first phase of the creation; namely, that Prajāpati's act of creating is a sexual act. For, as Walter Kaelber has noted, the act of "heating" (*√tap*) represents in the Vedic texts "the heat generating and generated by the sexual act which issues in biological birth."[110]

Prajāpati, following the model of the Ṛṣis, enters into the first phase of his creative activity by exerting (*√śram*) and heating (*√tap*) himself. Exhausted from this effort, Prajāpati first creates, or more precisely, first emits the *brahman*:

> That person (*puruṣa*) Prajāpati desired: "I should be manifold; I should procreate." He exerted and heated himself. He heated himself and was exhausted. The *brahman* was first emitted, the triple [body of] knowledge. That became a foundation (*pratiṣṭhā*) for him. Therefore they say: "The *brahman* is the foundation of this whole [universe]."[111]

There has been considerable scholarly discussion over the meaning of the term *brahman*, particularly of its meaning in the pre-Upaniṣadic period of Indian thought.[112] Mircea Eliade has summed up this discussion by noting that "the important fact is that, at all periods and on all cultural levels the *brahman* was considered and expressly called the imperishable, the immutable, the foundation, the principle of all existence . . . in other words, the *brahman* is the *Grund* that supports the world, is at once cosmic axis and ontological foundation."[113] In the Agnicayana myth the *brahman*, which is Prajāpati's first creation, is immediately identified with the triple body of the Veda (Ṛg, Sāma, and Yajus), speech (*vāc*), and Prajāpati's mouth.[114] Although the authors of this myth declare that "the *brahman* is the foundation of this whole [universe],"[115] it is the identification with the Veda that defines the way in which the *brahman* founds reality.

The authors of the Brāhmaṇas viewed the Veda as a repository of the spoken word coexistent with reality.[116] Moreover, in the Brāhmaṇas speech itself represents a potent means for penetrating the imperceptible relations of all existence.[117] (The seemingly interminable verbal identifications that dominate the discussions in these texts attest to the importance the Brāhmaṇic authors attributed to the potency of the word.) However, the reality that the word represents is insubstantial, and the reality that it embodies can be apprehended only by those possessing extraordinary powers of perception (exemplified by the Vedic Ṛṣis). The identification of the *brahman* with the Veda thus implies that the *brahman* founds not the gross cosmos but rather an intangible—albeit an underlying and essential—aspect of the cosmos's existence.

Following the creation of the *brahman*, Prajāpati again expresses his desire that "I should be manifold; I should reproduce."[118] And again Prajāpati exerts and heats himself to attain this goal. The result of this activity is the creation, or more precisely, emission of "foam" (*phena*): "he heated himself [and] was worn out. He emitted the foam. He knew that form indeed was that which is manifold."[119] As Wendy O'Flaherty has pointed out, foam "plays an important part in the creation by virtue of its ambivalence, half water and half air, mediating between matter and spirit."[120] In this instance the foam mediates between Prajāpati's creation of the underlying foundation, the *brahman*, and his creation of a gross foundation, the earth (*pṛthivī, bhūmi*), which follows the foam. Prajāpati enters into his creative activity of heating and exerting himself only three times: once to create the *brahman*, once to create the foam, and once to create the earth. However, unlike the *brahman* and the earth, the foam does not found any particular aspect of the creation. Its importance seems to lie in its intermediate character and, as such, in the possibility of a state of unification between two modes of existence.

Having created the foam, Prajāpati again exerts and heat himself. The resulting creation is distinguished by its plurality: "He exerted and heated himself . . . and being worn out he emitted clay, salt, the dry sea beds, gravel, stone, gold, plants and trees. By this [emission] the earth was covered."[121] The creation of the earth along with these several elements that cover it, indicates that the earth founds existence on the material level. This point is reiterated by elucidating the "etymologies" of the two common Sanskrit terms for earth, *bhūmi* and *pṛthivī*, in a way that shows they inherently represent a foundation that can be materially "spread out": "They say, 'This was (/*bhū*) indeed the foundation [so] it became the earth (*bhūmi*); he spread (/*prath*) that out [so] it became the earth (*pṛthivī*).' "[122]

The first phase of Prajāpati's creation ends with the establishment of the two foundations: the earth, and the *brahman*. Prajāpati begins the second phase of his creative activity by "uniting" (*mithunaṃ saṃ- /bhū*) with the earth; that is, by joining together with the material foundation he established in the first phase of the creation.[123]

The Sanskrit phrase *mithunaṃ saṃ- /bhū*, "to unite as a pair," bears the specific sexual connotation of copulation; in the Agnicayana myth the result of this activity is an egg (*aṇḍa*) that arises and hatches into the various constituents of the cosmos. However, the idea of "uniting as a pair" also expresses the dual nature of the cosmos. This duality is manifested in the idea that the essential nature of the various cosmic spheres are embodied in certain natural phenomena, represented as deities: the earth in fire (Agni); the atmosphere in the wind (Vāyu); the heavens in the sun (Āditya); and the quarters in the moon (Candramas).[124] In the Agnicayana's creation myth the dual nature of the material cosmos facilitates Prajāpati's creative activity of "uniting as a pair." Accordingly, to create each sphere of the cosmos Prajāpati employs successively the fire, sun, wind and moon as his agents of procreation. Beginning with the earth, with which Prajāpati unites by means of its corresponding natural phenomenon fire (Agni), Prajāpati's creative activity literally takes the form of "uniting as a pair" with the spheres of the cosmos. "Prajāpati desired: 'It should become manifold; it should procreate.' By means of Agni he united as a pair with the earth. From that an egg arose."[125] The egg that arises from this activity becomes the atmosphere (*antarikṣa*) and the wind (*vāyu*); that is, the region and its characteristic phenomenon, or deity, that in traditional Vedic cosmography are located above the earth: "That which was the embryo inside emerged as the wind (*vāyu*) . . . and that which was the shell became the atmosphere (*antarikṣa*)."[126] The distinction between the egg's shell and its embryo aptly reflects the distinction between the material planes of the cosmos and the natural phenomena that represent them. While the egg's shell becomes an aspect of the material cosmos—the atmospheric region—the embryo (*garbha*), "what is inside," becomes the phenomenon—the wind—that represents the essential (or, "inner") and animate aspect of that region.

This phase of the creation continues as Prajāpati unites with the atmosphere by means of the wind to produce another egg.[127] The shell and embryo of this egg become the heavens (*div*) and the sun (*āditya*), respectively; that is,the region and its phenomenon that are above the atmosphere. Prajāpati next unites with the heavens by means of the sun to produce another egg, and its shell and embryo become the quarters (*diś*) and the moon (*candramas*).[128] The cosmos that has been progressively established through this activity is the same as that which Puruṣa in the Ṛgvedic myth established through his dismemberment; that is, the three spheres of heavens, atmosphere and earth, and the ubiquitous quarters, or cardinal points.

Having created the various cosmic planes, Prajāpati turns to the creation of the beings who inhabit and animate those planes. Although Prajāpati's creative activity is still depicted as a process of "uniting as a pair," this stage of the creation is distinguished from the previous stage—that is, the creation of the cosmic planes—by its use of only two elements, speech (*vāc*) and mind (*manas*), elements that represent the inner or sensate aspect of existence and, in a previous phase of the creation, were identified with the *brahman*. Thus, in this stage of the creation Prajāpati is said to have "united as a pair with speech by means of mind."[129] The result of this activity is that Prajāpati himself becomes pregnant (*garbhin*). Here the absence of an egg, the shell of which constituted the *materia prima* of the cosmic regions, again evidences the subtle nature of this part of the creation.

As a consequence of his pregnancy, Prajāpati gives birth to the various deities who are associated with the four cosmic realms: the Vāsus, who are associated with Agni and the earth; the Rudras, who are associated with Vāyu and the atmosphere; the Āditvas, who are associated with the sun and the heavens; and the Viśvadevas, who are associated with the moon and the quarters.[130]

In Vedic thought the Vāsus, Rudras, and Ādityas personified the natural phenomena found on each of the three spheres of earth, atmosphere, and heavens, whereas the Viśvadevas seems to have personified the notion of universality[131] and thus are aptly identified here with the quarters, which are everywhere at once. In the Agnicayana creation myth the idea that these beings are engendered through speech and mind implies that they represent the inner or essential aspect of the cosmos. Their relationship to the various material spheres appears to be similar to that which the vital breaths have to Prajāpati's gross body; that is, they seem to embody the animate, and animating, aspect of the material cosmos.

To locate these "beings" within the various material spheres Prajāpati again utilizes the agency of the various natural phenomena, or deities, that represent the cosmic planes:

> Agni was created, the Vāsus were created in succession. He placed them on this one [the earth]. Vāyu [was created], the Rudras [were created in succession]. [He placed] them in the atmosphere. Āditya [was created], the Ādityas [were created in succession]. [He placed] them in the sky. Çandramas [was created], the Viśvadevas [were created in succession]. [He placed] them in the quarters.[132]

In facilitating the creation of the material planes of the cosmos, the role of Agni, Vāyu, Āditya, and Candramas seems to have been that of natural phenomenon. When the Vāsus, Rudras, Ādityas, and Viśvadevas are placed into the material cosmos, their role seems to be that of "deity"; that is, they are personified. The distinction between these two roles reflects the distinction between the two aspects of the creation: the gross and the subtle, the inanimate and the animate. However, the malleability of Agni, Vāyu, Āditya, and Candramas—that is, their easy transformation from deity to natural phenomenon—derives from the fact that in either of their roles they are intermediaries; mediating between the two aspects of the cosmic man and the two aspects of the cosmos.

Placing these various "beings" in the material planes completes Prajāpati's creation of the cosmos.[133] The animate and inanimate natures of Prajāpati's creation suggests the same sort of two-tier cosmic image that previously was seen in the Puruṣasūkta; that is, a cosmos that comprises the two aspects of human existence, represented by mind and body. However, in the Puruṣasūkta, the cosmos that arises from Puruṣa's dismemberment is ordered in direct correlation to the gross planes of the cosmic man's body and the subtle planes of his "head"; thus, the two-tier cosmos is at once cosmos and man. In the Agnicayana creation myth the relationship between Prajāpati and the cosmos he creates appears to be less immediate than that established as a result of Puruṣa's creative activity. In particular, the idea that Prajāpati's creative activity occurs through the agency of such intermediaries as Agni (fire), Vāyu (wind), Āditya (sun) and Candramas (moon) implies a sense of separation between the cosmic man and the cosmos.

In the discussions that follow the creation myth, the authors of the Śatapatha Brāhmaṇa's Agnicayana section represent the cosmos much in the same way as it is represented in the Puruṣasūkta; that is, the cosmos is imagined as being correlative to man. Thus, the gross planes of earth, atmosphere, and heavens are said to be the same as Prajāpati's feet, body, and head, respectively;[134] and Agni, Vāyu, Āditya, and Candramas—that is, the cosmos's animate aspect—are said to be the same as his speech, breath, eye, and mind.[135] In the discussions that accompany the Agnicayana ritual, Prajāpati is repeatedly equated with man, the sacrificer,[136] and this identity provides a model for the identification of man and cosmos. However, the authors of the Agnicayana do not conceive the identity of man and cosmos as a direct relationship but rather utilize the agency of the fire altar to establish this identity.[137] Just as the notion that Prajāpati, though he is equated with the cosmos, creates through the agency of Agni, Vāyu, Āditya, and Candramas suggests a relationship of both identity and separation to the cosmos; so, too, the fire altar stands between man and the cosmos with which he is supposed to be identical.

Conclusion: The Reenactment of the Cosmogony

Both the Puruṣasūkta and the Agnicayana's Prajāpati myth describe, through the event of the creation, the constitution and shape of the cosmos. And, as I have noted repeatedly in this chapter, the cosmos that arises through this event is conceived of as being correlative to man: its gross planes are equated with man's material body, while its subtle and essential nature is equated with the inner aspect of man's being. On the one hand, the Puruṣasūkta proposes this equation through directly relating Puruṣa's being to that of the cosmos; here the activity of the cosmogony, Puruṣa's dismemberment, facilitates the direct nature of this relationship. On the other hand, in the Agnicayana's creation myth, this equation between man and cosmos, though still apparent, is muddled by the cosmic eggs and various demigods that participate in the cosmogony. This myth lessens the directness of the relationship between man and cosmos, proposed by the Puruṣasūkta, as Prajāpati first emits a foundation (the *brahman* and the earth) and then unites with it to create the two aspects of the cosmos.

The differences between these mythologies mirrors a distinction in their orientations. Whereas the Puruṣasūkta clearly establishes the ideological basis of the innate relationship between man and cosmos, it does not address the problem of how man realizes that relationship; that is, how man becomes *saloka* with the cosmos that, according to the Puruṣasūkta, he so closely resembles. Though the Vedic ritualists acknowledged, in rituals such as the Puruṣamedha, that the model of Puruṣa's act of creating the cosmos could be reenacted through the death and dismemberment of the sacrificer, they do not ever seem to have taken this step in their ritual performances. For, in the Puruṣamedha the sacrificer, for whose benefit the ritual was performed, was not put to death but rather a large number of human victims were sacrificed in his place.

The Agnicayana's creation myth, although it also proposes an ideological basis for the identification of man and cosmos, exhibits at least an implicit awareness of the practical aspect of realizing this identity. The authors of the myth, employing the sort of tautological reasoning often seen in the Brāhmaṇas, thus declare: "Indeed that was the building up of [Prajāpati]; because [Prajāpati] was built up it was the building up of him. And now indeed this is the building up of the sacrificer (*yajamāna*); because he [will be] built up it is the building up of him."[138] In particular, just as Prajāpati first established the two foundations, the *brahman* and the earth, and then through them continued his creation, so too the sacrificer builds an altar that serves as the foundation for his (creative) ritual activity. And, following Prajāpati's model of uniting with his creation, the sacrificer generates himself into the cosmos through the agency of the fire altar,[139] with which the sacrificer is said to form a "pair" (*mithuna*). The sexual connotation of this union is expressed in the notion that the pair possesses the same generative capability as that required to produce sons.[140]

The mythology of Prajāpati's primordial creative activity at once represents a model *for* and a model *of* ritual action, for, in the Brāhmaṇas, myth and rite are inseparable. And, just as the transformation from the Ṛgvedic Puruṣa to the figure of Prajāpati in the Brāhmaṇas centers on a transformation from a "disjunctive" model (in which the cosmos arises from Puruṣa's dismembered body parts) to a "conjunctive" model (in which the cosmos arises from Prajāpati's act of "uniting as a pair"), so, too, the rituals, which this mythology underlies, exhibit an overwhelming concern with creating a format through which the sacrificer joins his own existence to that of the cosmos. These changes seem to have arisen as Vedic thought confronted the question of how man might realize the state of existence that the correlation of his own and the cosmos's own being held out to him.

Though many rites in the Vedic corpus reflect the cosmic man mythos, the building of the fire altar (*agnicayana*)—presented as the culmination of all the Vedic rites—stands out among the ritual analogues to the Prajāpati mythology. In fact, the most systematic Brāhmaṇic presentation of the Prajāpati mythology, that which accompanies the Agnicayana in the Śatapatha Brāhmaṇa, almost certainly seems to have originated in concert with the incorporation of this rite in the Vedic ritual corpus.[141] In the following chapter, I turn to an examination of this rite, for it represents the "other side" of the Vedic complex that culminates in the Upaniṣadic doctrine of karma; that is, standing on the ideological foundation of the cosmic man mythology, it proposes a *ritual* technique through which the sacrificer was supposed to become *saloka*.

3.

The Fire Altar (Agnicayana) as Man and Cosmos

The Problem of Sacrifice

J. C. Heesterman has succinctly characterized the nature of the sacrifice:

> When taken seriously sacrifice is, quite bluntly, an act of controlled death and destruction. This act purports to force access to the other world, the transcendent. The gap, the vacuum created by the sacrifice has to be filled by the other side with the opposite of death and destruction, that is the goods of life, in the most tangible sense of food and survival. Or in simple terms one must sacrifice a cow in order to obtain cows.[1]

In this basic form of offering "a cow for cows" the sacrificial ritual does not appear to be a problematic operation. However, when this principle of exchange is extended—in particular, from exchanging food for food to exchanging (human) life for (human) life—problems are rapidly encountered. The ideology of this extension, which seems to have been embraced by the Vedic thinkers, perceives the other world as the realm of life itself and, thus, seeks access to that world as a means of renewing one's life. In fact, this world was characterized as a realm of death; in creating the cosmos it is said that Prajāpati "over [this world] created death, who is the eater of men."[2] The way to life was through the sacrifice: "A man, being born, is a debt (*ṛṇa*), by his own self he is born to death, and only when he sacrifices does he extract himself from death."[3] Yet, the mechanism of the sacrifice would seem to require the sacrificer to give up his own life to attain this renewal. As A. B. Keith noted, "the perfect form of sacrifice should be suicide."[4]

Suicide of self-sacrifice does not appear in the Vedic texts as a ritual method. Although such an act might have fulfilled the theoretical demands of the sacrifice, its finality would have been contrary to the sacrifice's practical purpose; that is, the attainment of the goods of life from the other world. This attainment could not be realized though a single ritual event but required a lifetime of ritual performances (which is, of course, another way of sacrificing one's life): "A year should not pass without sacrificing; indeed the year is life, and life is this immortal state which he bestows on his own self."[5] Moreover, the texts make it clear that the individual who goes to the other world (perhaps through a self-sacrifice) before completing this process does not attain a full existence in that realm; the Śatapatha Brāhmaṇa thus describes the fate of those individuals who die before completing the lifelong process of performing sacrifices:

> Those who depart before the age of 20 they become attached to the world of the days and nights; those who [depart] above 20 and below 40 [become attached] to that [world of] the fortnight; those who [depart] above 40 and below 60 [become attached] to that [world of] the months; those who [depart] above 60 and below 80 [become attached] to that [world of] the seasons; those who [depart] above 80 and below 100 [become attached] to that [world of] the year. Now only that one who lives 100 years or more indeed attains the immortal state.[6]

Furthermore, the actual death of the sacrificer would have been contrary to the corporate nature of the Vedic rituals, as the sacrificer's ritual efforts were undertaken not only for his own benefit but also for the benefit of his ancestors and his offspring, who were not capable of sacrificing for their own selves: "For whosoever has offspring—when he goes by his own self to that other world—[his] offspring sacrifice in this world."[7] In the Śatapatha Brāhmaṇa this relationship between the sacrificer, his offspring, and his ancestors was described—just as the compulsion to sacrifice was—as the sacrificer's debt (*ṛṇa*), which the sacrificer could discharge only through a continuous process of sacrifice.[8]

Nevertheless, the ritualists were certainly aware that the sacrificer should be the object of the sacrifice. In part, the growth of the Vedic ritual into what has been called "the richest, most elaborate and most complete among the rituals of mankind,"[9] reflects the Vedic thinkers' attempt to circumvent the actual death of the sacrificer, while they strived to maintain the ideology of such an event, in the ritual performance. The attempt to resolve this practical difficulty was concentrated in two closely related areas: the use of substitute victims—such as goats, cattle, horses, and even men—in the place of the human sacrificer, and the employment of ritual specialists to perform the rites for the sacrificer's benefit.

The authors of the Śatapatha Brāhmaṇa explain the principle of substitution in the use of an animal victim for the human sacrificer: "Indeed, when he is offering, the sacrificial fires advance toward the flesh of the sacrificer; they think of the sacrificer, they desire the sacrificer . . . then when he sacrifices by means of the animal sacrifice indeed he ransoms his own self."[10] The substitution of an animal victim, however, raised its own unique set of problems. There was, in particular, a peculiar problem of identification. On the one hand, the ritualists had to establish a substantive identification between the sacrificer and the victim that stood in the sacrificer's place. For the most part, such an identification was established through correlating certain ritual implements to the sacrificer's physical proportions. Thus, the sacrificial stake (*yūpa*), the offering area, and the offering spoons were all constructed to the sacrificer's proportions.[11] In view of this correspondence the Brāhmaṇic authors asserted that "the man arranges the sacrifice to the same extent as a man; therefore, the sacrifice is a man,"[12] despite the fact that the victim was an animal or other substitute for man (the sacrificer).

The problem of identifying the sacrificer with the victim who stood in his place is also seen in several Brāhmaṇic discussions regarding the nature of the bond (*bandhu*) that existed between the sacrificer and the victim. In the basic form of offering a "cow for cows" the animal sacrifice was called *paśubandha*, "the binding (*bandha*) of the animal (*paśu*)," which apparently referred either to the manner in which the animal was slaughtered (it was strangled with a noose) or to its binding to the sacrificial post. However, in the Śatapatha Brāhmaṇa several passages suggest a subtle shift in the meaning of *bandha*, from the physical binding of the animal to that of a metaphysical binding of the animal to the sacrificer.[13] One passage in particular exhibits these two senses of binding—the physical binding of the animal to the *yūpa* and its metaphysical binding to the sacrificer—through its assertion of the equation between the sacrifice and the sacrificer: "The horse sacrifice is the sacrificer, and the sacrificer is the sacrifice; when he yokes the animals to the horse [in the horse sacrifice], indeed the sacrifice binds (/*rabh*) that [victim] to the sacrifice [i.e., the sacrificer]."[14] Here the equation between sacrifice and sacrificer (which is established in a somewhat convoluted syllogism through the middle term of a specific ritual event, the horse sacrifice) implies that the victims that are physically bound in the sacrifice become metaphysically bound to the sacrificer.[15]

On the other hand, however, the establishment of a very close identification between the sacrificer and the victim had certain negative connotations. As Hubert and Mauss observed, the sacrificer "needs to touch the animal in order to remain united with it, and yet is afraid to do so, for in so doing he runs the risk of sharing its fate."[16] The ambiguity of this situation is clearly reflected in one passage in the Śatapatha Brāhmaṇa:

> Now they say: "There [should] be no touching [of the victim] by the sacrificer (*yajmāna*); for they lead it to death. Thus he should not touch it!" But he should touch it; for what they lead by the sacrifice they do not lead to death. Thus he should touch it. For indeed when it is not touched he excludes his own self from the sacrifice; therefore he should touch it. It is touched in an imperceptible manner (*parokṣa*). The Pratiprasthātṛ [holds it] by means of the skewer; to the Pratiprasthātṛ [holds] the Adhvaryu; to the Adhvaryu the sacrificer. Thus it is held in an imperceptible manner.[17]

The ambiguity that the sacrificer experiences in the ritual killing of the victim may also be attributed to the general undesirability of death and destruction. The distance between the ritual exchange that brings new life into this world and a simple act of murder is not great; as Hubert and Mauss noted, "outside a holy place immolation is mere murder."[18] There is in the ritualists assertion that "what they lead by the sacrifice they do not lead to death" an implicit recognition of just how close the ritual killing is to an act of murder. The hint of discomfort expressed here over the killing of the sacrificial victim is, in fact, consistent with the tenor of several passages in the Brāhmaṇas that suggest the ritualists were unsure of the animals' willingness to die in the sacrificer's place. Thus, throughout the Brāhmaṇas there appear several brief narrative episodes that describe how the cattle, who were at first unwilling to submit to the role of victim, were convinced or coerced into accepting this fate.[19] Although, according to the Śatapatha Brāhmaṇa, the cattle eventually "condescended and became ready-minded for the [sacrificial] killing,"[20] before slaughtering the animal, the sacrificer still asks the permission of the victim's mother, father, and other relations.[21]

Closely related to the use of the substitute victim was the employment of ritual specialists, who actually performed the rite, in place of the sacrificer. On the one hand, the ritual specialists allowed the sacrificer to distance himself from the actual killing of the animal; thus, in the passage quoted earlier, the sacrificer's bond with the victim was established through holding on to the Adhvaryu (who was one sort of ritual specialist) who held on to the Pratiprasthātṛ (another specialist) who held on to the sacrificed animal.[22] On the other hand, the need for ritual specialists reflects the Brāhmaṇic concern for ritual exactitude. Ritual, by definition, is a strictly ordered series of events. And, because the outcome of the ritual performance depended on the ability to recreate precisely this series of events, it was necessary to employ specialists who were well versed in the techniques of the rites. However, this need for exactitude, and the employment of specialists to ensure its attainment in the rite, created a double bind for the sacrificer; as Sylvain Lévi noted:

> It takes an imperturbable confidence, hardly to be doubted, on the part of the faithful sacrificer to back up his decision to confront so many risks; it is not enough to admit the all-embracing power of the rites and formulas as dogma; one must entrust himself to the priests as though he were bound hand and foot, knowing that by an error or an act of negligence they could bring ruin or death upon him.[23]

The debt that the sacrificer incurred for this service was discharged through the form of strictly institutionalized sacrificial gifts known as *dakṣiṇā*. Similar to the rope (*bandha*), which the ritualists saw as the representative of an unseen bond between the sacrificer and the victim, the *dakṣiṇā* bound the sacrificer to the officiant: " 'Let there be a share for me in the world of the gods!' Whoever sacrifices, he sacrifices [for this reason]. That sacrifice of his goes to the world of the gods, after that goes the *dakṣiṇā* which he gives [to the officiants], and holding on to the *dakṣiṇā* is the sacrificer."[24] These gifts were not merely a form of payment used to induce the ritual specialists to carry out their office but were seen as a part of the ritual performance: "Thence he must give what should be given; no offering should be without a *dakṣiṇā*."[25] Without the giving of the sacrificial gift the sacrifice would not have been properly enacted and thus could not yield the results desired of it.

In the Brāhmaṇas the nature of the *dakṣiṇā* appears to be closely related to the specific benefits expected from the sacrificial performance. Thus, there is an emphasis on the giving of cows, the primary source of life among the Vedic people, and gold, symbol of immortality, as *dakṣiṇā*.[26] The giving of sacrificial gifts determined in this manner may not have been a problem in a sacrifice where the desired result is the winning of cows. It does, however, create a difficult situation in the rituals that seek new life for the sacrificer. Heesterman thus paraphrases a passage that implies that the sacrificer, having enacted the ritual to gain a rebirth, must give up his regenerated self to discharge his debt to the officiants:

> the sacrificer when distributing the *dakṣiṇās* is considered to give himself; to the *hotṛ* he gives his voice, to the *brahman* his mind (*manas*), to the *adhvaryu* his breath (*prāṇa*) to the *udgātṛ* his eye, to the *hotrakas* his hearing, to the *camarsādhvaryus* his limbs, to the *prasarpakas* the hairs on his body, and to the *sadasya* his trunk; for these parts of himself the *dakṣiṇās* are substituted.[27]

In this form of ritual activity that seeks not cows but new life for the sacrificer, the sacrificer finds himself in the position of having to give up, as sacrificial gifts, the benefits of the sacrifice that should have properly accrued to the sacrificer himself; namely, the sacrificer's regenerated self.

The Problem of Sacrifice and the Agnicayana

The chief problem raised by the ritual substitutes, both the animal victims and the officiating priests, appears to be one of distance; that is, how far could the sacrificer distance himself from the actual performance of the ritual and still expect to receive its benefits?[28] Hubert and Mauss thus describe the offering area: "I the outer circle stands the sacrificer; then come in turn the priest, the altar, and the stake. On the outer perimeter, where stands the layman on whose behalf the sacrifice takes place, the religious atmosphere is weak and minimal."[29] In fact, the Brāhmaṇic thinkers insisted on the sacrificer's (*yajamāna*) limited participation in the ritual performance. In one instance, Yājñavalkya, who is cited as the chief authority in the first five books of the Śatapatha Brāhmaṇa discusses the appropriateness of a prescription requiring the sacrificer to perform the simple action of averting his eyes at a certain moment in the ritual. Yājñavalkya is said to have responded to this point by asking, "Why do not the [sacrificer's] become Adhvaryus [i.e., officiating priests] themselves?" The sarcastic tone of this remark suggests that any activity on the part of the sacrificer was seen as an aberration.[30]

The Brāhmaṇic thinkers were aware of the problematic nature of this situation; that is, how the sacrificer's weak position in the actual performance of the rite might affect the benefits that accrue to him. In a key discussion that occurs at the end of the Śatapatha Brāhmaṇa's description of the Agnicayana ritual, the authors of the text distinguish between the sacrificer who performs the Agnicayana for his own self and the one who performs it for another.[31] In this discussion, performance for another is clearly disdained, as the authors describe the fate of such ritualists: "Now this [fire altar] is his divine undying self (*ātman*); those who complete it for another bestow their divine selves on those others, and thus only a withered trunk is left [for them] as a remainder."[32]

At the end of this passage Śāṇḍilya, who is the most frequently cited authority in the Śatapatha Brāhmaṇa's Agnicayana section, recounts a discussion, between the ancient sage Tura Kāvaṣeya and the gods, that seems to represent a recanting of this position regarding performing the rite for another. According to Śāṇḍilya, Tura Kāvaṣeya was asked by the gods, "Sage, they say the building of the fire [altar] is not conducive to heaven, then why did you build one [for another]?"[33] Tura Kāvaṣeya is then said to have replied:

> "What is conducive to heaven and what is not conducive to heaven?" The sacrificer is the body (*ātman*) of the sacrifice, the officiants are the limbs; where the body is, there are the limbs and

> where the limbs are, there is the body. Indeed, if the officiants are [in 'a state that is] not conducive to heaven, then indeed the sacrificer also is [in a state that is] not conducive to heaven. Both are equally heaven-winners.[34]

The idea presented here that the performers of the Agnicayana should continue to follow the traditional Vedic ritual format is supported by an additional statement by Tura Kāvaṣeya that "in the matter of the sacrificial gift (*dakṣiṇā*) there should be no discussion."[35] The *dakṣiṇā*, through which the sacrificer binds himself to the officiants (and, at the same time, the merit of the sacrifice), is, of course, given only in a ritual performance that employs ritual specialists; that is, a "performance for another."

The ambiguity that arises from these two contiguous discussions of performing the ritual for another is typical of many discussions that appear in the Śatapatha Brāhmaṇa's Agnicayana section. Although the origin of the Agnicayana ritual has not been precisely determined, it does not appear to have belonged to the early Vedic ritual corpus.[36] In fact, as Julius Eggeling noted, this rite "would seem originally to have stood apart from, if not in actual opposition to, the ordinary sacrificial system, but which, in the end, apparently by some ecclesiastical compromise, was added on to the Soma ritual as an important, though not indispensable, element of it."[37] Nonetheless, although it may not have been an indispensable element of the Soma rite, this association firmly established the Agnicayana within—in fact, at the highest level of—the Vedic ritual system.[38]

If the Agnicayana did indeed originate outside Vedic culture, then perhaps the ritualists used this circumstance, as they incorporated this rite into the Vedic tradition, to allow themselves a certain measure of freedom in addressing the traditional format of the Vedic rites. In any case, as part of the Vedic ritual system, the Agnicayana seems to have been elaborated in response to the problems raised by the format of these rites. Here the Agnicayana's unusual position—being at once part of the Vedic ritual system while (perhaps due to its external origins) addressing itself to the problems of that system—leads to contradictory statements in some of the discussions regarding the nature of this rite's performance. This is apparent in the passage quoted earlier, in which the

Brāhmaṇic authors seem to favor the notion that the ritual should be performed by an individual for his own benefit—an idea antithetical to the traditional ritual format—but then fail to support this extreme position. Accordingly, after denying the practice of performing for another they immediately cite the opinion of an ancient ritualist, Tura Kāvaṣeya, which firmly supports the continuation of the traditional relationship between the officiants and the sacrificer. This equivocation reflects the fine line the Agnicayana ritualists trod, as they attempted to alleviate the inherent problems of the Vedic ritual format. Working within the ritual system they had to temper their ideas, or at least their application in the rite, when these ideas bordered on destroying that system, as the displacement of the officiants would have done.

The most sensitive issue the Agnicayana ritualists addressed was the problem of death in the ritual. In view of the Agnicayana's emphasis on individual attainment, this problem was especially complex, for it seems to imply that the sacrificer must himself constitute the offering. On the one hand, the Agnicayana's conceptual framework addresses this problem in its modification of the cosmic man mythology; in particular, that achieved by transforming the Ṛgvedic figure of Puruṣa, and the event of his primordial dismemberment, into the Brāhmaṇic figure of Prajāpati, who creates largely through a process of sexual generation—both heating (*tapas*) and coupling (*mithunaṃ saṃ- /bhū*). The modifications established in the Prajāpati mythology are clearly represented in the actual performance of the Agnicayana ritual;[39] in replicating Prajāpati's primordial creative activity, the sacrificer generates—through the agency of the fire altar—the cosmos out his own self. The result of this activity is the sacrificer's attainment of a "unified, undecaying, and immortal" state;[40] that is, a state in which the sacrificer—like Prajāpati, who *is* the cosmos—realizes his identity with the cosmos.

On the other hand, the traditional Vedic ritual format presented several obstacles to the replication of the Prajāpati mythology. In particular, while the model established by Prajāpati's creative activity seems to circumvent the necessity of the sacrificer's death in the performance of Agnicayana, the basic structure of the ritual format yet demanded an exchange of life for life. In the Agnicayana the need to meet this demand is seen in the employment of five substitute victims. The Agnicayana ritualists redefine this act through assuming a unique view of the fate of the five victims. They propose that the animal victims are not killed but "healed" in the ritual, and so overshadow the event of their death (and the death of the human sacrificer that they represent) in the sacrifice. This notion of "healing" follows a concept firmly established in Vedic thought; namely, that all beings are born "dead" and come to life only through the performance of the rite.[41]

In the following section, I turn to the specific procedures of the Agnicayana ritual. In brief, the Agnicayana begins with the slaughter of the animal victims and then concerns itself with the construction, or generation, of an immense fire altar. This order of events reverses that of the traditional Vedic format, in which the sacrifice of the victim represents the culmination of the rite. This reversal is emblematic of how the Agnicayana ritualists alleviated the problem of the sacrifice. As Hubert and Mauss observed: "If he [the sacrificer] involved himself in the rite to the very end, he would find death, not life."[42] The reverse order of the Agnicayana leads the sacrificer, as he builds the altar and links his own existence to that of the cosmos, from the realm of death to the realm of life.

The Construction of the Fire Altar

The Agnicayana ritual consists of two phases: the building of the altar, and its utilization in a Soma sacrifice. According to the ritual system's classification, the Soma sacrifice constitutes the main part of the Agnicayana ritual, while the building of the fire altar represents an ancillary part of the rite.[43] The authors of the Śatapatha Brāhmaṇa's Agnicayana section exhibit an overwhelming concern with describing the construction of the altar and seem only nominally interested in describing the main Soma ritual. Thus, the Agnicayana section, which consists of four books (*kāṇḍa*), devotes three books to building the fire altar, and one to the Soma ritual.[44]

To a certain extent, this disproportionate emphasis on the Agnicayana's fire building rite reflects the considerable technical knowledge required to complete the altar. Frits Staal has recently estimated "that the extent of specialized knowledge needed to put the altar together ritually is on a par with the extent of technical knowledge required to build an aeroplane."[45] In general, however, the authors of the Brāhmaṇas did not concern themselves with detailed discussions of the technique of the ritual. As Jan Gonda has noted of the contents of these texts: "Though viewing almost all topics discussed from the ritual angle the authors generally supposed their audiences to be well acquainted with the course of the ritual, its terminology and technicalities. Many particulars are stated only in outline or omitted altogether."[46] Gonda rightly observes that the aim of the Brāhmaṇas is to "explain the origin, meaning, and *raison d'être* of the ritual acts to be performed."[47] Moreover, these explanations expound a unique world view; in them the ritual, when properly understood, can represent an otherwise unknowable reality.[48] And, because words represented the means for penetrating into the realm of truth and reality,[49] the discussions in the Brāhmaṇas often attain an inordinate length. Accordingly, in the Śatapatha Brāhmaṇa, the Agnicayana section's protracted discussion of the building of the fire altar appears primarily to be a reflection of what this rite reveals, at least potentially, about reality itself rather than an indication of its technical complexity. Similarly, the relatively brief discussion, which appears in the Agnicayana section, of the Soma sacrifice implies that for the Agnicayana ritualists this rite did not hold out the same sort of potentiality as that contained in the ritual construction of the altar.

While the building of the fire altar does not seem originally to have been part of the Vedic ritual corpus, its association with the Soma sacrifice, which belongs to the oldest stratum of the Vedic rites and stands at the highest level of the ritual system's hierarchy, placed this rite at the acme of the Vedic ritual system. However, the Śatapatha Brāhmaṇa's overwhelming emphasis on the "ancillary" rite of building the fire altar gives the main Soma sacrifice the appearance of an afterthought. In fact, even in the part of the text devoted to the Soma sacrifice, the authors are still preoccupied with the symbolism of the fire altar. Yet, to claim a position within the ritual system, the building of the fire altar had to be relegated to the position of an ancillary part of the Soma sacrifice, a problematic relationship given the ritualists' consuming interest in the fire altar. Accordingly, the Agnicayana's authors are painstaking in referring to the intimate relationship of the Soma ritual and the construction of the fire altar[50] and in asserting the precedence of the former over the latter.[51]

The unusual relationship between these two aspects of the Agnicayana rite is emblematic of the relationship between the fire altar rite and the Vedic ritual tradition in general. The act of constructing the fire altar proposes certain ideas that threaten to break out of the carefully delimited boundaries of the Vedic ritual form. Yet, the established ritual form represents the only means through which the Agnicayana's authors can express these new ideas. Here the attachment to the Soma ritual serves as a constant reminder of the fire altar's dependence on—though not subordination to—the Vedic ritual.

The building of the fire altar begins with a preliminary rite in which five animals are supposed to be sacrificed: a man, horse, sheep, bull, and goat.[52] These five animals are said to be "all the animals,"[53] a reference to the inclusion in this select group of the five prototypical animal victims used in the Vedic sacrifice. On the one hand, the sacrifice of this group of five clearly suggests that the Agnicayana represents the culmination of all the Vedic sacrifices. On the other hand, however, the use of these ritual substitutes, and the death and destruction to which they are subjected, represents the aspect of the Vedic ritual that the Agnicayana seems most anxious to overcome. This preliminary rite thus manifests the Agnicayana's peculiar conflict between the structure of the Vedic ritual form and its own unique ideas.

The parameters of this conflict manifest themselves immediately as the ritualists explore several alternatives to the actual killing of the five sacrificial animals. The first of these alternatives proposes the use of animals that are already dead.[54] However, those who adopt this procedure are said to become themselves "dead bodies," and to support this contention, the authors recall that there was an ancient ritualist by the name of Aṣāḍhi Sauśromateya, who followed this procedure and "died quickly after that."[55] This obviously undesirable result leads to the suggestion of another alternative, which proposes the substitution of five gold or clay models for the live animals.[56] In support of this practice the ritualists reason: "Of all that which has decayed [the earth is] the resting place, and these animals have decayed [in the past]; so from whence these animals have gone, we shall collect them."[57] However, this technique is disdained, as the authors declare that this practice is followed by "those who do not know the [correct] method and meaning regarding this [animal sacrifice]," and as a consequence of following this incorrect method, these ritualists are themselves said to "become decayed."[58] The discussion of these alternatives to the animal sacrifice expresses a fundamental principal of the Vedic ritual view: *the nature of the activity of the rite manifests itself in the results*. Thus, the use of an already dead animal in the ritual results in the immediate death of the sacrificer, and the use of decayed animals results in the sacrificer's own decay.

Having dismissed these two alternatives the ritualists explore a third option, which proposes the slaughter of one animal in place of all five. The ritualists choose the goat for this role, and thus they describe how the goat is equivalent to all the five sacrificial animals—man, horse, bull, sheep and goat:

> Regarding why he slaughters this animal: in this animal indeed exists the form of all animals. As it is hornless and beardless, so it has the form of a man, for man is indeed hornless and beardless; as it hornless and possessed of long hair, so it has the form of a horse, for the horse is indeed hornless and possessed of long hair; as it is eight-hoofed, so it has the form of a bull, for the bull is indeed eight-hoofed; as its hoof is sheep-like, so it has the form of a sheep; as it is a goat, so it [has the form] of a goat. Now when that [goat] is slaughtered by him, indeed all the animals are slaughtered.[59]

The Vedic animal sacrifice (*paśubandha*) normally utilized a single goat as its sacrificial victim;[60] in part, the reduction of the Agnicayana's five victims to one goat appears to be an attempt to represent the Agnicayana, at its outset, as the quintessence of the Vedic rites. And, because it accomplishes the original purpose of the rite—without too much bloodshed—the ritualists accept the sacrifice of the single goat as an alternative to the sacrifice of all the five animals.[61]

The peculiar relationship between the two aspects of the Agnicayana rite—the building of the fire altar and the Soma sacrifice—leads the ritualists to question how this preliminary animal sacrifice relates to the rest of the rite. Although the Soma ritual includes an element of the animal sacrifice,[62] in the Agnicayana this preliminary rite occurs before the main action of the Soma sacrifice and cannot be correlated with the Soma ritual's animal sacrifice.[63] In the Śatapatha Brāhmaṇa the ritualists are depicted as asking if the animal sacrifice represents a complete sacrifice (that is, a Paśubandha wholly separate from the Soma sacrifice), which would then require the giving of a sacrificial gift (*dakṣiṇā*),[64] or if it is a preliminary (that is, an aspect of the initiation [*dīkṣā*]) to the Soma ritual, which would then require the sacrificer to abstain from both eating meat and having sexual intercourse.[65]

This sort of questioning is a subterfuge; in fact, the Agnicayana's preliminary animal sacrifice, having apparently originated outside the sphere of the classical ritual, is neither a Paśubandha nor a Soma initiation. However, by calling upon these two categories of the classical ritual, the ritualists create an either-or situation to which the only answers, a Paśubandha or a Soma initiation, lie within the larger structure of the ritual system.

The Agnicayana's animal sacrifice resembles the Paśubandha more closely than it does the Soma rite's initiation, which does not include an animal sacrifice.[66] However, if this preliminary event is represented as a Paśubandha, and thus a complete sacrifice, then an untenable situation arises: the Agnicayana ritual, which has hardly begun, would be abruptly ended. In the words of the ritualist: "Lest in the beginning [of the ritual] I should dismiss the gods; lest I should cause the [entire rite] to be completed."[67] And, to emphasize the preliminary nature of this animal sacrifice the ritualists prohibit at this time the giving of a *dakṣiṇā*,[68] without which any single ritual event is said to be incomplete.[69] Thus, the outward resemblance of the preliminary animal sacrifice to the classical Paśubandha is another subterfuge. What appeared to be an either-or situation does not present a real choice; for the Agnicayana ritual to continue the animal sacrifice must be viewed as an initiation.

Yet, the preliminary animal sacrifice does not appear to have any of the characteristics of the classical Soma initiation, a situation that leads the Agnicayana ritualists to declare: "In no way is this a *dīkṣā*; for there is no girdle and no black antelope skin."[70] The purpose of an initiation is to place the sacrificer, who is on his way to being transformed in the ritual, in a liminal state;[71] in the case of the Vedic ritual this is partly accomplished by the prohibitions against eating meat and engaging in sexual intercourse.[72] The Agnicayana ritualists meet the requirements of the Vedic initiation by declaring that the performer of this preliminary rite must refrain from sexual intercourse. However, in this instance, the prohibition against eating meat is modified to a prohibition against eating honey,[73] and thus the ritualists acknowledge that this preliminary animal sacrifice is distinct from the usual initiation rite. Moreover, this modified prohibition ensures that the animal sacrifice does not interfere or is not confused with the proper *dīkṣā* that, as a part of the Soma sacrifice, will occur later in the course of the Agnicayana performance.[74] Thus, despite its formal dissimilarity to the Vedic initiation rite, the preliminary animal sacrifice becomes a sort of "preinitiation" initiation rite; its prohibitions replicating the function of the initiation, without infringing on the place of this rite in the performance of the Agnicayana's Soma ritual. At the same time, by transforming this animal sacrifice into an initiation, the ritualists have, in a certain sense, removed this preliminary rite from the realm of animal sacrifices; for, as already noted, the Soma initiation does not include an animal sacrifice. Through subtly redefining this preliminary rite the Agnicayana ritualists have once again bridged the problem of death in the sacrifice.

The second phase in the construction of the fire altar is fashioning the fire pan (*ukhā*).[75] Although the fire pan is used in several ways in the Agnicayana, its principle function is to transfer the consecrated fire (*agni*) from the old ritual fireplace, which is used for lesser rites, to the newly built fire altar.[76] As the vehicle of the fire the fire pan is identified as the "self" (*ātman*) of the fire altar.[77] And, as such, the fire pan is said to give birth to the altar.[78] The integral relationship of these two is expressed concretely in the burying of the pan within the bottom layer of the altar.[79] Of equal importance to this relationship is the relationship between the sacrificer and the fire pan, for the fire pan is also identified with the sacrificer; after it is fashioned and before the altar is built, the sacrificer straps the fire pan to himself for a period of one year.[80]

The Śatapatha Brāhmaṇa likens fashioning the fire pan to a birth process. The first stage of this process is that of an impregnation, as a lump of clay is dug up and then placed in a hole for "this [earth] is a womb, and that [clay] is seed."[81] The clay is then dug out of the hole and placed in a black antelope skin,[82] which in many Vedic rituals symbolizes the covering of the womb. Thus, in one ritual, when the sacrificer seats himself on a black antelope skin with the statement "I touch you," the Śatapatha Brāhmaṇa tells us that he actually means, "I enter into you," and instructs the sacrificer to close his hands, for "embryos have [their] hands closed."[83] In another ritual context, that of the cremation rite, the body of the deceased is placed on a black antelope skin: "Thus he is caused to be born from [his] own [sacrificial] womb."[84]

The lump of clay and its antelope skin covering are then placed on a lotus leaf, which, like the antelope skin, represents the covering of the womb:[85] "He puts it on a lotus leaf; indeed the lotus leaf is a womb, and thus the seed is emitted in the womb. When the seed is emitted in the womb that becomes procreative."[86] The lump of clay is then worked with water and foam, since "it was emitted from these forms in the beginning, from these it is now born."[87] These three elements—water, foam, and earth (represented in the lump of clay)—represent the two foundations of the cosmos's existence, and the intermediate or unifying state between them. Fashioning the fire pan thus replicates the events of the cosmogony.[88]

With the same clay that the sacrificer uses to make the fire pan, the sacrificer's wife fashions the first eight bricks for the fire altar.[89] Whereas the use of this clay first used to fashion the fire pan establishes an essential connection between the altar and the fire pan, the employment of the sacrificer's wife to perform this act establishes an intimate relationship between the sacrificer and the altar; for, the bricks that will be used to build the altar now become the sacrificer's "offspring": "Now he makes the fire pan; he makes it to be his own self. Then he makes the 'all-light' bricks; the 'all-light' bricks are his offspring. . . . That which is clay he makes from his self, then he creates these offspring . . . he makes these offspring manifest from his [own] self."[90]

Although for the most part, the sacrificial ritual was a male enterprise, the ritualists occasionally refer to a man's "incomplete" nature, which apparently refers to his inability to procreate by himself. Thus, in one of the few instances in which the wife participates in the rite, the Brāhmaṇic authors explain: "The wife is indeed half of his self; for as long as he does not obtain a wife, is how long he is not born, and for that long he is not whole. Now when he obtains a wife then he becomes whole."[91] In Vedic mythology, the half nature of man is explained as having resulted from the cleavage of an androgynous primordial being, whose two halves then became husband and wife.[92] In the Bṛhadāraṇyaka Upaniṣad, Yājñavalkya is reported to have commented that, as a result of the division of the primordial being, "this own [body] is like a half portion, and so a woman fills this space."[93] Through joining together with his wife in the fashioning of the bricks and the fire pan, the sacrificer recreates the androgynous state of the primordial being. However, with this one act the active participation of the sacrificer's wife in the construction of the fire altar is ended; and thus, it seems that man, the sacrificer, having attained this state of primordial androgyny, is capable of (ritually) procreating on his own. This notion finds support in one passage in the Taittirīya Saṃhitā, which states that when building the fire altar the sacrificer should not engage in sexual intercourse, at least with women, for the text intimates the sacrificer is engaged in a sexual act with the altar.[94]

The fire pan is then placed on the old offering fire (*gārhaptaya*). Here, the fire pan is described as a maiden (*yoṣā*) and the fire as a potent male (*vṛṣan*): "Indeed the fire pan is a maiden and the fire is a potent male; when the male heats thoroughly in the maiden then the seed is placed in her."[95] The fire pan is here identified as a womb, with *muñja* grass and hemp as its inner and outer membrane; ghee apparently as its embryonic fluid; and the kindling stick as its embryo.[96] The coals of the old offering fire cause these highly flammable materials to ignite. Creating the consecrated fire in this way again points to this rite's connection with the larger body of the Vedic rituals, as the new fire is born out of the old ritual fire. However, at the same time, being newly created this fire expresses the Agnicayana's distinct identity.

A one year hiatus in the ritual proceedings follows the creation of the fire pan and the fire. During this time the sacrificer, who has now placed a gold plate around his neck, carries the lit fire pan.[97] The year is a gestation period,[98] at the end of which the altar will be born with its characteristic bird shape: "He now forms (*vi- √kṛ*) that [matter in the fire pan] into that having wings and a tail; in whatever manner the seed forms it in the womb, so it is born, and what he there forms into having wings and a tail will be born in the future as having wings and a tail."[99]

The year is also identified with death,[100] and one of the goals of the construction of the fire altar is to reach beyond all that is governed by the year to the immortal world.[101] The one year hiatus in the ritual, which takes the sacrificer beyond the year, thus represents a way of exceeding the realm of death. At this stage of the ritual, however, the sacrificer has not entirely gone beyond death but may be said to be at the threshold of this attainment. In particular, wearing the gold plate, which represents the sun, suggests that the sacrificer now stands "in between" the mortal and immortal realms. In the Śatapatha Brāhmaṇa, the sun, which measures the year, is depicted as the point of bifurcation between the mortal and the immortal sphere: "Indeed, that one who burns there is death; therefore, those people who are on this side die; but those who are on the other side are the gods, and therefore immortal."[102] Accordingly, while the sun is identified with death, it is said to be "within the immortal [realm]."[103] As the ritual continues, the sacrificer will cross this threshold to that which is on the other side of the sun.

The next phase of the ritual is the construction of a "domestic hearth" (*gārhapatya*), which represents a reconstructed version of one of the three hearths (*ahavanīya, dakṣiṇāgni, gārhapatya*) used in all the Vedic *śrauta* rites. The construction of this hearth is again likened to a birth process. Here, the womb is said to be the earth, and the embryo inside the womb is identified as having both the shape of a man and the shape of a bird, which is the shape of the completed fire altar.[104] The Gārhapatya thus represents the earthly foundation of man and the fire altar, both of which will be (ritually) born during the course of the Agnicayana's performance. To express this connection the Gārhapatya, which traditionally has a round shape, is made to the same measure as a man or the distance between a man's outstretched arms (*vyāmamātra*), and its shape is said to symbolize the roundness both of the womb and the earth.[105] However, the text makes it clear that there is a generative relationship between the sacrificer, the Gārhapatya, and this world, which goes beyond this symbolic correspondence in size, as the sacrificer (*yajamāna*) is said to emit his "real semen" (*retas bhūta*) into the fire pan: "Then this sacrificer emits [his] real semen, [his] self, into the fire pan, the womb. Indeed the fire pan is the womb. In one year a foundation forms for him. In it he causes this world here to be born—indeed the Gārhapatya is this world."[106] Through emitting his semen into the fire pan—a union that yields the Gārhapatya—the sacrificer invests his own self into the earth, which the Gārhapatya represents.

During the course of the ritual the sacrificer will be going forth—at least symbolically—into the unknown cosmos. However, because the sacrificer is not yet ready to permanently leave this world (a situation desirable only at death), he must ensure that he will be able to return at the end of the ritual performance. This sort of journey and return is a characteristic of many Vedic rites,[107] and as a reflection of the dangerous nature of journeying into the unknown, it is sometimes called the *difficult ascension* (*dūrohaṇa*).[108] In these rites the sacrificer depends on the officiating priests to guide his return to this world.[109] The image—presented in the Śatapatha Brāhmaṇa—that exemplifies this is that of the sacrifice as a heaven-bound ship with the priests as its oars.[110] However, the Agnicayana's emphasis on individual performance implies that the sacrificer will not be able to depend on the officiants to guide him back to this world. Here, the sacrificer's act of emitting his semen into the fire pan—which establishes an inextricable relationship between an aspect of the sacrificer's own self and the Gārhapatya that is created by this act—releases the sacrificer from this dependence on the officiants. The Gārhapatya, which represents the earth, is said to serve as the sacrificer's foundation, ensuring that he does not become lost during his journey outward into the larger cosmos:

> Now regarding why he stands just there; indeed, the Gārhapatya is this world. The foundation is this [earth] and indeed the Gārhapatya is the foundation. Now when he goes in that direction, it is that which is without a path as it were. But he stands on his world, that which is the foundation, this [Gārhapatya]. Thereby he returns to this [earth]; so he establishes himself on this foundation.[111]

Following the construction of the Gārhapatya, the sacrificer prepares the site upon which the fire altar will be erected. The sacrificer first plows eight furrows: two from west to east, one from east to west, two south to north, one north to south, one northwest to southeast, and one southwest to northeast.[112] After the furrows are plowed, the sacrificer pours jars of water on the altar site; "thus he puts rain on it."[113] And, following the water, all types of seeds are sown on the site.[114] The plants that arise from these seeds are said to provide not only food but also medicine (*bheṣaja*), which serves to "heal" (*/bhiṣaj*) the altar.[115] The chief purpose of the fire altar is to effect a unification between man and cosmos. The wholeness achieved through this process recreates Prajāpati's primordial state and, as such, represents the realization of man's original state. As medicine, the plants assist in "healing" this relationship.

The Śatapatha Brāhmaṇa's authors preface the actual construction of the fire altar with the enigmatic statement that the sacrificer "inciting the fire [altar] takes [it] into [his own] self; indeed, from [his own] self he causes him to be born, and how he sees (*/dṛś*) it, it is born now having just that appearance."[116] As a result of this process, the sacrificer ensures that he does not "give birth to a man from a man, to a mortal from a mortal," but "having taken the fire [altar] into his own self . . . he gives birth to the immortal from the immortal."[117] The ritualists here express the idea that the mental process, as the sacrificer takes the altar into his own self and views it in his mind's eye, represents a level of perfection that far exceeds that which can be accomplished in the physical construction of the altar. And, in fact, the altar that is about to be built bears little physical resemblance to the cosmos and the cosmic man (Prajāpati) that it is supposed to represent. Henceforth in the rite, this mental picture, which presents the altar in its ideal form, will guide the sacrificer in establishing the identity of the fire altar.

The construction of the altar proper begins with placing a lotus leaf in the center of the altar site.[118] As noted earlier, the lotus leaf represents a womb, and in placing it on the altar site the authors identify it as such.[119] On top of the lotus leaf the sacrificer places the gold plate that he has been wearing around his neck for the past year. And, on top of this he places a gold man (*hiraṇya puruṣa*). The gold man is identified as both Prajāpati and the sacrificer (*yajamąna*), as well as the fire altar (Agni).[120] The primary identification, however, is between the gold man and the sacrificer, and thus the sacrificer "sings over the [gold] man and [so] puts [his own] virility (or semen) (*vīrya*) into the man."[121] The sacrificer then places two offering spoons, which are said to represent arms, next to the gold man.[122] Along with the offering spoons he places two bricks that are identified as "seed-shedders" (*retaḥsic*).[123] These bricks are said to be the (sacrificer's) testicles. To whatever new existence the construction of the fire altar leads the sacrificer, with his offering spoons and testicles, he will at least be able to continue his characteristic (and closely related) activities of performing the Vedic rites and procreating.[124]

On top of the gold man the sacrificer places the first of the "naturally perforated" bricks (*svayamātṛṇṇā*). In the completed altar there will be three of these bricks, one each placed on the first, third, and fifth levels. These three bricks are identified with the three levels of the Vedic cosmos: earth, heavens, and atmosphere. The perforations in these three bricks allow the sacrificer to pass through the otherwise solid altar in his symbolic ascent through the cosmos. In this first layer of the altar the sacrificer also places a tortoise, which represents the heavens (the upper shell), the earth (the lower shell), and the atmosphere (what is inbetween the two shells); the fire pan, which represents a womb; and a mortar and pestle, which represents a penis in the womb.[125] Along with these various objects the sacrificer places bricks in specific areas, and the shape of the altar begins to manifest itself. The authors describe this shape as that of an animal, with certain bricks representing its head, neck, breast, back, and hips, and thus they declare: "That animal which is the fire [altar], even now has a form complete and whole."[126]

The sacrificer next places in the fire pan the heads of the five sacrificial animals—goat, sheep, cow, horse, and man—or, if the sacrificer followed the alternative procedure, the head of the single goat that represents them. The sacrificer then throws seven gold chips in each head: "The vital airs (*prāṇa*) are gold, and from these ritually slaughtered animals the vital airs went out; when he throws these chips [into the heads], he puts the vital airs [back] in them."[127] This act thus represents the sort of reuniting or "healing" that is the particular aim of the Agnicayana. And, because in Vedic ritual thought the animals stand in the place of the sacrificer, the placement of the gold chips in the mouths of the animals also represents the "healing" of the sacrificer.

Placing the vital breaths into the sacrificial animals is enacted on a larger scale as the sacrificer puts down a series of bricks that are identified as the "breath-holders" (*prāṇa-bhṛt*).[128] These bricks represent the vital breaths that, in the Agnicayana's creation myth, were said to arise as a result of the Ṛṣis' exertions. These vital breaths came together to form Prajāpati's body and then, in their essential forms, "removed themselves upwards" to form Prajāpati's head.[129] In the creation myth this sequence of events apparently occurred *in illo tempore* and initiated the conditions necessary for Prajāpati's, and hence the cosmos's existence. As a part of the altar's first layer, and thus its foundation, the placement of the *prāṇa-bhṛt* bricks seems to serve this same purpose; in particular, the placement of the vital breaths will provide an animating force for the otherwise lifeless bricks of the fire altar: "These limbs the vital breath does not reach . . . indeed that becomes withered, it decays. Therefore he should place the [breath-holder bricks] in contact with the [altar's] enclosing stones."[130]

After this point, the construction of the altar entails the continued placing of bricks until all five levels are completed. The fire altar described in the Śatapatha Brāhmaṇa requires 10,800 bricks: 1,950 bricks on each of the first, second, third and fourth layers, and 3,000 bricks on the fifth layer.[131] Many of these bricks are individually identified, either as parts of Prajāpati's body (fingers, toes, vital breaths, and so forth) or as parts of the cosmos (the seasons, quarters, worlds, deities, and so forth). These identifications define each layer in relationship to the spheres of the cosmos and to the cosmic body of Prajāpati. The basic image presented here correlates the altar's five levels to Prajāpati's feet, legs, waist, chest, and head and to the pentadic cosmos of earth, intermediate space, atmosphere, intermediate space, and heavens (see Figure 1).[132] And because the sacrificer generated the altar out of his own self, these identifications between altar, cosmos, and cosmic man are implicitly identifications to the sacrificer's own being.

A significant expression of the relationship between the altar, Prajāpati, and the cosmos is seen in the location of the two foundations, the material earth and the immaterial *brahman*, in the fire altar. The first level of the fire altar, which is correlative to the earth and to Prajāpati's feet, is also said to be Prajāpati lying on his back.[133] The placement of the tortoise, which represents the three spheres of the cosmos, on this level implies that Prajāpati founds all material existence on this level, a notion supported by

Altar	*Prajāpati*	*Cosmos*
	All the worlds extend "inwards and outwards" on the fifth level	
Level 5	Head	Heavens
brahman (above)		Death (below)
Level 4	Chest	Intermediate
	Prajāpati curled around the altar's central axis	
Level 3	Waist	Atmosphere
Level 2	Legs	Intermediate
	Prajāpati lying on his back as the foundation of the altar	
Level 1	Feet	Earth

Figure 3.1 The five levels of the fire altar and their relationship to the body of Prajāpati and the cosmos.

the identification of this level as a "complete" animal. On the other hand, immaterial existence appears to be founded on level four, which is identified with the *brahman*. The cosmic man mythology (that of both Puruṣa and Prajāpati) represents this immaterial level of existence through the image of the head, which seems to contain the entire cosmos in its animate and essential form.[134] In the symbolism of the fire altar this notion of an all-inclusive realm is expressed in the fifth level—that is, the level that rests on the *brahman*—which is identified as the head of the altar.[135] The all-inclusive nature of this level is seen as it appears to contain all the worlds, seasons, regions, and so forth that are apportioned vertically on the first four levels of the cosmos.[136] On the fifth level these various elements are said to extend "inwards" (*arvāñc*) and "outwards" (*parāñc*), an image that clearly exceeds the boundaries of any sort of material representation of the cosmos.[137]

The relationship between the "head" and the "body" of the fire altar is exemplified in the notion that the fourth level is not only the *brahman* but also death (*mṛtyu*).[138] In passing above the fourth layer, the sacrificer exceeds material existence, with its inevitable decay, and enters the realm of immortality. The nature of this journey and the difficulty of the passage from one realm into the other is expressed in a myth found in the Jaiminīya Upaniṣad Brāhmaṇa, a text roughly contemporary with the latest stratum of the Śatapatha Brāhmaṇa.[139] The myth first describes how, after death, an individual travels through the various realms of the cosmos: earth, atmosphere, seasons, quarters, moon, and so forth. At each stop on this journey the sacrificer receives an aspect of his own being—a process that obviously reverses the cosmogony, in which the primordial man created the cosmos out of his own self (and implicitly reverses the activity of the Agnicayana rite, in which the sacrificer, following Prajāpati's model, generates himself into the cosmos). He receives his "foundation" from the earth, his hearing from the quarters, the joints of his body from the months, and so forth, as he continues his journey. When the deceased reaches the moon he asks to be taken to the world of *brahman*, which is apparently the highest station. Instead of granting his request, he is taken to the sun, where he had been before going to the moon, and so he asks again: "He says to the sun: 'Carry me forth.' 'To what?' 'To the world of *brahman*.' It carries him forth to the moon. He thus wanders to and fro between these divinities (*devata*). This is the end. There is no carrying forth beyond this."[140] The individual remains within this lower cosmos and, according to the text, eventually descends to the earth and another birth (and consequently, another death).[141]

In the world of the ritual, the sacrificer does not encounter this problem of denial during his passage into the higher realm of the cosmos. The controlled environment of the Agnicayana allows the sacrificer to complete his ascension vertically through the cosmos as he completes the construction of each level of the altar. Thus, with the completion of this fifth level, "the sacrificer, having covered completely all these worlds, enters the heavenly world (*svarga loka*)."[142]

Conclusion: Man and Cosmos in the Fire Altar

At the outset of the Śatapatha Brāhmaṇa's Agnicayana section the authors of the text pose the question, "To [attain] what object (*kāma*) is the fire [altar] built?" The initial response to this is that the altar "having become a bird shall convey me [the sacrificer] to heaven."[143] This statement indicates that the bird-shaped fire altar was seen as a representation of the Vedic sun-bird, who was occasionally identified with Agni and who would thus be capable of conveying the sacrificer to the heavenly realm in which it had its abode.[144] And, in fact, in constructing the fire altar the sacrificer establishes this identification with the Vedic sun-bird on several levels; a gold disk, which is identified with the sun, is placed in the base of the altar; the altar is itself oriented so it is "towards the right, [because] the sun moves around these worlds from there;"[145] and, most obviously, the altar is built in the shape of an eagle, which seems to have been the type of bird meant by the Vedic sun-bird.

However, in this same discussion of the object of constructing the fire altar, the authors of this text disparage the sacrificer "who should think in this manner," believing that the altar is merely a bird that might convey him to the heavenly realm. They state that the sacrificer should build the birdlike altar to attain the same form as Prajāpati, for it was in the form of a bird that he became immortal (*amṛta*).[146]

This discussion reflects the underlying conflict of the Agnicayana; that is, the problem generated by its need to remain within the boundaries of Vedic ritual thought, while striving to express its own unique ideas regarding the purpose of the rite. Thus, the choice of an eagle shape is clearly a concession to the norms of Vedic thought; though the Śatapatha Brāhmaṇa mentions other shapes—such as those of a bucket, a chariot wheel, or a heron—for the construction of the altar, the authors disdain their use.[147] Moreover, through endorsing only a single form for the altar—namely, the eagle shape that undoubtedly represents the Vedic sun-bird and would certainly be recognized as such by the performers of the rite—the Agnicayana's authors establish this ritual within the mainstream of the Vedic tradition. Yet, they are not interested in applying what would appear to be the traditional function of the sun-bird to their definition of the larger purpose of the Agnicayana. Thus, rather than assert that the altar is built with the expectation that it might fly the sacrificer to the heavenly world, as its representation in the form of the Vedic sun-bird would seem to imply, the ritualists declare that the altar is built to attain the same form that Prajāpati had when he created the cosmos, which incidentally was that of a bird.

The authors of this text thus make it clear that the innovative nature of this rite lies in its potentiality to recreate the conditions of Prajāpati's being. To understand what these conditions are and how the Agnicayana ritualists perceived the construction of the fire altar to lead to their attainment, it is necessary to return briefly to the creation myth that initiates the Śatapatha Brāhmaṇa's discussion of the Agnicayana ritual.

After Prajāpati completes his creation of the cosmos, he is said to "fall apart," (*vi- / srams, /srams*).[148] The chief characteristic of this state appears to be the loss of Prajāpati's vital airs (*prāṇa*): "From him fallen apart, the vital airs [that were] amidst him went out, [when the vital airs] in him went out, so too the gods left."[149] Although in the Agnicayana's creation myth, the vital airs are represented as constituting both aspects of Prajāpati's being—after emerging from the Ṛṣis they first transform themselves into the gross parts of Prajāpati's body and then, in their essential form, concentrate themselves in his head[150]—they chiefly represent the inner or animate aspect of existence. And, the gods referred to here apparently are those beings (Agni, Vāyu, Āditya, and Candramas) Prajāpati employs as his agents in placing the animate and essential aspect of existence into the cosmos.[151] The notion that Prajāpati "falls apart" after the creation thus seems to express a notion of disjunction that applies specifically to Prajāpati's separation from the inner or animate aspect of existence, in terms not only of his own being but also in relationship to his creation, the cosmos.

As a result of Prajāpati's condition he asks Agni to restore him. Although the details of this restoration are obscure, this process seems to entail the replacement of Prajāpati's vital airs:

> He [Agni] said: "What do I place [you] on?" He [Prajāpati] replied: "On the foundation (*hita*)." The vital airs are the foundation; indeed the vital airs are the foundation of all that lives. And just as he placed him on the foundation, so people [now] say: "I will place [it]; I am placing [it]; I place [it]."
>
> They say: "What is the foundation (*hita*), and what is [its] condition (*upahita*)?" Indeed the vital airs are the foundation and speech is the

condition. This speech is indeed founded on the vital airs. And so too the vital airs are the foundation and the limbs are the condition; for indeed on this foundation of the vital airs the limbs are founded.[152]

The symbolism of the fire altar clearly reflects this replacement of the vital airs in Prajāpati; for, the vital airs are preeminent among the various entities with which the sacrificer identifies the bricks and other implements used to construct the altar.[153]

Although the event of Prajāpati's reconstruction presents a paradigm for man's own attainment of wholeness, it poses the troubling question of why Prajāpati, whose being seems to represent an ideal state, falls apart as a result of his creative activity. In particular, what does Prajāpati's "falling apart" mean for the human sacrificer who reenacts the cosmic man's activity in his own ritual performance?

To answer this question it is important to delineate clearly the stages of Prajāpati's career. In the first stage, Prajāpati creates the cosmos; the correlation between his own being and that of the cosmos represents a state of wholeness. In the second stage, Prajāpati falls apart; his separation from the vital airs and the gods represents a state of fragmentation, the polar opposite of his original state of wholeness. And, in the third stage, Prajāpati is restored; the reunification with his vital airs implies the reattainment of his original state of wholeness. These stages suggest the cycle of generation, death, and regeneration that characterizes the Vedic ritual; as Heesterman has noted: "In the sacrifice are summed up the two opposite poles of the cyclical rhythm of the cosmos: birth and death, ascension and descent, concentration and dispersion."[154] In reenacting the cosmic man's primordial activity through the construction of the fire altar, the human sacrificer may be said to approach the ritual in a state of fragmentation—that is, already at what in the creation myth is the second stage of Prajāpati's career—and only through completing the altar does he attain a state of wholeness.

In the performance of the Agnicayana, these ideas are partly expressed through the peculiar sequence of the ceremony, which places the animal sacrifice (which is a beheading) before the actual construction of the altar. The main part of the ritual thus employs animals described as being already detached from their vital airs,[155] and reconnecting these vital airs represents an important aspect of the ceremony.[156] The Vedic ritual tradition links inextricably the animal victims to the human sacrificer; they are, in fact, his representatives, and the sacrificer's career mirrors that of the victims. Accordingly, the sacrificer's state, as he embarks on the construction of the altar, may be said to be one of fragmentation; that is, detached from the vital airs that represent the essential aspect of his being.

The notion that the sacrificer approaches the ritual performance in a state of fragmentation reflects the Vedic notion that man is born into this world as an incomplete being; as Brian Smith has observed: "The creation of an ontologically viable person is the result of ritual work, the constructive activity which makes form out of formlessness."[157] The ritual performance was thus said to represent the sacrificer's second birth,[158] a process that completed what was left unfinished by the sacrificer's natural birth: "As long as a man does not sacrifice, for that long he remains unborn (*ajāta*). It is through the sacrifice that he is born; as an egg broken too early (*prathama*), that is how he is [before sacrificing]."[159] To express this notion that the ritual represents a process of birth, during the ceremony the sacrificer assumes several attributes of an embryo;[160] thus, the sacrificer imitates an embryo's mode of existence as he restricts his movements,[161] remains in a womblike enclosure,[162] and keeps his hands closed, "since embryos have their hands in a closed manner."[163]

When the sacrificer emerges from this embryonic state, he is ready to embark on the ritual journey to the world of the gods. This attainment represents the goal of the Vedic rituals:[164] "Whoever sacrifices, he sacrifices [saying], 'Let there be a share for me in the world of the gods!'."[165] To accomplish this goal the sacrificer makes an offering—which is in lieu of his own self—to please the gods: "He who sacrifices pleases the gods with this sacrifice . . . and having pleased the gods becomes one cohabiting among them."[166] The offering, which in the symbolism of the ritual is bound to the sacrificer, leads him to the world of the gods.[167] However, the relationship between the sacrificer and the offering is not a direct one, but one that is mediated through the officiants: "that sacrifice of his goes to the world of the gods, after it goes the *dakṣiṇā*, and holding on to the *dakṣiṇā* which he gives [to the officiants] is the sacrificer."[168]

In presenting itself as a rite that should not be performed for another, the Agnicayana unravels this circuitous route to the heavenly world. The Agnicayana ritualists thus excise one of the elements—namely, the employment of the various ritual specialists—that distances the sacrificer from the ritual performance and, of course, from its benefits. Moreover, the traditional notion that the sacrificer attains the heavenly realm through "pleasing" the gods, as he exchanges life—in the form of a victim—from this world for life in the other world is not apparent in the Agnicayana ritual. In fact, if the construction of the fire altar is separated from the Soma sacrifice, to which it is attached for what appear to be only formal reasons, then it becomes apparent that there is no real "sacrifice" in this ritual. In other words, there is no victim that, when the altar is completed, serves as an offering to please the gods. Although the slaughtering of the animals at the outset of the ceremony presents a semblance of an offering, their death is not viewed as an exchange that brings new life into this world, but rather, like the bricks, they are simply a part of the altar's construction. Without any real offering, the construction of the fire altar, unlike those rituals that call on and require the participation of the gods, is a self-contained activity. Based on the paradigm of Prajāpati's creative activity, building the altar seeks to re-create the anthropomorphic cosmos that signifies a state of wholeness and immortality.

In both the Agnicayana and the traditional Vedic ritual format, man, the sacrificer, is represented as being in an incomplete state. And, in both instances, this state seems to be attributed to the loss of an original wholeness. In the mythology underlying the traditional Vedic rituals, this state of wholeness is represented as a time when men and gods coexisted, a relationship that, for certain reasons, was broken: "In the beginning the gods and men were here together. And whatever there was that was not for the men, those [men] importuned the gods, 'This is not ours, give it to us!' Then those gods, disliking these requests, disappeared."[169] The traditional Vedic format attempts to bring man back into contact with the gods: "Indeed, [by the sacrifice] both gods, men and fathers drink [together]; this is their meeting. In the past they drank [together] in a visible manner; now they [drink] invisibly."[170]

In the Agnicayana, on the other hand, Prajāpati presents the paradigm for man's original state of wholeness. Here, wholeness is defined through a correlation to the existence of the cosmos; that is, the unique events of the cosmogony define an original state of existence wherein man and cosmos are equated on both the planes of "outer" (the physical body, the spheres of the cosmos) and "inner" (the mind and senses, the animate constituents of the cosmos) existence. These two planes represent two poles of existence, the mortal and the immortal: "In the beginning Prajāpati was both mortal and immortal; his vital airs (*prāṇa*) indeed were immortal and [his] body (*śarīra*) was mortal."[171] That Prajāpati "falls apart" after his creation—that is, his vital airs, his "immortal part," leave his material body, and he is cut off from the larger cosmos—reflects the notion that Prajāpati is paradigmatically a man. For man, whose realm is the material earth, is characterized by his mortal nature.[172] The purpose of constructing the fire altar is to reunify man's material being with the essential aspect of existence and thereby regain the original state of wholeness: "By this ritual work, by this proceeding, he [the sacrificer] makes his own self (*ātman*) uniform, undecaying, and immortal."[173] The Śatapatha Brāhmaṇa's many discussions of the symbolism of the fire altar make it clear that the self (*ātman*) that the sacrificer constructs in the ritual act is "uniform, undecaying and immortal," because it not only brings together the two aspects of human existence but also because it brings together the two aspects of the cosmos's existence; and thus "the sacrificer becomes founded in this all."[174]

The construction of the fire altar represents a "ritual" solution to the problem of sacrifice, for it still contains its activities within the abstract world of the ceremony. As J. C. Heesterman has noted: "The place of the sacrifice is conceived of as a replica of the universe and the course of the sacrifice corresponds to the course of the universe;"[175] accordingly, the attainments of the sacrifice are merely replication (though in the case of the Agnicayana it is replication enacted on a scale of enormous complexity), symbolic of a larger experience.

The occasion on which the sacrificer finally moves out of the limited sphere of the ritual is his death. For the sacrificer, however, the event of death has already been defined by the ritual experience, which, as the replication of the universe itself, enacts—in its limited arena—all experience. And, this definition by ritual leads in the earliest stratum of Upaniṣadic thought to the articulation of the karma doctrine.

4.

From Death to Rebirth

Mircea Eliade, echoing a view that has long been held among Indologists, observed that "the Vedic and Brāhmaṇic conceptions concerning postexistence in the beyond are complex and confused."[1] In part, the apparent confusion that surrounds these notions is a reflection of the peculiar nature of the Vedic cosmography, which, over centuries of development, variously depicted the number of spheres and their relationship to one another in the cosmos.[2] These depictions ranged from the bipartite cosmos of heavens and earth, which was prevalent in the earliest period of the Ṛgveda's composition, to the multileveled cosmos consisting of such diverse members as units of time (days, months, seasons, and so forth) and the many worlds that are defined through their association with a particular group of inhabitants (gods, fathers, *gandharvas*, and so forth), which is seen in the Brāhmaṇas.[3] The Vedic cosmography was further complicated by the fact that these various cosmic images were not mutually exclusive; for example, the older bipartite and tripartite cosmic images were never entirely abandoned, but were incorporated in the newer pentadic and heptadic images in such a way that their presence was still strongly manifested.[4] (This peculiar sort of consolidation is exemplified in the imagery of the fire altar, which at once represented a heptadic, pentadic, and tripartite cosmos.)[5] The confusion that arose from the superimposition of the various cosmic images is apparent in one passage in the Śatapatha Brāhmaṇa, which discusses a reference to the phrase "in the highest heaven" (*adhi nāka*), a phrase that may have been drawn from a text that still employed a simpler depiction of the cosmos. Because the *highest heaven* might refer to any one of several spheres in the multileveled Brāhmaṇic cosmos—in particular, either the realm of the gods or the realm of the fathers—the authors of the text emend this reference by adding that "what he means to say is 'amongst the gods' (*devatrā*)."[6]

The expansion of the cosmos from a single otherworld, the heavens, to a multiplicity of otherworldly spheres, coincided with an increase in the number of places to which the deceased might go after leaving this world. And, just as this development in cosmography made it difficult to distinguish specific otherworldly realms, so, too, this increase made it difficult to ascertain precisely where the deceased went after leaving this world.[7] This problem is apparent in a discussion that appears in the Bṛhadāraṇyaka Upaniṣad, in which Yājñavalkya is questioned regarding the afterlife fate of the Pārikṣitas, who were known in Vedic legend as performers of the horse sacrifice.[8] Yājñavalkya's reply consists of an obscure description of this world and the next, after which he discloses the fate of the Pārikṣitas:

> [He said:] "This world (*idam loka*) is [equivalent to] thirty-two of a day's journey of the [sun] god's chariot; around that, covering twice as much [area], is the earth (*pṛthivī*); around that, covering twice as much [area], is the sea. Then as much as is the edge of a blade, or as much as is the wing of a bee, so much is there a space inbetween. Indra, having become a bird, delivered them [the Pārikṣitas] to the Wind (*vāyu*). The Wind, having placed [the Pārikṣitas] in its own self, led them there where the performers of the horse sacrifice abide."[9]

Although Yājñavalkya's narrative implies a specific otherworldly realm exists to which the performers of the horse sacrifice go, it does not disclose its location or present precise cosmographic information that might distinguish it from the other realms in the cosmos. This lack of precision is especially apparent in the final statement of this passage, which purports to describe the place where the Pārikṣitas abide. This description rests chiefly on a tautology, as Yājñavalkya tells his audience that the Pārikṣitas, who were well-known as horse sacrificers,[10] went "there where the performers of the horse sacrifice abide."

On the level of cosmography this description of the afterlife seems to exemplify the "complex and confused" character of these beliefs in late Vedic thought. However, on another level—namely, that concerned with the attainments of the afterlife—the outlines of a coherent eschatology emerge from Yājñavalkya's narrative. In particular, Yājñavalkya's tautological description of where the

Pārikṣitas went expresses the notion that individuals attain specific otherworldly realms as the result of specific sorts of activities. This principle suggests that the various afterlife realms can be distinguished, or ordered, on the basis of the types of (ritual) activities that individuals perform before death. As such, this description of the Pārikṣitas' fate may be said to represent an early formulation of the doctrine of karma, for it combines the traditional Brāhmaṇic definition of karma as ritual action, while adding to it the notion, which appears prominently in the Upaniṣads, that the effects of ritual actions are realized in the conditions of the afterlife. Significantly, Yājñavalkya's discussion of the fate of the Pārikṣitas immediately follows his statement of the doctrine that "one becomes good by good action and bad by bad [action]," widely considered to be the earliest formulation of the karma doctrine in the Upaniṣads.[11] Although this statement is depicted as a "secret" teaching, Yājñavalkya's discussion of the Pārikṣitas' fate seems to represent a "public" declaration of the same doctrine.

The notion that certain acts lead an individual to attain a specific world in the afterlife is prefigured in the ritual sphere. This relationship between act and world is especially evident in a discussion of the results of the initiation, as the sacrificer—through the activity of the rite—is said to make (/kṛ) a world for his own self: "When he performs the initiation, he makes for it [his own self] that world beforehand (*purastāt*); and when he becomes initiated he is born to that made world. Therefore they say: 'Man is born to the world that is made [by his own self]'."[12]

The statement that occurs at the end of this passage, "man is born to the world that is made [by his own self]," has been interpreted by several scholars as a reference to the attainments of the afterlife. Julius Eggeling thus noted that this passage meant "man receives in a future state the reward or punishment for his deeds during this life."[13] And though Jan Gonda observes that Eggeling's interpretation is "properly speaking, not the purport of the text,"[14] he nevertheless states that this passage indicates that "in the future one will receive that form of existence and those circumstances in life which one has gained or brought on oneself before that future birth."[15]

The context in which this statement occurs implies that the sacrificer's "rebirth" follows not his physical death, but rather the sort of symbolic death associated with the ritual performance. The Jaiminīya Upaniṣad Brāhmaṇa clearly distinguishes between the event of an individual's actual death and his "death" in the ritual sphere—in particular, as an aspect of the initiation rite: "This [man] indeed dies for the first time when the emitted seed is produced. . . Then he dies for the second time when he becomes initiated. . . Then he dies for the third time when he dies."[16] In the symbolism of the Vedic ritual, the initiation represents a death to the world of ordinary experience, out of which the sacrificer is "born" into the world of the rite.[17] This notion of a new birth is expressed through the identification of the sacrificer, as he undergoes the initiation rites, with an embryo.[18] The "beforehand world," which man makes when he is initiated and into which he is born, is the world of the ritual. This world is prepared for the sacrificial performance—just as man is—through the preliminary event of the initiation rite.

Nevertheless, the interpretation put forth by Eggeling and Gonda that the statement, "man is born to the world that is made [by his own self]," refers to the attainments of the afterlife is not entirely incorrect. This notion of rebirth bears an obvious resemblance to the later formulations of the karma doctrine and, as already noted, seems to prefigure the principle by which the Pārikṣitas attained the afterlife realm of the horse sacrificers; namely, that the nature of an individual's afterlife existence is determined by the sorts of ritual activities that he performs during the course of his life. Moreover, the death and subsequent rebirth that occurs in the initiation must be viewed as a part of a continuum of death experiences, which, according to the Jaiminīya Upaniṣad Brāhmaṇa passage quoted earlier, begins with conception and ends with the physical death that ends a single lifetime. In each instance, the principle that governs this experience—namely, the attainment of a world created through a certain set of acts—remains the same. Thus, although this statement that "man is born to the world that is made [by his own self]" is clearly intended to refer to the sacrificer's symbolic death in the initiation rite, there is little to distinguish it, *in principle*, from what occurs on the event of the physical death that marks the end of a single lifetime.

The idea that death does not occur once but rather several times in an individual's lifetime is an important factor in interpreting the late Vedic notions of the afterlife. In particular, the symbolic death that the sacrificer experiences in the ritual provides a model for the physical death that marks the end of his lifetime; the factors that lead the sacrificer to specific attainments in the ritual sphere operate in the same fashion when the individual embarks on his final journey to the otherworld. Moreover, this final journey is itself brought about through a ritual event, the funeral rites, aptly named the *final sacrifice* (*antyeṣṭi*). As David Knipe has pointed out, this final rite is also an initiation, through which the deceased enter the otherworld and join the community of the gods and ancestors.[19]

The ritual journey to the otherworld, although it is said to place the sacrificer on a dangerous path,[20] can be faced with a greater degree of certainty than that which the individual confronts as a result of the final sacrifice. Although the sacrificer (*yajamāna*) depended on a number of ritual specialists (*ṛtvij*) to actually perform the sacrifice, he yet retained a measure of control through his active presence at the ordinary (i.e., nonfuneral) *śrauta* rites. In the final sacrifice, however, the *yajamāna*, who is now on the funeral pyre, is limited to an entirely passive experience in the ritual performance. For the deceased the level of danger—that is, the possibility of not attaining a good existence in the otherworld—is thus markedly increased over that experienced in his other ritual activities. In this final sacrifice ritual mistakes cannot be corrected; that which previously was realized symbolically in the ritual gives way to a real and final experience in the otherworld.

The problem raised by the individual's lack of control in this final sacrifice is tempered by the amount of preparation he undergoes in life. This preparation consists of performing the *śrauta* rituals, which, at least symbolically, lead the sacrificer to the otherworld. The attainments achieved through the ordinary sacrifices thus create a model for the attainments of the afterlife. However, the *śrauta* sacrifices are not all the same but rather exist in a specific hierarchy so that "a person is in general only eligible to perform a later ritual in the sequence, if he has already performed the earlier ones."[21] This ritual hierarchy resulted in a hierarchy of rewards, and these are clearly reflected in the attainments of the afterlife. However, the sequential nature of the Vedic rites meant that only those who had lived to a greater age could perform the higher rites, and attain their greater rewards; thus, a passage in the Śatapatha Brāhmaṇa correlates specific afterlife existences to the age at which the sacrificer dies:

> Those who depart before the age of 20 they become attached to the world of the days and nights; those who [depart] above 20 and below 40 [become attached] to that [world of] the fortnight; those who [depart] above 40 and below 60 [become attached] to that [world of] the months; those who [depart] above 60 and below 80 [become attached] to that [world of] the seasons; those who [depart] above 80 and below 100 [become attached] to that [world of] the year. Now only that one who lives 100 years or more indeed attains the immortal state.[22]

The one who lives and, of course, sacrifices for 100 years effectively sacrifices his life away, and so he attains what in theory is the goal of the Vedic sacrifice. Because the Agnicayana stood at the zenith of the Vedic ritual hierarchy it is clear that the one who lives and sacrifices for 100 years would have performed this rite as his penultimate sacrifice (the final sacrifice was the funeral rite). The final sacrifice for one who had in life completed the Agnicayana possessed its own distinctive nature: called the *building of the burial place* (*śmaśānacayana*), it was said to complete the building of the fire altar (*agnicayana*). As such it exemplifies the continuum between the ritual and the final journey to the otherworld.

In the following section, I examine how the *śrauta* rites prepared the sacrificer for his journey to the otherworld and how they represented the model for this otherworldly attainment. This relationship is exemplified in the performance of the Śmaśānacayana; for it reenacts the Agnicayana. I then draw from this relationship some general principles regarding the movement from death to rebirth.

The Agnicayana and the Śmaśānacayana

Scholars have often noted the similarity between the construction of the Vedic fire altar (*agnicayana*) and the construction of the burial place (*śmaśānacayana*) for one who has built the fire altar.[23] In fact, the many features shared by these two structures have even led to a modicum of discussion regarding the identity of several mounds constructed of bricks and clay—that is, whether they represented the remains of fire altars or tumuli—excavated at a pre-Mauryan site.[24] However, other than the observation that the fire altar and the burial place bear a remarkable resemblance, few suggestions have been made regarding the nature of the relationship between the two ritual complexes, the funeral rites and the ritual construction of the fire altar, which contextualize these structures.

Wilhelm Caland, who did consider the nature of the relationship between these two events, suggested that the Śmaśānacayana constituted a sacrifice to the fathers, whereas the Agnicayana constituted a sacrifice to the gods.[25] Caland's suggestion is a reasonable one, in view of the intimate association between the fathers and the funeral rites in Vedic thought.[26] In the Ṛgveda this association appears to define the limits of the fathers' participation in the sacrificial ritual.[27] Thus, although the fathers are called on to partake of the sacrificial offering in terms similar to those applied to the gods, the Agni who carries the oblation to them is the cremation fire (the "flesh-eating Agni") and is clearly distinguished from the Agni who carries the oblation to the gods.[28]

The fathers' well-defined and delimited role in the Ṛgveda contrasts with their ubiquitous presence in the Brāhmaṇas, which causes the authors of these texts to discuss the necessity both of keeping away from the fathers and maintaining a clear distinction between them and the gods—even at rituals that traditionally do not appear to have been within the fathers' domain. Several passages in the Śatapatha Brāhmaṇa thus warn the sacrificer to avoid the southern quarter of the ritual area "for that is the quarter of the fathers . . . and then the sacrificer would go quickly to the otherworld."[29] The fathers' presence at the nonfunerary rites led to a certain degree of confusion; the dual presence of the gods and the fathers blurs the traditional distinction between the oblations that call forth the fathers and the oblations that call forth the gods. In one instance this dual presence leads the ritualists to question the nature of fasting during the ritual.[30] After performing the Agnihotra the sacrificer was apparently permitted to take his evening meal; however, the ritualists wonder if this is improper, since the gods, who have been drawn to the ritual area by the activity of the sacrifice, may not yet have partaken of the oblation, which is their "food": "Now it would be improper if one were to eat before [other] men who had not eaten; but what then [the impropriety] if one ate before gods who had not eaten. Therefore, one should not eat."[31] As Yājñavalkya then points out, fasting is a feature of sacrifices to the fathers—or of the funeral rites—and thus, "if he does not eat [the sacrificer] becomes one who is sacrificing to the fathers."[32] To resolve this conflict between offending the gods (by eating before them) and entering upon a sacrifice to the fathers (by fasting), Yājñavalkya proposes that "one should eat that which is eaten [when] fasting."[33] Although it is not entirely clear what type of food Yājñavalkya refers to here,[34] the entire discussion underscores the confusion in Brāhmaṇic thought between the role of the gods and the role of the fathers in the ordinary *śrauta* rituals.[35]

This change in view—from that of the Ṛgveda where the fathers' role is limited to the funeral rites to that of the Brāhmaṇas, which sees them as being present at all types of rituals—seems to be a part of a larger concern with the nature of death in the sacrifice. In particular, several passages in the Brāhmaṇas suggest a certain discomfort over the necessary killing of the sacrificial victim. Among these are the story of Bhṛgu in the otherworld, where Bhṛgu sees cattle eating men, apparently in revenge for man's use of them as both food and the sacrificial offering,[36] and the several myths that describe how cattle and men, who each possessed the sort of skin that the other one now has, exchanged their skins, for which the cattle—getting the more durable skin—agreed to allow men to use them for both food and the sacrificial offering.[37] Such myths reflect what J. C. Heesterman has referred to as the Brāhmaṇas' "obsessive concern about *hiṃsa*, the killing required by sacrifice."[38] This preoccupation suggests a discomfort that might only be resolved through the elimination of death and destruction from the sacrificial ritual.

According to Heesterman the elimination of death from the sacrifice was achieved through the "contrivance of ritual"; that is, by replacing the reality of death with a carefully constructed system of abstract identifications.[39] As a result of this ritual solution, Heesterman notes, "the ritualists found themselves confronted with the problem of meaning; that is, they had to construct a way back to the lived-in world of mundane reality."[40] The ubiquitous presence of the fathers at the Brāhmaṇic rites implies that one method of reintroducing the reality of death back into the ritual was the identification of the death element, at whatever level of abstraction it may have been present, in all sorts of rituals, with the real death that was the subject of the funeral rites, the proper sacrificial domain of the fathers. In other words, by their presence at the ordinary *śrauta* rites, the fathers made felt the reality of death in a sphere where death, though it was an essential part of the sacrificial experience, had largely been reduced to an abstraction.

The merging of the funeral rites with the ordinary *śrauta* rites may underlie the close resemblance of the Agnicayana and the Śmaśānacayana.[41] Although the Śmaśānacayana does exhibit an overwhelming concern with the fathers, it is important, in view of its similarity to the Agnicayana, to question the precise nature of the relationship between these two rites. At the very least, the characterization that Caland suggested, that one of these rites constituted a sacrifice to the fathers while the other a sacrifice to the gods, does not seem to reflect adequately the many nuances of the relationship between them. The Śatapatha Brāhmaṇa specifically states that the construction of the burial place completes the Agnicayana ritual.[42] In view of this relationship it seems unlikely then that these two rites would have such markedly different orientations; that is, one to the gods, the other to the fathers. However, the two rites are clearly not the same, for they represent a continuum, as one rite leads into the other. This relationship between the Śmaśānacayana and the Agnicayana is clearly expressed in one passage in the Śatapatha Brāhmaṇa:

> He makes the burial place of the one who has performed the fire altar building ceremony after the form (*vidhā*) of the fire [altar]. When the sacrificer builds the fire [altar], by [this] sacrifice he completes a self for that other world. But, this sacrificial act [the Agnicayana] is unenduring if the burial place is not completed. Whoever makes the burial place of the one who has performed the fire altar building ceremony after the form of the fire altar he alone causes the fire altar to be completed.[43]

Here the idea that the burial place is made after the form (*vidhā*) of the fire altar, apparently refers to the employment of several ritual techniques used in the Agnicayana, such as sweeping the burial site,[44] using enclosing stones,[45] plowing and sowing seeds on the burial site,[46] and finally, placing a series of bricks to form a bird's shape, "just like that of the fire [altar]," according to the Śatapatha Brāhmaṇa, to form the burial mound.[47] Just as such ritual techniques seem to have been used in the ordinary rites to lessen the reality of death, so, too, in this funeral rite these techniques temper the harshness of the situation by introducing an element of familiarity and control into an otherwise unknowable experience. However, unlike the ordinary rites, where—through the contrivance of ritual—death seems to have remained merely an abstraction, in the funeral rites the reality of death could never be fully abrogated. This contrast between the funeral rite and the ordinary rite expresses how the Śmaśānacayana "completes" the Agnicayana. Whereas in the Agnicayana the sacrificer's death can only be symbolically realized, the Śmaśānacayana confronts this death as a concrete event.

Funeral rites concerned with burial (and not just cremation), other than the Śmaśānacayana, are referred to in the Ṛgveda and the Brāhmaṇas.[48] In these rites the burial represents a secondary funeral rite that reconstructs, for an otherworldly existence, the body destroyed in an earlier cremation rite.[49] The burial rite for those who in life performed the Agnicayana differed from the rite for those who had not undertaken the ritual construction of the fire altar. In particular, the burial mound for one who performed the Agnicayana was constructed out of bricks, with which the deceased's bones were interspersed, and formed into the shape of a bird;[50] the tumulus for those who had not performed the Agnicayana was constructed out of an apparently formless mound of pebbles.[51] The invention of a burial rite that so closely follows the Agnicayana, and the limitation of its use to those who had performed this rite, implies that the specific purpose of the Śmaśānacayana is to reenact the Agnicayana and thereby to re-experience the otherworldly attainments and rebirth that the sacrificer experienced through it. In other words, the Śmaśānacayana was made to resemble the Agnicayana to ensure that the same otherworldly attainments experienced—albeit on a symbolic level—through the ritual building of the fire altar are actually attained through this final ritual.

The journey to the otherworld, and a resultant state of rebirth, represents a central aspect of the Vedic *śrauta* rites.[52] Thus, the sacrificer's experience in performing the various rites may be said to represent the "empirical" evidence of the attainments that he hopes to realize again—though in a final way—at the end of his lifetime. There are certain general principles on which the sacrifice operates that attest to the journey to the otherworld and the rebirth that results from it. In the Brāhmaṇas there are several references to a cycle of generation and regeneration that starts with the smoke of the sacrifice rising upward to the otherworld. There the smoke becomes clouds, and returns to this world in the form of rain. The rain falls to the ground where it is transformed into plants. When the plants are eaten they become semen, and thus creatures arise. The creatures are then offered in the sacrificial fire, and continuing the cycle of generation, they rise to the otherworld in the form of smoke: "From this world this seed pours forth (/*sic*) as smoke, and that becomes rain in the otherworld. From there that [rain pours forth] as this rain. By this [going] between [creatures] are produced."[53]

This theory does not represent an impersonal process. The oblation, whether it was a goat or a human being, was intimately identified with the sacrificer; at least symbolically, it was the sacrificer's own self that rose up to the otherworld in the smoke of the sacrifice. The effect this theory had on late Vedic afterlife beliefs is clearly seen in the Upaniṣadic description of the *pitṛyāna*, which describes how the deceased is transported to the otherworld in the form of smoke (from the funeral pyre) and then becomes in turn a cloud, rain, rice and other grain, and semen.[54]

Another principle of the Vedic rituals that appears to set a precedent for the attainments of the afterlife is the idea that the sacrifice was a birth process. I already noted that, to express this idea of birth in the ritual, the sacrificer in the course of the ritual performance assumes the attributes of an embryo. Just as this act of assuming an embryonic state suggests that birth from the mother's womb represents the model for the sacrificer's rebirth in the ritual, so it seems that the ritual rebirth stands as the model for the deceased's rebirth in the funeral rite. A passage in the Śatapatha Brāhmaṇa thus refers to the continuum of a man's three births:

"Indeed man is born three times. First he is born from his mother and father. Then that one who sacrifices, when the sacrifice is disposed (*upa- /nam*) to him, he is born a second time. And then when he dies, and they place him on the fire and when he arises from that he is born a third time."[55]

In another passage the performance of a specific *srauta* rite is represented as a middle term linking an individual's natural birth with his birth from the funeral pyre: "When he dies and when he puts him on the [cremation] fire, then Agni burns his body, and from Agni that one is born. Just as he is born from his mother and father, so he is born from Agni. But whoever does not offer the Agnihotra, indeed, he does not arise; therefore, one must offer the Agnihotra."[56] Thus, while the cremation rite is likened here to the birth process, this similarity can only be realized through the performance—during the course of one's life—of the *śrauta* rites, in this case the Agnihotra. Without establishing a precedent for a sacrificial birth, the individual cannot attain a rebirth from the final sacrifice.

These notions that, on the one hand, the sacrificer attained a new birth in the ritual sphere and, on the other hand, that he entered into a cycle of generation as the smoke of the fire became rain, were linked in the ritual process in the idea that the sacrifice was a journey to the otherworld.[57] As noted earlier, in the Agnicayana the construction of the Gārhapatya served to orient the sacrificer in undertaking this journey and thus ensured his return to this world. In fact, the return, or descent, from the otherworld represented an essential component of the ritual journey. As Brian Smith has noted: "The Brāhmaṇas are quite blunt in their warnings to those who spurn a round trip ticket and do not descend from the *svarga loka*."[58] Smith rightly points out that the return from the otherworld is necessitated by the human condition; unlike the immortal, or more precisely, "undying" (*amṛta*) gods, who long ago made the journey to the otherworld and remained there, the mortal sacrificer would have to give up his life in the ritual to remain in the otherworld.[59]

Although the return to this world is characterized as a return from the state that the gods enjoy to the state of being a man,[60] the mechanism of the sacrifice implies that the sacrificer emerges from this journey to a new state of existence or rebirth. In particular, the two processes of the sacrificer's symbolic transformation into an embryo and the physical transformation of the oblation—as it turns into smoke and then rain—with which the sacrificer is identified, complement this journey to the otherworld. There the sacrificer realizes a state of original wholeness, which according to Brāhmaṇic mythology is achieved either through uniting with the gods or through the realization of one's own identity with the cosmos.[61] Yet, this transformation appears to be a matter of degree, as the sacrificer, after his descent from the otherworld, is still much the same—at least in terms of his physical being—as he was before his journey.

There is one situation that would seem not to necessitate a descent from the otherworld; that is, the event of the sacrificer's death. Yet, although the (deceased) sacrificer is now free to remain in the otherworld, the model of ascent and descent, which was established through a lifetime of sacrificial performances, seems to remain effective in this final experience. The possibility of a return from the otherworld, after the event of the sacrificer's death, is seen in a passage in the Jaiminīya Upaniṣad Brāhmaṇa that describes the journey of the deceased. After journeying to the many spheres of the cosmos (including the worlds of the months, the seasons, the years, the *gandharvas*, the apsarases, the sun, and the moon), the deceased finds himself at the "end" (*anta*):

> There is no carrying forward beyond this point. And all the worlds beyond this which have been discussed [here] are obtained; they are conquered. In them all he, who knows thus, moves as is his desire. If he should desire: "Let me be born here again," in whatever family he directs his attention, either the family of a brahman or the family of a king, into that he will be born. Indeed to this world he goes ascending (*abhy-ā- /ruh*) again, as one knowing.[62]

The return to another birth in this world seems to represent one of two types of existence after death that the deceased might pursue, for the text also implies that the deceased might remain in some sort of otherworldly state. The distinction between attaining a rebirth in this world and remaining in the otherworld, suggests (it may, in fact, be a precursor of) the Upaniṣadic notion of the two paths—the *devayāna* and the *pitṛyāna*—open to the deceased. The *devayāna* leads the sacrificer to an indefinite sojourn in the world of Brahmā, and the *pitṛyāna* leads the sacrificer to a rebirth in this world.[63]

Although these notions of the rain cycle, the attainment of a new birth in the sacrifice, and the journey and descent to the otherworld express principles that appear to operate in all types of *śrauta* rituals, it is clear that the Vedic thinkers understood the performance of specific rites within the *śrauta* corpus as leading to specific otherworldly attainments. In particular, the Śatapatha Brāhmaṇa seems to suggest a general distinction between the performance of the bulk of the *śrauta* corpus and the Agnicayana. Thus, in one passage the Śatapatha Brāhmaṇa carefully delineates all the various *śrauta* rites, while it declares that "this building of the fire [altar] rite is that which is all these sacrifices"[64]—a notion implying that it absorbs and perhaps transcends all the other rites. This distinction is also seen in the attainments of the afterlife, as the one who performs the Agnicayana is alone said to achieve a state of immortality:

> Now regarding the vigor (*vīrya*) [gained] from the sacrifice. Whoever performs the Agnihotra eats daily in the otherworld; that is how much empowerment there is in this sacrifice. The Darśapūrnamāsa sacrificer eats every half-month; the Cāturmāsya sacrificer every four months; the Paśubandha sacrificer every half year; and the Soma sacrificer every year. The one who builds the fire altar [eats] every century, as is his desire. In this way, according to his desire [he does] not [eat] for one hundred years—as much as is immortality, unending, everlasting. Indeed whoever knows this, his [state] is immortality, unending, everlasting.[65]

This state of immortality reflects the symbolic attainments of the Agnicayana performance. Thus, in constructing the fire altar the sacrificer is said to make "his own self, uniform, undecaying, and immortal."[66] To ensure that, on the event of his actual death, the performer of the Agnicayana again attains this state of immortality—albeit as a concrete attainment—the Śmaśānacayana for the performer of the Agnicayana recreates the fire altar: the tumulus is built of brick and shaped in the form of a bird.[67] Yet, unlike the fire altar, the bricks of which only symbolically represent the sacrificer, the funeral mound actually incorporates the deceased sacrificer, for the mound is built up through interspersing bricks with the bones of the deceased.[68] This final event thus realizes the goal of the Agnicayana (and so, as the text expresses it, it "completes" the Agnicayana); that is, in its construction man and fire altar become a single entity: the bond between man and cosmos attained symbolically in the construction of the fire altar is now concretely and finally realized by the sacrificer in the burial mound.

At the same time, the symbolic bond between man and altar that the Agnicayana first establishes leads to the assertion that the attainments, in the afterlife, of this rite exceed the attainments of all the other *śrauta* rites. For, unlike the other *śrauta* rites, the connection between the Agnicayana and the Śmaśānacayana is established on the basis of a particular type of knowledge. In contrast to this, the general Brāhmaṇic principle that the performance in life of specific *śrauta* rites leads after death to the attainment of specific afterlife realms suggests that the sacrificer need not concern himself with understanding precisely where the ritual will lead him, for the correct performance of the rite ensures its own attainments. A passage in the Śatapatha Brāhmaṇa exemplifies the unimportance of the sacrificer's knowing where he will go, since the ritual act, when correctly performed, imparts its own knowledge: "[At the Aśvamedha] they hold the tail [of the horse] from behind to [gain] knowledge for the attainment of the heavenly world. Man indeed does not know [the way to] the heavenly world, but the horse truly knows [the way to] the heavenly world."[69]

For the Agnicayana ritualist, the ceaseless mental identifications that establish the correlations between cosmos, cosmic man, sacrificer, and altar establish a precedent for the final event in which the sacrificer becomes joined physically with the funeral mound. Just as, in constructing the fire altar, the altar's physical form is superceded by the sacrificer's vision of the altar: "how he sees it, it is born now having just that appearance"[70]—and in this way a nearly shapeless mound (its bird shape was covered by layers of earth) becomes the cosmic man—so, too, in this final experience, the sacrificer can expect to attain a state that exceeds the funeral mound's physical form. In the Agnicayana the particular knowledge that allows the sacrificer to move beyond the ritual form—to see in it the existence of the cosmos—allows the sacrificer in the Śmaśānacayana to move beyond an afterlife existence based strictly on that form and thus to achieve a state of coexistence with the cosmos.

The notion that the performance of specific rites in life leads the sacrificer, upon death, to the attainment of specific afterlife realms seems to underlie the several Upaniṣadic passages identified as the earliest formulations of the doctrine of karma and rebirth. Thus, the Upaniṣadic description of those who follow the *devayāna* and those who follow the *pitṛyāna* centers on a distinction between two types of ritual activity. On the one hand, those who after death attain the *devayāna* are said to "worship in the forest thinking 'faith is austerity',' on the other hand, those who attain the *pitṛyāna* are said to "worship in the forest thinking 'giving [to the priests who perform the sacrifice] is [for the purpose] of storing sacrificial merit in the other world'."[71] However, the afterlife attainments described here are not based on specific ritual activities, but rather on a general principle that distinguishes two *types* of ritual activities. The performance of what has been called the *interiorized sacrifice*, which follows the model of Prajāpati's primordial creative activity and centers on the individual sacrificer, leads to the attainment of the *devayāna*, whereas the performance of what may be termed the *traditional sacrificial format*, which employs ritual specialists on behalf of the sacrificer to call on the gods, leads to the attainment of the *pitṛyāna*. Similarly, Yājñavalkya's statement that "one becomes good by good action (*karman*), bad by bad [action]" describes the fate of the individual not on the basis of a specific ritual act but as the result of a type of ritual activity: here, the notion of the dissolution of the deceased on the funeral pyre—the breath into the air, the eye into the sun, the mind into the moon, and so forth—suggests the cosmic man paradigm.[72] In these Upaniṣadic passages the notion, found prominently in the Brāhmaṇas, that specific rites lead the sacrificer to the attainment of specific afterlife realms is transformed into a general principle; that is, the attainments of the afterlife follow a type of activity: one type based on the traditional sacrificial format, another type based on the format modeled on Prajāpati's primordial sacrifice.

The distinction presented in the oldest Upaniṣads between the two types of ritual activity, which then lead to two types of afterlife existences (*pitṛyāna*, *devayāna*) represents the first stage in generalizing the *Brāhmaṇic* doctrine of the afterlife effects of specific ritual acts into what may be termed a *doctrine* of karma. The bridge between the specific and general principles expressed here may be found in the Agnicayana's emphasis on coupling performance with knowledge. Here a certain type of knowledge allows the sacrificer to move beyond the limitations of the ritual form; in Upaniṣadic thought this principle leads to the view that any rite in the Vedic corpus (and even mundane actions such as eating and breathing) when properly understood allows the sacrificer to reenact the events of the cosmogony. The contrast between those who possess this knowledge and those who do not, seems in Upaniṣadic thought to underlie the general distinction between those who follow the traditional sacrificial format, and accordingly attain one type of afterlife existence (*pitṛyāna*), and those who follow the model of Prajāpati's sacrifice, and accordingly attain another type of afterlife existence (*devayāna*). The emergence in the Upaniṣads of the attainment of two generalized afterlife paths, the *devayāna* and the *pitṛyāna*, thus represents a watershed in Vedic thought, for it elicits from the wealth of ritual structures established in Brāhmaṇic thought a view of the relationship between an act in this life and its effects in the afterlife that could be, and finally was, extended beyond the ritual sphere. In the form of the karma doctrine, these principles pervaded nearly all subsequent Indian thought.

Conclusion: The Karma Doctrine in the Context of Brāhmaṇic Thought

In the first chapter of this book, I noted that A. B. Keith distinguished the thought of the Upaniṣads from that of the Brāhmaṇas by the presence, in one of these textual milieus, of a doctrine of transmigration:

> The distinction [between the Brāhmaṇas and the Upaniṣads] corresponds, we may fairly say, in the main to a change of time and still more to a change of view. The Upanishads hold in some degree at least the doctrine of transmigration, and though not in a developed condition the pessimism which follows on it: these views are not those of the Brāhmaṇas, which, taken all in all, know not transmigration.[73]

Keith's view reflects the biases that pervaded the work of many nineteenth century Indologists, as these scholars attempted to discount the significance of Brāhmaṇic thought in the development of doctrines first articulated fully in the Upaniṣads, an enterprise in which the doctrine of karma and rebirth was of especial importance. In an odd circular argument this doctrine was, by its supposed moral content, separated from the thought of the Brāhmaṇas, while, by its supposed moral content, it delineated the thought of these two textual milieus. A reevaluation of this perspective is long overdue; as David Knipe has remarked: "It is imperative for historians of religion to review the Vedic substrata and perceive essential religious structures and meanings, especially since large areas of the Vedic corpus have lain fellow, neglected by hermeneutics, after a rough century's harvesting with the implements of the textual critics."

In the case of the Upaniṣadic karma doctrine the essential structures that must be attended to in the Vedic substrata are the Brāhmaṇic notions of the ritual process that leads the sacrificer, during the course of the ritual performance, to the attainment of specific otherworldly realms, for the correlations that are established in the ritual world—albeit on a symbolic level—eventually lead the sacrificer, upon death, to the attainment of an afterlife existence in the real cosmos. The distinctions between these two levels of attainment—the symbolic attainments of the ritual world and the actual attainments brought about by the individual's death—may represent the primary distinction between the Upaniṣadic doctrine and the Brāhmaṇic principles that precede it. While the Brāhmaṇas exhibit an overwhelming concern with the ritual world, the Upaniṣads look outward to the larger cosmos. The Upaniṣadic thinkers did not, however, abandon the principles that are the hallmark of Brāhmaṇic thought: to look outward from the carefully delimited boundaries of the ritual world, they simply extended the principles that governed the ritual. This extension is exemplified in a passage in the Chāndogya Upaniṣad that describes the various aspects of a person's life (eating, procreating, and so forth) as a participation in the sacrifice: "When one hungers and thirsts, and when that one has no pleasure, these are his initiatory rites. And when one eats and drinks, and when that one enjoys pleasure, he undergoes the Upasada ceremonies. Then when he laughs and eats, and has sexual intercourse, then he joins in the chants and recitations."[75]

This passage concludes by relating the sacrificer's death to the final bath,[76] for, as the event that concluded the ritual performance, the bath represents the conclusion of a life understood as the sacrifice itself. Underlying this correlation is the key to how the Upaniṣadic thinkers moved from the carefully delimited world of the Brāhmaṇic ritual to the larger cosmos. In the Brāhmaṇas the overwhelming concern with death led to the development of innumerable ritual devices, exemplified, in particular, in the immensely detailed technique of the Agnicayana rite. These ritual devices allowed the Brāhmaṇic thinkers to transform the necessary event of an actual death in the sacrifice into an abstract and largely symbolic experience. The institution of such devices seems to have allowed the Upaniṣadic thinkers to confront the realities outside the world of the ritual sphere. Here, the correlation between death and the final bath of the ritual implies that for the Upaniṣadic thinkers the event of one's death could be faced with a certain degree of assurance; as this otherwise unknowable and dangerous experience was seen to be merely an aspect of the ritual performance, and thus one that had been experienced—at least, symbolically—many times. The Brāhmaṇic abstraction of death in the ritual sphere thus seems to have provided the Upaniṣadic thinkers with the ability to confront death, in whatever context it may have occurred, in the same "unreal" way in which it was experienced in the context of the ritual performance. This ability, which also allowed the Upaniṣadic thinkers to move beyond the specific confines of the ritual arena, reflects a process of generalization, as the structures, paradigms, and principles long established in that arena, were carried outward to a larger world of experience.

J. N. Farquhar once remarked of the Brāhmaṇas that "It seems as if the men who composed these interminable gossiping lectures had left realities far behind them, and were living in a dreary realm of shadowy gods and men and topsy-turvy morality and religion, in which nothing belongs to the world we know except the sacrificial meats, drinks, and the fees paid to the priestly dreamers."[77] To the nineteenth century Indologists, whose views Farquhar here represents, the concern with the sacrificer's real death in the Upaniṣadic karma passages may have signified a movement away from this supposed dream world. The karma doctrine, however, operates on the same principles as those that underlie the Brāhmaṇic ritual theories, merely extending them from the ritual world outward to a larger world of experience. Thus, rather than a movement away from the ritual orientation of the Brāhmaṇas, the Upaniṣadic concern with the sacrificer's actual death may simply reflect an absorption of reality itself into what Farquhar called the "dream world" of Brāhmaṇic ritual thought.

Abbreviations of Vedic Texts

AB .... Aitareya Brāhmaṇa
ĀpŚS .... Āpastamba Śrauta Sūtra
AV .... Atharva Veda (Saṃhitā)
BĀU .... Bṛhadāraṇyaka Upaniṣad
CU .... Chāndogya Upaniṣad
HŚS .... Hiraṇyakeśin Śrauta Sūtra
JB .... Jaiminīya Brāhmaṇa
JUB .... Jaiminīya Upaniṣad Brāhmaṇa
KāṭhB .... Kāṭhaka Brāhmaṇa
KāṭhS .... Kāṭhaka Saṃhitā
KāṭhU .... Kāṭha Upaniṣad
KB .... Kauṣītaki Brāhmaṇa
KBU .... Kauṣītaki Brāhmaṇa Upaniṣad
MS .... Maitrāyaṇī Saṃhitā
MuU .... Muṇḍaka Upaniṣad
PB .... Pañcavimsa Brāhmaṇa
ṚV .... Ṛg Veda (Saṃhitā)
ŚB .... Śatapatha Brāhmaṇa
SV .... Sāma Veda (Saṃhitā)
TB .... Taittirīya Brāhmaṇa
TS .... Taittirīya Saṃhitā
VS .... Vājasaneyi Saṃhitā
VŚS .... Vaitāna Śrauta Sūtra
YV .... Yajur Veda (Saṃhitā)

Notes

Introduction

1. Heesterman, *The Inner Conflict of Tradition*, p. 3.
2. O'Flaherty, *The Origins of Evil in Hindu Mythology*, p. 227. The notion of the world egg is already intimated in the Ṛgveda (10.121), and is well established in the mythology of the Śatapatha Brāhmaṇa (see, e.g., 11.1.6.1–2; 6.1.2.2 ff.).
3. O'Flaherty, *Dreams, Illusion, and Other Realities*, p. 203.
4. See Hubert and Mauss, *Sacrifice*, pp. 28–29.
5. ŚB 7.2.1.4; 9.2.3.4.
6. In Hindu thought death represents a necessary prelude to any sort of creation; cf. Wendy O'Flaherty's remark that "all the karma texts on rebirth *begin with death*, and then proceed to describe birth" ("Karma and Rebirth in the Vedas and Purāṇas," p. 5).
7. See, Heesterman, "The Ritualist's Problem," passim.
8. BĀU 3.2.13.
9. See, e.g., the interpretations of BĀU 3.2.13 set forth by Deussen, *Philosophy of the Upanishads*, p. 330 and Keith, *The Religion and Philosophy of the Veda and Upanishads*, p. 573, and cf., Hume's suggestion that the doctrine presented here was Buddhist in origin (Hume, *The Thirteen Principle Upanishads*, p. 6). In a recent treatment of this passage David Knipe emphasizes its relationship to the Vedic cosmogony of the primeval anthropomorphic sacrifice (Knipe, "*Sapiṇḍīkaraṇa*," p. 113).
10. Dumont, *Homo Hierarchicus*, p. 23.
11. See the section, "The Upaniṣads and the Vedic Origins of the Karma Doctrine" in Chapter 1.
12. As Paul Horsch points out this lack of understanding is seen in the impasse (*Sackgasse*) scholars reached during the past 150 years in their research into the origins of karma (Horsch, "Vorstufen der Indischen Seelenwanderungslehre," p. 99).
13. By this statement I do not mean to imply that the origins of karma are to be found only in the Vedic ritual sphere. See "The Vedic Origins of the Karma Doctrine," later in this Introduction.

14. See, especially, Eggeling, *The Śatapatha Brāhmaṇa*, pt. 4, p. xiii.

15. Heesterman, "Veda and Dharma," p. 87.

16. See, e.g., ŚB 1.3.1.25; 7.4.2.22.

17. O'Flaherty, *Karma and Rebirth*, p. xvii.

18. Ibid.

19. Nineteenth century scholars generally believed that the early Vedic texts contained a level of Indo-European belief closely related to that of their own ancestors, a notion that, according to one scholar "might readily strike disagreeably one who, living among the late posterity of such an ancestry, has to struggle against their weaknesses and vices" (Von Roth, "On the Morality of the Veda," p. 333). The transformation of the Indian tradition was attributable to the increasing admixture of Aryan and non-Aryan. Certainly, the ancient texts, which represent the Aryan viewpoint in what was believed to be a pristine form, were of greater interest to nineteenth century Indologists than was India itself, which represents a thorough mixture of Aryan and non-Aryan. Edward Said writes that "it is reported of some of the early German Orientalists that their first view of an eight-armed Indian statue cured them completely of their Orientalist taste" (Said, *Orientalism*, p. 52).

20. See ŚB 7.4.2.22; cf., 1.3.1.25.

21. Collins, *Selfless Persons*, p. 32.

22. Both the Śatapatha Brāhmaṇa and the Bṛhadāraṇyaka Upaniṣad are attached to the White (*śukla*) Yajurveda. The Yajurveda, which comprises two textual traditions, the Black (*kṛṣṇa*) and the White (the former has attached to it several Brāhmaṇa texts; the latter only the Śatapatha Brāhmaṇa), is the "Veda of ritual *par excellence*" (Staal, *The Science of Ritual*, p. 10).

23. Weber, *History of Indian Literature*, p. 116.

24. Gonda, *Vedic Literature: Saṃhitās and Brāhmaṇas*, p. 352.

25. Although European libraries had already acquired many of these texts in manuscript form, it was not until after 1870 that critical editions of a significant number of Brāhmaṇas were published. A notable exception, however, was Albrecht Weber's excellent Sanskrit edition of the Śatapatha Brāhmaṇa, which was published in 1855.

26. Müller, *A History of Ancient Sanskrit Literature*, p. 204.

27. Müller, *Chips from a German Workshop*, pp. 113. This remark was made in a review of Martin Haug's translation of the Aitareya Brāhmaṇa, published with the Sanskrit text in 1863, and thus one of the first editions of a Brāhmaṇa that would have been available to a general readership.

28. Müller, *Chips from a German Workshop*, p. 114.

29. Müller, *A History of Ancient Sanskrit Literature*, p. 204.

30. Müller's legacy regarding the Brāhmaṇas is discussed further in Chapter 1. See also, Wendy O'Flaherty's discussion of the views held by Müller

and his contemporaries and their "tendency to parrot one another's terms of abuse," in their discussions of these texts (O'Flaherty, *Tales of Sex and Violence*, p. 5).

31. Eggeling, *The Śatapatha Brāhmaṇa*, pt. 1, p. ix.

32. O'Flaherty, *Śiva*, p. 12.

33. Müller, *Chips from a German Workshop*, p. 113.

34. The Sacred Books of the East Series, fifty volumes edited by Max Müller, employs a particularly unusual system of transliteration, the so-called Missionary Alphabet (each volume contains a table explaining the system). W. D. Whitney remarked that the system was "a mixture too awkward and ugly to be tolerated" and that "it was certainly a grave error of judgement on Müller's part to impose its use upon the wealthy Clarendon Press" (Whitney, "Eggeling's Translation of the Śatapatha Brāhmaṇa," p. 410).

35. In a review of Eggeling's translation, W. D. Whitney pointed out that Eggeling often bridges the Śatapatha Brāhmaṇa's many lacunae (a feature of its style) with interpolations of uncertain origin. Whitney generously attributed this to the possibility that Eggeling had in his possession either an unpublished commentary, or another recension of the text (Whitney, "Eggeling's Translation of the Śatapatha Brāhmaṇa," pp. 396, 403). These interpolations are, for the most part, superfluous additions to the Sanskrit text, and thus, the translations from the Śatapatha Brāhmaṇa in this book do not make use of them.

36. A. B. Keith's biography illustrates this. Eggeling's student at Edinburgh and Macdonell's student at Oxford, Keith is reported to have outdistanced any previous candidate in the Home and Indian Civil Service Examination by over a thousand marks. His prodigious record of Indological publications (critical editions, translations, treatises on Indian philosophy, drama, literature and mythology, and the monumental India Office Library Catalogue of Sanskrit and Prakrit manuscripts) was matched by a remarkable output of works on British constitutional law (Keith was for the last thirty years of his life Great Britain's leading expert on constitutional law). (*Dictionary of National Bibliography, 1941–50*, s.v., "Keith, Arthur Berriedale.")

37. Müller, *A History of Ancient Sanskrit Literature*, p. 4.

1. The Problem of Karma and the Textual Sources

1. Dubois, *Hindu Manners*, pp. 556–57. Dubois cites what he calls the *Bhagavata* here; it is not clear whether he refers to the Purāṇa or to some other popular text.

2. See, Dubois, *Hindu Manners*, pp. 401–15, 173. Though Dubois died in 1848, as Max Müller noted in a prefatory note to the third edition of

Hindu Manners: "The Abbé belongs really to the eighteenth century" (ibid., p. v); that is, to the period before Indologists began to study systematically the Hindu textual tradition.

3. See, e.g., Dasgupta, *A History of Indian Philosophy*, p. 71.

4. Sharma, "Theodicy and the Doctrine of Karma," p. 359.

5. Cf. Wendy O'Flaherty's report of the proceedings of a series of conferences devoted to the notion of karma: "Much of our time at the first conference . . . was devoted to a lively but ultimately vain attempt to define what we meant by karma and rebirth. The unspoken conclusion was that we had a sufficiently strong idea of the parameters of the topic to go ahead and study it, in the hope that perhaps *then* we would be able to see more clearly precisely what we had studied . . . " (O'Flaherty, *Karma and Rebirth*, p. xi).

6. A. L. Basham, "The Indian Doctrine of Transmigration," lecture delivered at the University of Chicago on April 29, 1983.

7. See, O'Flaherty, *Karma and Rebirth*, p. xi, and Horsch, "Vorstufen der Indischen Seelenwanderungslehre," p. 100. Also cf. Chapple, *Karma and Creativity*, p. 3, which discusses a recent (though decidedly minority) trend among some scholars to view karma and rebirth as wholly discrete terms.

8. The importance of context in the interpretation of karma is especially apparent in the several studies collected in O'Flaherty, *Karma and Rebirth*. See also Gerow, "What Is Karma (Kim Karmeti)?" which explores karma chiefly as a grammatical problem (though one that establishes a paradigm for many other aspects of Indian thought).

9. See "The Earliest Notice of the Doctrine of Karma and Rebirth in the Bṛhadāraṇyaka and Chāndogya Upaniṣads."

10. Whitney, *Oriental and Linguistic Studies*, p. 61.

11. Horsch, "Vorstufen der Indischen Seelenwanderungslehre," p. 99; cf. O'Flaherty, *Karma and Rebirth*, pp. xi–xii.

12. H. T. Colebrooke's essay, "On the Vedas or Sacred Writings of the Hindus," (first published in 1805) was the first realistic depiction of the Vedic texts to appear in the West. (For British scholarship on the Vedas prior to Colebrooke, see Marshall, *The British Discovery of Hinduism in the Eighteenth Century*, pp. 19–20.) The next clear account of the Vedic texts by a Western scholar was Rudolph von Roth's *Zur Litteratur und Geschicte des Weda* (published in 1846). This hiatus of several decades following the appearance of Colebrooke's essay has been attributed to several factors; in particular, the generally poor quality of the Indian manuscripts (containing many corrupt readings, omissions, and often in a state of material deterioration) and the sudden death in the 1830s of the first Western scholar to attempt a translation of the Vedic hymns, Frederich Rosen. Colebrooke's essay, the first to depict the Vedic texts with any degree of accuracy, has often been cited as an important factor contributing to the lack of

progress in the first half of the nineteenth century in Vedic studies. Colebrooke concluded his essay by stating that the Vedas "are too voluminous for a complete translation of the whole; and what they contain would hardly reward the labor of the reader; much less that of the translator" (Colebrooke, "On the Vedas," p. 476). In the opinion of W. D. Whitney (and this view has been repeatedly expressed by Indologists): "This prophecy was doubtless in some measure the cause of its own fulfillment" (Whitney, "On the Main Results of the Later Vedic Researches," p. 292). However, Colebrooke has been unfairly burdened in this matter; after all, his remarks were also directed to the Upaniṣads, which, even without an accurate translation, were embraced by Western scholars during the first half of the nineteenth century.

13. Published in Paris in 1801, the *Oupnek'hat* was based on a Persian translation of fifty Upaniṣads and other apparently Upaniṣadic-like texts (among them Ṛgveda 10.90), which were first translated into Persian in the seventeenth century. (For the history of the Persian text and a specimen of Anquetil-Duperron's translation, see, Müller, *The Upanishads*, pt. 1, pp. lvii–lix.) Anquetil-Duperron first translated the Persian into French and then into Latin. Nineteenth century scholars thus had before them a text that could have been only a shadow of the original. Despite this, in attestation to its popularity, in 1882, the *Oupnek'hat* was translated into German and so represented an edition of the Upaniṣads four times removed from the original Sanskrit.

14. While attending Schelling's lectures at Berlin in 1844, and apparently under Schelling's influence, Max Müller undertook his first studies of the Upaniṣads. (Müller, *The Upanishads*, pt. 1, p. lxv.) Schopenhauer's influence on later Vedic studies is clearly seen in the work of Paul Deussen, whose *Die Philosophie der Upanishad's*, though no longer considered to be authoritative, has not been surpassed as a detailed examination of Upanisadic thought.

15. Schopenhauer, *Welt als Wille und Vorstellung*, p. xiii, cited by Müller, *The Upanishads*, pt. 1, pp. lix–lx. Cf. Bloomfield, *The Religion of the Veda*, pp. 55–56.

16. Said, *Orientalism*, p. 150.

17. Müller, *Natural Religion*, p. 18. This is Müller's account of a conversation with Schopenhauer. While the early Vedic texts were not available to scholars in the West at this time, the journal of the Asiatic Society of Bengal, *Asiatick Researches*, as well as several of Colebrooke's books were available, and these seem to have been especially popular among German scholars (Kopf, *British Orientalism*, pp. 34, 88).

18. Whitney, "On the Main Results of the Later Vedic Researches," p. 316.

19. Von Roth, "On the Morality of the Veda," p. 347. This view of an ancient people whose behavior differs markedly from India's contemporary inhabitants is in accord with what David Kopf has called, "the Jones-

Colebrooke portrayal of the Vedic age to which a Müller would add the finishing touches, and which today is widely accepted" (Kopf, *British Orientalism*, p. 41). Cf., also, Dubois, *Hindu Manners*, p. 105.

20. Dubois' *Hindu Manners*, published in 1816 with the sanction of the East India Company and recommended by one colonial governer as "the most correct, comprehensive and minute account extant in any European language . . . of the Hindus" (Dubois, *Hindu Manners*, p. xiv), exemplifies the colonial experience of Hinduism. Although Dubois described all Hindus in terms of their "untrustworthiness, deceit and double dealing," he was especially contemptuous of the Brahmans: "The priests of the Hindu religion, although too enlightened to be blinded by the follies which they instil into the minds of their weak fellow-countrymen, are none the less zealous in maintaining and encouraging the absurd errors which procure their livelihood, and which keep them in that high estimation which they have wrongly usurped" (ibid., p. 575; cf., p. 292).

21. Von Roth, "On the Morality of the Veda," p. 346.

22. In part, these scholars seem to have modeled their approach to the history of ancient India on the cyclical interpretation of history that was characteristic of eighteenth century classicism. David Kopf notes that: "To the men of the Enlightenment . . . the history of civilizations did not show uninterrupted progress toward Utopia, but was, on the contrary, cyclical in its discontinuous movements from greatness to decline" (Kopf, *British Orientalism*, p. 24). Having glorified the antique past, these eighteenth century historians were profoundly sensitive to the decline of the classical world. However, this decline represented a necessary event in the cycles of history; it was only after a period of decline that the spirit of the golden age of antiquity could reemerge in a Renaissance, an event for which these scholars were "exuberantly optimistic" (ibid., p. 24). There is an obvious correspondence between this view of history and the views of the nineteenth century Indologists, who saw a golden age in the beliefs of the Ṛgveda, its decline in the Brāhmaṇic period, and a Renaissance in the thought of the Upaniṣads.

23. Whitney, "Hindu Eschatology and the Kāṭha Upanishad," p. 13.

24. This notion is most often associated with Max Müller, who "believed that religion was subject to inevitable decline under the dead hand of institutionalism" (Sharpe, *Comparative Religion*, p. 39). The belief, held by several Indologists, that the rise of the priesthood in the Brāhmaṇic period had a deadening effect on the Vedic religion suggests this same view of priestcraft; see Whitney, "On the Main Results of the Later Vedic Researches," p. 314; Barth, *Religions of India*, p. 44; Hopkins, *Religions of India*, p. 199.

25. Hopkins, *Religions of India*, p. 199.

26. Ibid., p. 181; cf. Keith, *Religion and Philosophy*, p. 586.

27. Some Western interpreters even refused to believe that the sacerdotalists who composed these texts were entirely serious in the treatment of

their subject. Keith thus remarked that the Brāhmaṇas "abound in their explanations of rites with all sorts of absurdities, which we need not accuse the priests of being so foolish as not to recognize as absurdities" (Keith, *Religion and Philosophy*, p. 440). Cf. Hopkins, *Religions of India*, p. 188.

28. See Eggeling, *The Śatapatha Brāhmaṇa*, pt. 4, pp. xiv–xv; and Gonda, *Vedic Literature: Saṃhitās and Brāhmaṇas*, p. 389.

29. Gonda, *Vedic Literature: Saṃhitās and Brāhmaṇas*, p. 339. Cf. Tsuji, "On the Relation between Brāhmaṇas and Śrautasūtras," p. 187; and Burnell, *Sāmavidhānabrāhmaṇa*, p. ix.

30. See Chapter 3; and also Gonda, *The Haviryajñah Somāh*, pp. 71–73.

31. Bloomfield, *Religion of the Veda*, p. 44. These sentiments have been expressed repeatedly by Western Indologists (see especially, the numerous citations compiled by Gonda, *Vedic Literature: Saṃhitās and Brāhmaṇas*, p. 342, n. 17). Whitney, e.g., remarked that: "While they contain valuable fragments of thought and tradition, they are in general tediously discursive, verbose and artificial, and in no small part absolutely puerile and inane . . . they contain no elaborated and consistent system, either of religious or of philosophical doctrine" (*Oriental and Linguistic Studies*, pp. 68–70). See also, Eggeling, *The Śatapatha Brāhmaṇa*, pt. 1, p. ix (quoted earlier, in the Introduction); Hopkins, *Religions of India*, p. 210; and Farquhar, *An Outline of the Religious Literature of India*, p. 27.

32. Hopkins, *Religions of India*, p. 210.

33. This view of the Brāhmaṇic period as an ancient Indian dark age seems to have led scholars to question whether or not the Brāhmaṇas should even be preserved, let alone studied. Thus, Müller remarked that "there is much curious information to be gathered from these compilations. In spite of their general dreariness, the Brāhmaṇas well deserved to be preserved" (Müller, *A History of Ancient Sanskrit Literature* p. 225). In fact, scholars seemed to believe that before their own "discovery" of the Brāhmaṇas, the Indians themselves had little concern with the perpetuation of these texts, attributing their preservation to "priestly folly." As E. W. Hopkins commented: "There is some compensation on reading such trash in the thought that all this superstition has kept for us a carefully preserved text, but that is an accident of priestly foolishness, and the priest can be credited only with the folly" (Hopkins, *Religions of India*, p. 201).

34. Müller, *Chips from a German Workshop*, p. 113. This is the well-known passage (repeated in almost the same words in his *A History of Ancient Sanskrit Literature*, pp. 204–205) in which Müller refers to the Brāhmaṇas as "twaddle, and what is worse theological twaddle."

35. Müller, *A History of Ancient Sanskrit Literature*, p. 228. Cf. Whitney, *Oriental and Linguistic Studies*, p. 69; and Lévi, *La Doctrine du Sacrifice*, p. 7.

36. Lanman, *A Sanskrit Reader*, p. 357.

37. Farquhar, *Outline of the Religious Literature of India*, p. 27.

38. Max Müller remarked that: "It is only when the divine and infallible character of the whole Veda had been asserted by the Brahmans, and when the Brāhmaṇas also, in which these claims were formulated, had been represented as divinely inspired and infallible, that a protest, like that of the Buddhists, becomes historically intelligible" (Müller, *Lectures on the Origin and Growth of Religion*, p. 138; and cf. *A History of Ancient Sanskrit Literature*, p. 17).

39. Müller, *Lectures on the Origin and Growth of Religion*, p. 340. Cf. Deussen, *Philosophy*, p. 396.

40. See, Deussen, *Philosophy*, pp. 62–63, 396–97; and Keith, *Religion and Philosophy*, pp. 513–14.

41. BĀU 1.4.10.

42. Deussen *Philosophy*, p. 396, referring directly to this passage; cf. Müller, *Lectures on the Origin and Growth of Religion*, p. 396.

43. ŚB 11.2.6.13–14.

44. Nonetheless, Keith and Deussen, attempting to show the Upaniṣadic authors' implicit derision of offering to the gods, discussed the comparison of such sacrificers to animals (*paśu*) at BĀU 1.4.10 by translating the Sanskrit term, which generally indicates cattle but can mean any domestic or sacrificial animal, as "housedogs." According to Keith: "with a certain mockery . . . the relation of the ordinary worshipper is compared with that of housedogs" (Keith, *Religion and Philosophy*, p. 514; cf. Deussen, *Philosophy*, p. 62). Similarly, Deussen noted that the use of *paśu*, which he translates "brute beasts," at BĀU 3.9.6 to describe the essence of the sacrifice "sounds very contemptuous" (Deussen, *Philosophy*, p. 62). Even in the Brāhmaṇas, however, the sacrifice is likened to the sacrificial animal; see, e.g., ŚB 2.2.4.13.

45. See, e.g., Müller, *A History of Ancient Sanskrit Literature*, p. 166; Deussen, *Philosophy*, pp. 4, 23. The correspondence between Upaniṣad and Brāhmaṇa is that generated by the existence of separate Vedic schools (*śākhā*). Thus, e.g., both the Bṛhadāraṇyaka Upaniṣad and the Śatapatha Brāhmaṇa belong to the school of the White Yajur Veda. See, further, Winternitz, *History of Indian Literature*, pp. 217–18.

46. See, Deussen, *Philosophy*, p. 4.

47. Cf. Keith, *Religion and Philosophy*, p. 492, regarding Deussen's view.

48. Deussen, *Philosophy*, p. 4.

49. E.g., the Upaniṣad of the Śatapatha Brāhmaṇa, which is extant in two recensions, is titled *Bṛhadāraṇyaka-upaniṣad* in the Kāṇva recension and was also known as *Vajasaneyi-brāhmaṇa-upaniṣad* (Colebrooke, "On the Vedas," p. 36). The colophon to the Mādhyaṃdina recension of the text, however, refers to the Upaniṣad portion as the *Mādhyaṃdina Śatapatha-brāhmaṇa-upaniṣad*, and in the colophon to Dvivedaganga's commentary,

it is called the *Mādhyaṃdina-āraṇyaka*. Also cf. the title of the Jaiminīyas' (a school of the Sāmaveda) Āraṇyaka, *Jaiminīya-upaniṣad-brāhmaṇa*, and the name of the Kauṣītakins' (a school of the Ṛgveda) Upaniṣad, *Kausītaki-brāhmaṇa-upaniṣad*.

50. BĀU 5.2.1.

51. BĀU 5.2.2–3.

52. ŚB 2.4.2.1.

53. ŚB 2.4.2.4–5.

54. The existence of a set of terms specific to the Brāhmaṇic-Upaniṣadic milieu was long ago recognized by Franklin Edgerton; see, his proposal for an "Index of Ideas of Vedic Filosofy" (Edgerton, "Sources of the Filosophy of the Upanisads," p. 203).

55. Such passages occur with great frequency; see, e.g., BĀU 3.9.1 ff.; CU 3.5.1 ff.; ŚB 10.3.3.1 ff.

56. Such lists tracing the line of tradition occur at BĀU 2.6; 4.6; 6.3.7–12; 6.5; CU 3.11.4; MuU 1.1.2. The link these lists establish between the Upaniṣads and the Brāhmaṇas is perhaps incidental to their larger purpose; namely, to place the Upaniṣadic teachings as an integral part of the body of the "heard" Vedic texts (*śruti*) and hence establish them as a part of reality itself. Thus, BĀU 2.6.3 ultimately traces the teaching of the doctrine to Brahmā; BĀU 6.5.4, to Prajāpati and Brahmā.

57. According to the list of teachers that appears at BĀU 6.5.3 (cf. 6.3.7), Yājñavalkya received the doctrine from Uddālaka Āruṇi, who is referred to as an authority on ritual matters throughout the ŚB. See, further, Macdonell and Keith, *Vedic Index*, s.v. "Uddālaka Āruṇi."

58. Although a definitive chronology regarding the composition of the Vedic texts has not been established (see Winternitz, *History of Indian Literature*, pp. 272–88, and Gonda, *Vedic Literature: Saṃhitās and Brāhmaṇas*, pp. 20–25), it is possible to estimate the relative ages of the Brāhmaṇas and Upaniṣads, based on differences in style, language, and content.

59. Hume, *The Thirteen Principal Upaniṣads*, p. 7.

60. Macdonell and Keith, *Vedic Index*, s.v. "Yājñavalkya." Cf. Hermann Oldenberg's remark that Yājñavalkya's teachings in the Bṛhadāraṇyaka Upaniṣad, "falschlich auf ihn ubertragen sein" (Oldenberg, *Buddha*, p. 33, n. 1).

61. Deussen, *Philosophy*, p. 17; cf. p. 396.

62. Cf. Keith, *Religion and Philosophy*, pp. 494–95; Winternitz, *History of Indian Literature*, pp. 213–14; Farquhar, *Outline of the Religious Literature of India*, p. 53; Dasgupta, *History of Indian Philosophy*, p. 31. As early as 1916 Edgerton advanced arguments he thought might put an end to "the strange theory advanst by Garbe and accepted by Deussen, that the filosofic thot of the Upaniṣads is a product of the warrior caste and is geneti-

cally unrelated to the ritualistic speculations of the Brahmans" (Edgerton, "Sources of the Filosofy of the Upaniṣads," p. 202). Nonetheless, the idea of a Kṣatriya origin still appears in discussions of the origins of the Upaniṣads; see, e.g., Collins, *Selfless Persons*, p. 34; Frauwallner, *History of Indian Philosophy*, p. 34.

63. Deussen, *Philosophy*, p. 396.

64. Ibid., p. 21.

65. Keith, *Religion and Philosophy*, p. 515.

66. Müller, *The Upanishads*, pt. 2, pp. xix–xx.

67. Ibid., p. xix.

68. Keith, *Religion and Philosophy*, p. 441.

69. Ibid., pp. 441–42.

70. See Hopkins, *Religions of India* p. 530, n. 3; Griswold, *The Religion of the Rigveda*, p. 313; Keith, *Religion and Philosophy*, p. 571.

71. ṚV 10.16.3 (O'Flaherty, *The Rig Veda*, p. 49); cf. AB 2.6, which discusses the fate of the sacrificial victim; ŚB 10.3.3.6–7, which discusses the fate of the sacrificer, apparently after death.

72. See *Encyclopedia of Religion and Ethics*, s.v. "Transmigration," by Garbe; Barth, *The Religions of India*, pp. 23–24; and Keith, *Religion and Philosophy*, p. 571.

73. Barth, *Religions of India*, p. 23; cf. *Encyclopedia of Religion and Ethics*, s.v. "Transmigration."

74. *Encyclopedia of Religion and Ethics*, s.v. "Transmigration."

75. Barth, *Religions of India*, p. 24.

76. Cf. Bloomfield, *The Religion of the Veda*, p. 254.

77. Keith, *Religion and Philosophy*, p. 405.

78. See especially, ŚB 13.8.3.1 ff.; cf., ŚB 10.3.3.6–7; AB 2.6.

79. Keith, *Religion and Philosophy*, pp. 571–72. Cf. Deussen, *Philosophy*, pp. 315–16, 410; Bloomfield, *The Religion of the Veda*, pp. 255–59.

80. Deussen, *Philosophy*, p. 329.

81. See JB 1.45; cf. ŚB 11.6.2.6–10.

82. Keith, *Religion and Philosophy*, p. 575.

83. Ibid., p. 573; Deussen, *Philosophy*, pp. 329–30; Farquhar, *Outline of the Religious Literature of India*, p. 34; Oldenberg, *Die Lehre der Upanishaden und die Anfangen der Buddhismus*, p. 109.

84. The CU is roughly contemporary with the BĀU and so represents the same strata of Upaniṣadic literature. (See Weber, *History of Indian Literature*, p. 71). In fact, a considerable amount of material is common to these texts: parallel passages can be found, e.g., in BĀU 1.3.1–21 and CU 1.2; BĀU 1.3.22 and CU 1.6.1. See further Haas, "Recurrent and Parallel Passages in the Principal Upaniṣads and the Bhagavad-gītā," pp. 522–35.

85. BĀU 3.2.10–13.

86. This motif first appears at ṚV 10.16.3. As David Knipe has pointed out, the dissolution of the deceased into the various parts of the cosmos "is an obvious reversal of the cosmogonic process outlined in the Puruṣasūkta (ṚV 10.90.13)" (Knipe, "*Sapiṇḍīkaraṇa*," p. 113). As such, this Upaniṣadic passage has its most important antecedents in Brāhmaṇic ritual theory, according to which the sacrificer replicates the cosmogonic activity of Prajāpati (the Brāhmaṇic equivalent of Puruṣa) in his own ritual activity. As noted earlier, in their discussions of the origins of the Upaniṣadic karma doctrine, scholars tended to dismiss the importance of this Ṛgvedic passage and related passages in the Brāhmaṇas, seeing in them an indication of animistic belief.

87. BĀU 3.2.10.13.

88. BĀU 3.2.13: puṇyo vai puṇyena karmaṇā bhavati pāpaḥ pāpena.

89. Deussen, *Philosophy*, p. 330; Keith, *Religion and Philosophy*, pp. 573–74.

90. Deussen, *Philosophy*, p. 330.

91. Keith, *Religion and Philosophy*, pp. 468–81.

92. Ibid., p. 468.

93. Ibid., p. 476; cf. p. 338.

94. See Mackie, *Ethics*, p. 59.

95. ŚB 2.3.4.18.

96. Mackie, *Ethics*, p. 106.

97. ŚB 1.3.1.21. Cf. Macdonell and Keith, *Vedic Index*, vol. 1, p. 480, for a discussion of the meaning of *paraḥ puṃsā* in this passage.

98. Lévi, *Doctrine du Sacrifice*, p. 10. At least one passage in the Śatapatha Brāhmaṇa implies that it is better to sacrifice, even if done incorrectly, than not to sacrifice at all. Thus, the sage Āruṇi is quoted (ŚB 4.5.7.9): "Why should he sacrifice who would think, 'Worse [am I] by the miscarriage of the sacrifice.' Indeed, I think I am better even by the miscarriage of the sacrifice."

99. Keith, *Religion and Philosophy*, p. 479.

100. Farquhar, *Outline of the Religious Literature of India*, p. 35.

101. BĀU 3.2.13.

102. Gonda, *Vedic Literature: Saṃhitās and Brāhmaṇas*, p. 389.

103. Ibid. See also Eggeling, *The Śatapatha Brāhmaṇa*, pt. 4, p. xv; cf. Knipe, "*Sapiṇḍīkaraṇa*," p. 113.

104. Gonda, *Loka*, pp. 115–30, has conducted an exhaustive survey of these terms in the Vedic literature.

105. Ibid., p. 125.

106. Ibid., pp. 126 ff.

107. Cf. TB 3.3.10.2, where the world of merit (*sukṛtasya loka*) is equated with good deeds (*puṇyaṃ karman*). Gonda, in regard to this TB passage, notes that: "The only question which it not explicitly answered is that as

to the character of the 'good karma,' how and by what activities it was acquired. The context itself points, of course, in the direction of ritual performances" (Gonda, *Loka*, p. 129).

108. See, e.g., Horsch, "Vorstufen der indischen Seelenwanderungslehre," p. 100; cf. Farquhar, *Outline of the Religious Literature of India*, p. 34.

109. See Keith, *Religion and Philosophy*, p. 573; cf. Deussen, *Philosophy*, pp. 330–31.

110. BĀU 4.4.4. The Mādyhaṃdina version (ŚB 14.7.2.5) adds man (*manuṣa*) to this list.

111. BĀU 4.4.5.

112. Gonda, *Loka*, p. 56. An important aspect of the connection with the sacrifice here is that this text refers to seven spheres of beings: that of man, the fathers, *gandharvas*, gods, Prajāpati, Brahmā, and others. (Cf. the Mādhyaṃdina text, ŚB 14.7.2.5. The Kāṇva [BĀU 4.4.4] omits man, but, this sphere is obviously assumed as the fate of man is under discussion here.) What appears to be an arbitrary list of beings here may have been arrived at to fulfill the Brāhmaṇic notion that equates the body of Prajāpati with seven spheres of the cosmos. This equation is established in the Agnicayana rite, which dominates the ŚB (the text to which the BĀU is appended). In this ritual the seven layers of the altar represent the totality of the cosmos, which is the body of Prajāpati. ŚB 9.5.2.8, e.g., equates seven worlds of the gods with the seven layers of the fire altar.

113. Gonda, *Loka*, p. 113.

114. O'Flaherty, "Karma and Rebirth in the Vedas and Purāṇas," p. 18, quoting from the Mārkaṇḍeya Purāṇa. Despite the absence of this notion in BĀU 4.4.4, Keith asserted "clearly they [evildoers] would take on at best the forms of beings inferior to themselves, perhaps men of lower degree, animals, etc." (Keith, *Religion and Philosophy*, p. [illegible]). This assertion reflects Keith's view of the scope of karma, in its early appearances in the Upaniṣads, as an ethical system applying to all actions.

115. Gonda, *Loka*, pp. 126–29.

116. Deussen, *Philosophy*, p. 328; cf. Keith, *Religion and Philosophy*, p. 575.

117. BĀU 6.2; CU 5.3–10.

118. BĀU 6.2.9–14; CU 5.4–9. The minor differences between the BĀU (in both the Kāṇva and Mādhyaṃdina recensions) and the CU are pointed out by Deussen, *Sechzig Upanisad's des Veda*, p. 138.

119. BĀU 6.2.9–16; CU 5.10.

120. ŚB 11.6.1.6–10; JB 1.45–6. These are the Brāhmaṇas to which the BĀU and the CU are most closely related. The BĀU is physically appended to the ŚB and, although the CU and the JB are not of the same schools (*śākhā*)—the CU belongs to the Kauthuma school, the JB to the Jaiminīya school—they are both Sāmavedic texts. That the CU and the JB

are not of the same Sāmavedic school is not a significant factor in evaluating the proximity of their thought. The CU perhaps stood independently in the Sāmavedic tradition; the term *chāndogya* does not refer to a particular Sāmavedic school but, in a general sense, to those who chant the Sāmaveda. Moreover, the text to which the CU is appended appears to be a late and artificial Brāhmaṇa, the Mantra Brāhmaṇa, which contains mantras for special domestic rites.

121. The first three levels correspond to the tripartite Vedic cosmology of heaven, atmosphere, and earth. See Macdonell, *Vedic Mythology*, pp. 8–10. On the addition of man and woman as the fourth and fifth spheres of the cosmos, see Knipe, "One Fire, Three Fires, Five Fires," pp. 29–31.

122. CU 5.4.1, 5.8.1; cf. BĀU 6.2.9, 6.2.13 (and the Mādhyaṃdina recension, ŚB 14.9.1.12); ŚB 11.6.1.6; JB 1.45. In the CU, BĀU, and JB each of the five fires is represented by a similar pentadic symbol (fuel, flame, smoke, spark, and coal). (For a comparison and analysis of these three texts, see Bodewitz, *Jaiminīya Brāhmaṇa* I, 1–65 pp. 110–13.) The ŚB alone uses a triadic symbolism (offering fire, fuel, and pure libation) but presents the same basic motifs found in the other texts in relating the sacrificial fire to a particular sphere (e.g., the sun as an aspect of the sacrificial fire of the heavens, the womb as an aspect of the sacrificial fire of the woman).

123. Earlier expressions of this doctrine appear in ŚB 4.6.7.12; 1.3.1.25.

124. See BĀU 6.2.14; JB 1.46. This contrast between a "real" sacrifice and a symbolic event is seen in the Brāhmaṇas in the distinction between the funeral rites and the nonfuneral rites (e.g., the *śmaśānacayana* and *agnicayana* as they are described in the ŚB) that both take man, the sacrificer, as the material of the offering. Since in the ordinary rites this would entail the death of the sacrificer, the ritual becomes a largely symbolic event. Only upon the sacrificer's death can a real sacrifice be enacted, the ritual at this point being a funeral. See further, Chapter 4 passim.

125. CU 5.10.1: tad ya ittham viduḥ ye ceme 'raṇye śraddhā tapa ity upāsate. Cf. BĀU 6.2.15.

126. CU 5.10.3: atha ya ime grāma iṣṭāpurte dattam ity upāsate. Cf. the parallel passage at BĀU 6.2.16: "they conquer those worlds [of the *pitṛyāna*] by sacrificial gifts (*yajñena dānena*)." For an analysis of the term "*iṣṭāpurta*," see Muir, *Original Sanskrit Texts*, p. 293.

127. See Eliade, *Yoga*, pp. 111–14.

128. See ŚB 1.9.3.1; 4.3.4.6; 4.2.5.9.

129. See, e.g., ŚB 9.5.2.12–16.

130. See further, Chapter 3 passim.

131. CU 5.10.5.

132. KB 15.1; ŚB 4.3.4.5–6; 4.5.1.11–12. See Heesterman, "Reflections on the Significance of the Dakṣiṇā," pp. 241–45.

133. ŚB 4.3.4.6; 1.9.3.1.

134. BĀU 6.2.16; CU 5.10.3. A discussion in the JUB of the path followed by the deceased, which closely replicates the description of the *pitṛyāna* in these Upaniṣadic passages, supports this notion of the interaction of the priests and the sacrificer in the attainments of the afterlife; thus, according to this text, the journey to the otherworld begins when "the priests having placed the sacrificer in this [sacred] syllable, carry him up together to the heavenly world" (JUB 3.19.7).

135. See, e.g., ŚB 1.8.1.31; cf. ŚB 1.7.2.1, which describes the relationship between offspring and ancestors as a (sacrificial) debt (*ṛṇa*).

136. JB 1.46 (cf. 1.18), translation from Bodewitz, *Jaiminīya Brāhmaṇa* I, 1–65, p. 116.

137. BĀU 6.2.16; cf. CU 5.10.4.

138. CU 5.10.5.

139. CU 5.10.1; BĀU 6.2.15; cf. the role of knowledge in JB 1.50, 1.18.

140. See Eliade, *Yoga*, pp. 114–17.

141. ŚB 10.5.4.16.

142. JB 2.113; cf. ŚB 2.6.4.8: "who offers the Varuṇa *praghāsa* becomes Varuṇa, then indeed, he attains a world, closely united, together with Varuṇa." See also Gonda, *Loka*, pp. 113–14.

143. BĀU 3.4.1.

144. BĀU 1.5.23.

145. CU 2.24.1–16.

146. BĀU 3.2.13; cf. 5.10.1.

147. BĀU 4.4.4.

148. There appears in the Upaniṣads an equation between the impersonal Brahman (a term sometimes linguistically indistinguishable from the term used to refer to the figure of Brahmā—see, Monier-Williams's *A Sanskrit-English Dictionary*, s.v., "Brahman," "Brahmā") and the figure of Puruṣa-Prajāpati; see especially CU 3.18.2 ff., which presents a cosmology that replicates the Puruṣasūkta (ṚV 10.90) replacing the figure of Puruṣa with Brahman.

149. CU 5.10.2. Radhakrishnan translates the phrase *brahma gamayati* as "he leads [him] to Brahmā" (*Principal Upanisads*, Radhakrishnan, p. 431). However, *brahma*, which is in the accusative case here, is neuter and thus may refer to the impersonal Brahman, rather than to the world of Brahmā (generally expressed as a masculine substantive); cf. CU 4.15.5.

150. ŚB 2.3.3.7–8. The point of bifurcation between these two realms is the sun (accordingly, the sun is both immortal and mortal; see ŚB 10.5.2.4); hence, the *pitṛyāna* leads the sacrificer to the sun but not beyond it (see, CU 5.10.3; cf. JUB 3.27–28) to the year, which is the immortal world (see, ŚB 10.2.6.3–5; cf. 11.1.2.12).

151. ŚB 10.1.3.2.; cf. 6.1.2.11.

152. Gonda, *Vedic Literature: Saṃhitās and Brāhmaṇas*, p. 389.

153. See, e.g., ŚB 1.1.1; cf., 1.9.3.23. Even in the Brāhmaṇas, however, the idea is expressed that "whatever exists here on earth, all that takes part in the sacrifice" (ŚB 3.6.2.26). As R. S. Murthy has noted: "A patient perusal of the Brāhmaṇa reveals that the concept of sacrifice extends beyond the mere ritualistic form" (Murthy, "Vedic Sacrifice—A Conspectus," p. 116).

154. CU 3.16.1–5; cf. 3.17.

155. This passage occurs only in the CU and does not appear in the parallel text in the BĀU. A similar passage, embedded within a discussion of the deceased sacrificer's journey afterlife, does occur in the JUB (JUB 3.28.4).

156. CU 5.10.7.

157. See, e.g., the description in the Mārkaṇḍeya Purāṇa (quoted by O'Flaherty, "Karma and Rebirth in the Vedas and Purāṇas," p. 18) of how an individual "accompanied by his remaining sins and merits" is born in one of the four castes, a higher being, or an inferior being.

158. The term *caraṇa* (from the root *car* meaning "to move about, to conduct one's self") does occur in the Brāhmaṇas referring to the performance of the sacrifice. As a past participle *carita* the term is sometimes compounded with *su-* and *duṣ-* to indicate the "right" and "wrong" performance of the sacrifice (see, e.g., ŚB 3.3.3.13). However, the terms *ramaṇīya*, "pleasant," and *kapūya*, "stinking," used in CU 5.10.7 suggest a valuation of action that exceeds "right" and "wrong" (ritual) conduct.

159. See ŚB 11.2.6.13–14; 9.5.2.12–13; cf., 1.3.1.26.

160. ŚB 11.2.6.13.

161. ŚB 9.5.2.12–13.

162. As Heesterman notes: "The single sacrificer incorporates alone the whole universe, articulating by himself the cosmic process, like his prototype Prajāpati, who is at the same time sacrificer, victim, and recipient of the sacrifice" (Heesterman, *The Inner Conflict of Tradition*, p. 50).

163. This is in accordance with the notion that, in Brāhmaṇic thought, the result of the poorly performed sacrifice seems to have been the diminution of the sacrificer's otherworldly *loka*. (See Gonda, *Loka*, pp. 128–29.) This passage thus implies that the sacrifice performed for another was simply incorrect.

164. CU 5.10.7. Cf. JUB 3.28.4, which describes the deceased (who, according to JUB 3.19.7, had been led to the otherworld by the priests; i.e., followed the traditional sacrificial format) as returning to this world after a journey through the various cosmic spheres (in which he is denied the world of Brahman): "If he should wish: 'May I be born here again, in whatever family he fixes his thoughts, either a *brahman* family or a king's family (*rāja-kula*),' into that he is born."

165. Deussen, *Philosophy*, p. 332.

2. The Cosmos as Man: The Image of the Cosmos in Vedic Thought

1. See, e.g., ŚB 2.2.4.18; 2.6.4.8; 3.7.1.25; 5.2.2.14; 11.4.4.2; 11.6.2.2; cf. JUB 3.20.6 ff.; Gonda, *Loka*, p. 114.

2. ŚB 2.6.4.8.

3. Gonda, *Loka*, p. 49.

4. ŚB 7.2.1.4; 9.2.3.4. Cf. TB 1.5.9.4.

5. Cf. Mircea Eliade's well-known observation that: "Every mythical account of the origin of anything presupposes and continues the cosmogony . . . the cosmogony becomes the exemplary model for the creation of every kind" (Eliade, *Myth and Reality*, p. 21).

6. See Gonda, *Vedic Literature: Saṃhitās and Brāhmaṇas*, p. 389. Eggeling, *The Śatapatha Brāhmaṇa*, pt. 4, p. xix.

7. The motif of the creation of the cosmos from the body of a primordial man first appears in ṚV 10.90. The Ṛgveda's tenth book (*maṇḍala*) contains, for the most part, material that was composed much later than that found in the other books of this collection; see, further, Gonda, *Vedic Literature: Saṃhitās and Brāhmaṇas*, pp. 11–13.

8. See further Kuiper, "The Basic Concept of the Vedic Religion," pp. 110–11.

9. See, e.g., ŚB 2.2.4.1; 4.1.1.16.

10. Eggeling, *The Śatapatha Brāhmaṇa*, p. xix; cf. Heesterman, *The Ancient Indian Royal Consecration*, p. 224–25, regarding the coordination of the older rites in the creation of the Rājasūya.

11. See, e.g., Edgerton, "The Upaniṣads: What Do They Seek, and Why?" p. 99.

12. Eggeling, *The Śatapatha Brāhmaṇa*, pt. 4, p. xvi.

13. See, e.g., ṚV 1.162.6.

14. See Hubert and Mauss, *Sacrifice*, p. 29; cf., p. 98.

15. TS 6.3.4.1. Cf. ŚB 1.3.2.1; 3.1.4.23; 3.9.32; all of which identify the sacrifice (*yajña*) as being the same size as man. See also Hubert and Mauss, *Sacrifice*, p. 27.

16. Gombrich, "Ancient Indian Cosmology," p. 112.

17. See especially ṚV 1.160, 1.185, 6.70. (Translations of these hymns appear in O'Flaherty, *The Rig Veda*, pp. 203–207.) Several references to the cosmic image of heavens and earth in the Vedic literature are cited by Macdonell, *Vedic Mythology*, pp. 126–27.

18. The many references to this image in the ṚV are cited by Macdonell, *Vedic Mythology*, pp. 8–10.

19. W. N. Brown, "Theories of Creation in the Rig Veda," p. 23; Gombrich, "Ancient Indian Cosmology," p. 112; Macdonell, *Vedic Mythology*, p. 125.

20. Macdonell, *Vedic Mythology*, p. 10.

21. The atmosphere is also known as *rajas*, "[the sphere of] vapor or mist," which may refer to either the clouds or the dust particles that reflect the sunlight; see Wallis, *Cosmology of the Rigveda*, p. 113.

22. See, e.g., ṚV 5.60.6; 1.108.9–10; Wallis, *The Cosmology of the Rigveda*, p. 114; Macdonell, *Vedic Mythology*, p. 9.

23. ṚV 6.9.1; 7.80.1; 5.8.4; Macdonell, *Vedic Mythology*, p. 10; Wallis, *The Cosmology of the Rigveda*, pp. 115–17.

24. Cf. Bodewitz, "The Waters in Vedic Cosmic Classifications," p. 45. On the significance of three in Ṛgvedic thought, see Hopkins, "Numerical Formulae in the Veda and Their Bearing on Vedic Criticism," pp. 276–77; and Gonda, "Triads in Vedic Ritual," pp. 17 ff. Cf. also the speculative study by Stella Kramrisch, "The Triple Structure of Creation in the Rgveda," pp. 140–75; 256–85.

25. This image is especially apparent in the Agnicayana section of the Śatapatha Brāhmaṇa, books (*kāṇḍa*) 6 through 10. This section of the ŚB also refers to a seven-level cosmos (e.g., 8.4.7.12, 19) apparently as an elaboration of the image of the pentadic cosmos.

26. ŚB 8.2.1.2: yad ūrdhvaṃ pṛthivyā arvācīnam antarikṣād.

27. ŚB 8.4.1.2: yad ūrdhvaṃ antarikṣād arvācīnam divas.

28. ŚB 9.2.3.13, 29.

29. Again, I refer primarily to the Agnicayana section of the ŚB, which describes the construction of the fire altar and its metaphysical implications. However, myths and legends that express the importance of the pentad are not limited to the text's Agnicayana section; see, e.g., ŚB 1.5.4.6–16.

30. Cf. Gombrich's remark that "the most discouraging feature of traditional Indian cosmology is not its fantastic and uncritical character but its complexity," as he notes that the most comprehensive study on this subject, Kirfel's *Die Kosmographie der Inder*, "has over 400 large pages with hardly anything more than bare quotations and tables" (Gombrich, "Ancient Indian Cosmology," pp. 110–11).

31. Gonda, *Loka*, p. 110; cf. Gombrich, "Ancient Indian Cosmology," p. 116. A notable exception to this view is seen in the work of W. N. Brown, who, in several articles, presented the idea that the cosmology of the Ṛgveda is ordered around the central opposition of the two realms of the Existent (*sat*) and the Nonexistent (*asat*). See Brown, "The Creation Myth of the Rig Veda," pp. 85–98 passim; idem, "The Rigvedic Equivalent for Hell," p. 79; and cf. idem, "Theories of Creation in the Rig Veda," p. 24. Among recent studies, see Wendy D. O'Flaherty, "The Ethical and Non-Ethical Implications of the Cosmogonic Myth of the Separation of Heaven and Earth in Indian Mythology," which examines the influence of the problem of evil on the shape of the cosmos.

32. Knipe, "One Fire, Three Fires, Five Fires," p. 35.

33. Ibid.

34. Ibid., pp. 33–36. Similarly, J. C. Heesterman has observed that, in the formation of the numbers that in Vedic thought symbolize such entities as the cosmos, "the outstanding feature is the principle of the element added to a totality," and that in many instances this extra element "summarizes and encompasses the totality of the number to which it is added" (Heesterman, *The Ancient Indian Royal Consecration*, p. 35).

35. O'Flaherty, *Dreams, Illusion, and Other Realities*, p. 143.

36. BĀU 3.1.3–10.

37. ṚV 10.90.4.

38. ṚV 10.129.1.

39. ṚV 10.90.2: puruṣa evedam sarvaṃ yad bhūtaṃ yac ca bhaivam.

40. ṚV 10.90.7.

41. ṚV 10.90.11.

42. ṚV 10.90.11.

43. ṚV 10.90.14.

44. See Macdonell, *Vedic Mythology*, pp. 8–11.

45. In general, the Vedic world view expressed itself in terms of a triadic symbolism, whereas later Indian (or, as it is usually designated, Hindu) thought emphasized the fourfold nature of existence. (See, e.g., *Encyclopedia of Religion and Ethics*, s.v. "Numbers [Aryan]" by Keith.) Although these two symbolic complexes are considered to represent two dissimilar Indian traditions, their synthesis (or, at least, the attempt to achieve their synthesis) is seen throughout the history of Indian thought. (See Potter "Karma Theory and Its Interpretation in Some Indian Philosophical Systems," p. 266). On the most basic level, this synthesis was achieved through adding a fourth member to original Vedic triads. Thus, e.g., Hindu tetrads such as the four *varṇa*, the four ends of existence, and the four Vedas, represent simple extensions of Vedic triads. (See Ingalls, "Dharma and Mokṣa," p. 45). Though the Puruṣasūkta is a Vedic hymn, it expresses itself in terms of a fourfold symbolism and includes several themes that are characteristically Hindu: e.g., the four *varṇa* (10.90.12); the four Vedas (10.90.9). However, its superimposition of Puruṣa's fourfold body on the Vedic tripartite cosmic image of earth, atmosphere, and heavens seems to be a case of a simple extension of the Vedic image and, thus, appears to have been made with the intention of synthesizing the two world views of the *trivarga* and the *caturvarga*.

46. See e.g., ŚB 8.2.1.8; 8.6.1.14 (which refers to five directions).

47. ṚV 10.90.13.

48. See Macdonell, *Vedic Mythology*, s.v., "Agni," "Vāyu." In early Vedic mythology, the moon does not seem to have been associated with any particular region of the cosmos (see Keith, *Religion and Philosophy*, pp. 122–23). However, in the Brāhmaṇas the moon is associated with the quarters (see, e.g., ŚB 6.1.2.4). Indra's association with Agni and Puruṣa's mouth appears to be an anomaly here; in Vedic mythology Indra is associated

with the atmosphere. Indra's appearance in the Ṛgvedic myth may be a concession to his importance in this text. Thus, Indra is not mentioned in the VS version of the Puruṣasūkta, and Agni alone is depicted as arising from Puruṣa's mouth (VS 31.12).

49. The relationship of the winds to either the ear or the nose is seen in variant readings of this verse. The VS version of the Puruṣasūkta replaces the ṚV's statement that "from his breath (*prāṇa*) the winds were born" with "from his ear breath (*prāṇa*) and wind were born" (VS 31.12). The KāṭhB replaces *ear* with *nose* (see Whitney, *The Atharva Veda*, p. 905). However, the difference between these three statements is not great; in Vedic thought the term *breath*, *prāṇa*, might represent either the ear, eye, nose, or mouth (see Macdonell and Keith, *Vedic Index*, s.v. "Prāṇa"). Since the eye and mouth are already mentioned in ṚV 10.90.13, the *prāṇa* that relates to the wind must be either the nose or the ear.

50. Various passages in the Brāhmaṇas and Upaniṣads indicate the Vedic thinkers distinguished between the inner workings of the mind and the senses and the gross features of the body (see, especially, CU 6.5.1–3; cf. ŚB 10.1.3.4). Although the Vedic texts do not exactly represent the former as being "immaterial" and the latter as being "material," the inner or essential nature of the mind and senses is contrasted to the gross nature of the body.

51. Eliade, *Myth and Reality*, p. 32.

52. Kuiper, "The Basic Concept of Vedic Religion," pp. 110–11; cf. Brown, "The Creation Myth of the Rig Veda," pp. 92–97. The Ṛgveda does not contain a single and consistent exposition of Indra's creative activities; Kuiper and Brown "reconstruct" the Indra mythology from several Ṛgvedic myths that refer to his exploits.

53. Kuiper, "The Basic Concept of Vedic Religion," p. 111.

54. Ibid., p. 115; Heesterman, "Brahmin, Ritual and Renouncer," pp. 2–4: "Veda and Dharma," pp. 87 ff.

55. Though many older beliefs were displaced in the late Vedic period, as J. C. Heesterman has observed, beneath these new rituals "a different older pattern can be discerned" (Heesterman, *Inner Conflict of Tradition*, p. 27).

56. See, especially, Eggeling, *The Śatapatha Brāhmaṇa*, pt. 4, p. xv; Gonda, *Vedic Literature: Saṃhitās and Brāhmaṇas*, p. 389.

57. Gonda, *Viṣṇuism and Śivaism*, p. 27.

58. Keith, *Religion and Philosophy*, p. 459; cf. Lévi, *La Doctrine du Sacrifice*, pp. 132–33.

59. Keith, *Religion and Philosophy*, p. 459.

60. See ŚB 1.7.2.1–6; 3.6.2.25; and cf. TB 6.3.10.5; and Lévi, *La Doctrine du Sacrifice*, p. 133: "Les Brāhmaṇas ignorent le suicide, peutetre de propos delibere; une forme si brutale du sacrifice rompait violemment avec ces rites minutieux que les Brahmanas se plaisent a exposer."

61. Shende, "The PuruṣaSūkta (ṚV 10.90) in the Vedic Literature," p. 45, cites the many occurrences of ṚV 10.90 in the ritual literature as an accompaniment to the Puruṣamedha; e.g., ŚB 13.6.2.12; VŚS 37.19; ĀpŚS 16.28.3; 20.20.2; 24.10.

62. Keith, *Religion and Philosophy*, p. 347; idem, *The Veda of the Black Yajus School*, pp. cxxxvii–cxl; Eggeling, *The Śatapatha Brāhmana*, pt. 5, pp. xl–xlv. Gonda notes: "Whereas the *brāhmaṇa* literature does not speak of the actual slaying of a man for ritual purposes, the human sacrifice (*puruṣamedha* in ŚB 13, 6) being a mythical and symbolical rite, and TB 3, 4 (cf. VS 30, 5–22) confining itself to enumerating the victims, some *śrautasūtras*, viz., the comparatively recent ĀpŚS (20, 24, 1–25, 2) and HŚS (14, 6, 1–14), works that have much in common, describe it as a ritual reality, the arrangements of which are closely related to those of the preceeding horse sacrifice" (Gonda, *Vedic Literature: The Ritual Sutras*, p. 495).

63. Keith *Religion and Philosophy*, p. 347.

64. Eliade, *Yoga*, p. 111.

65. On the nature of the breaths, see Ewing, "The Hindu Conception of the Function of Breath," pp. 250–308 passim; Macdonell and Keith, *Vedic Index*, s.v., "Prāṇa."

66. CU 5.19–20.

67. CU 5.21–23.

68. ŚB 13.6.1.10–11.

69. ŚB 13.6.2.7–8.

70. See Gonda, *Die Religionen Indiens*, pp. 186–87.

71. Eggeling, *The Śatapatha Brāhmaṇa*, pt. 4, xv, this point has been noted repeatedly by scholars. See, e.g., Keith, *The Veda According to the Black Yajus School*, pp. cxxv–cxxvi (cf. idem., *Religion and Philosophy*, pp. 442–43); Gonda, *Vedic Literature: Saṃhitās and Brāhmaṇas*, p. 389; Staal, *Agni*, 1:115.

72. See especially, Gonda, "The Popular Prajāpati," p. 147; Staal, *Agni*, 1:113–25.

73. Gonda, "The Popular Prajāpati," pp. 135–43.

74. Ibid., pp. 147–48.

75. See, especially, Eggeling, *The Śatapatha Brāhmaṇa*, pt. 4, p. xiii; and also Gonda, *Vedic Literature: Saṃhitās and Brāhmaṇas*, pp. 388–89.

76. See Staal, *Agni*, 1:73–166.

77. ŚB 10.5.2.20.

78. Eggeling, *The Śatapatha Brāhmaṇa*, pt. 4, p. xv. See also Keith, *Religion and Philosophy*, pp. 442–43; cf. Staal, *Agni*, 1:115–16; Gonda, *Die Religionen Indiens*, pp. 186–87.

79. Gonda, *Vedic Literature: Saṃhitās and Brāhmaṇas*, p. 369, referring to ŚB 10.5.5.1.

80. Gonda, *Notes on Names and the Name of God in Ancient India*, p. 7; cf. Gonda, "The Etymologies in the Ancient Indian Brāhmaṇas," p. 78.

81. Eggeling, *Śatapatha Brāhmaṇa*, pt. 4, xv; Gonda, *Vedic Literature: Saṃhitās and Brāhmaṇas*, p. 389; Staal, *Agni*, 1:115.

82. Various passages which identify the sacrificer with Prajāpati are found throughout the ŚB; see, e.g., ŚB 4.5.5.1–2; 7.2.1.6; 7.4.1.15. (In the fire altar building ritual, this identification is achieved through the medium of the altar; see e.g., ŚB 6.4.1.3; 6.4.4.18; 6.7.3.12; 8.3.4.11–13.) The ideology of this identification is clearly expressed in the oft-repeated phrase in the Brāhmaṇas, "This [ritual act] done now is that which the gods did then [in the beginning]" (see, e.g., ŚB 9.2.3.4). Cf. Coomaraswamy "Átmayajña: Self-Sacrifice," p. 359; Keith, *Religion and Philosophy*, p. 459; Gonda, *Vedic Literature: Saṃhitās and Brāhmaṇas*, p. 389; and Eliade, *A History of Religious Ideas*, p. 230.

83. Eggeling, *The Śatapatha Brāhmaṇa*, pt. 4, pp. xv–xvi. Eggeling's views are endorsed by Keith, *The Veda of the Black Yajus School*, p. cxxvii.

84. This aspect of the Prajāpati mythology seems to have led the great Indologist A. B. Keith to the conclusion that "The details of these stupid myths [of Prajāpati's primordial activity] are wholly unimportant" (Keith, *Religion and Philosophy*, p. 442).

85. ŚB 6.1.1.1–6.1.3.20.

86. For example, the ŚB myth includes such cosmogonic motifs as the nonexistent (*asat*) (ṚV 10.129), heat (*tapas*) (ṚV 10.190), and the cosmic embryo (*hiraṇyagarbha*) (ṚV 10.121).

87. Wendy O'Flaherty has suggested that the authors of the Ṛgveda intentionally assumed a style of poetic discontinuity—the Ṛgveda's "one universal semantic feature" (O'Flaherty, *The Rig Veda*, p. 18). This poetic style obscures the Ṛgveda's mythology, as individual hymns often contain a seemingly random assortment of brief mythological episodes. Thus, as O'Flaherty notes, although it may be founded on a solid mythological corpus, due to its peculiar style, the Ṛgveda itself "has no true mythology" (p. 18). (Cf. Louis Renou's suggestion that the Ṛgveda represents a "mythology in the making" [Renou, *Religions of Ancient India*, p. 12]; and see also Winternitz, *A History of Indian Literature*, p. 67.) The verboseness of the Brāhmaṇas, on the other hand, is a natural corollary of their authors' purpose, which is "to understand the at first sight unintelligible bonds by which the various entities, beings, provinces of nature are united with the unseen world, and to gain an insight into the mystic relations of all existence," much of which resided in words and names (Gonda, "Etymologies in the Ancient Indian Brāhmaṇas," p. 78). The verboseness of these texts also seems to have resulted from their synthetic nature. The process of assimilating the culturally diverse beliefs and practices, which converged in the late Vedic period, was for the Brāhmaṇic authors a verbally arduous

one, involving the repetition of myths with only slight differences in each version, and a seemingly endless series of forced identifications.

88. Although the Puruṣasūkta is cited as the model for a number of ritual activities, it does not appear to have been composed for a single ritual purpose.

89. ŚB 6.1.1.1: asad vā idam agre āsīt.

90. This motif is most clearly represented in ṚV 10.129.1: in the beginning, "There was neither nonexistence nor existence." Even in the Brāhmaṇas, which are dominated by the Prajāpati cosmogony, this thought-provoking motif was capable of generating a unique (non-Prajāpati) creation myth; see especially, JB 3.360–61 (the problematic Sanskrit text is reconstructed and translated into German by Karl Hoffman, "Die Weltenstehung nach dem Jaiminīya Brāhmaṇa," pp. 59–67); and also CU 6.2.1 ff.

91. ṚV 10.129.3.

92. In the final two verses of the hymn (ṚV 10.129.6–7) the poet agonizes over the fact that the universe's original state of nonexistence denies the possibility of knowing the events of the creation and, finally, admits to a complete agnosticism: "Who really knows? Who will here proclaim it? Whence was it produced? Whence is this creation? The gods came afterwards, with the creation of this universe. Who then knows whence it has arisen?"
"Whence this creation has arisen—perhaps it formed itself, or perhaps it did not—the one who looks down on it, in the highest heaven, only he knows—or perhaps he does not know" (O'Flaherty, *The Rig Veda*, pp. 25–26).

93. ṚV 10.129.4. O'Flaherty, *The Rig Veda*, p. 25. Cf. ṚV 7.76.4, which, as Sukumari Bhattacharji has noted, presents the idea "that all creation would have lain enveloped in darkness had not the true-speaking Angirases . . . sung out the right kind of praise" (Bhattacharji, *Literature in the Vedic Age*, p. 19).

94. Whereas the ŚB creation myth refers to the Vedic sages as Ṛṣis, ṚV 10.129.4 refers to them as *kavi*. However, *kavi* seems to have been a common designation for a Ṛṣi; e.g., Kavi Uśanas (see, Macdonell and Keith, *Vedic Index*, s.v. "Uśanas Kavya").

95. ŚB 6.1.1.1.

96. See, e.g., ŚB 6.1.1.8.

97. See, e.g., ŚB 6.1.2.12.

98. ŚB 6.1.1.1. The idea of primeval nonexistence appears to be assumed in the Puruṣasūkta; see, ṚV 10.90.2.

99. The heptadic symbolism employed here is an extension of the Agnicayana's more typical pentadic symbolism. This extension is a reflection of the nature of the fire altar, which was essentially a construct of five layers of brick. However, two extra layers, one of soil and one of gold

chips, bring the altar to seven layers. These two layers represent respectively either of the two aspects (mortal [soil] and immortal [gold]) that characterize the altar as a whole.

100. Macdonell and Keith, *Vedic Index*, s.v. "Ṛṣi."

101. Ibid., s.v., "Prāṇa," citing Sāyana's commentary on the Aitareya Āraṇyaka 1.3.7. Cf. Ewing, "Hindu Conceptions of the Functions of Breath," p. 249.

102. See Macdonell and Keith, *Vedic Index*, s.v. "Prāṇa."

103. The authors of the Śatapatha Brāhmaṇa do not seem to have ever precisely defined the vital airs, perhaps because the subtle nature of their composition prohibited further definition. Thus, e.g., in ŚB 8.1.3.1 the question, "What are the vital airs?" receives the answer, "The vital airs are just the vital airs." Nevertheless, that the sense organs were referred to both as "vital airs" (*prāṇa*, literally "breath") and as physical entities (eye, ear, etc.) implies that the Brāhmaṇic thinkers distinguished the physical organs from their "essences," or their animate aspect, which they denoted with the term *prāṇa*.

104. ŚB 6.1.1.2.

105. ŚB 6.1.1.3. The shape of this body appears to be that of a bird, which is the shape that the fire altar will take in the ritual.

106. ŚB 6.1.1.4; cf. 6.1.1.7.

107. ŚB 6.1.1.5: sa eva puruṣaḥ prajāpatir abhavat.

108. ŚB 6.1.1.8.

109. Cf. Lévi, *La Doctrine du Sacrifice*, p. 18.

110. Kaelber, "*Tapas*, Birth, and Spiritual Rebirth in the Veda," p. 348.

111. ŚB 6.1.1.8.

112. See Narahari, *Ātman in Pre-Upanisadic Vedic Literature*, pp. 23–43, for a discussion of the views held by scholars such as Bopp, Haug, Deussen, Keith, Oldenberg, Hillebrandt, Hertel, Charpentier, and Dumezil regarding the meaning of *brahman*. A less detailed (though more substantial) review appears in Gonda, *Notes on Brahman*, pp. 3–8.

113. Eliade, *Yoga*, p. 115.

114. ŚB 6.1.1.8–10.

115. ŚB 6.1.1.8: brahmā asya sarvasya pratiṣṭhā.

116. See Gonda, *Vedic Literature: Saṃhitās and Brāhmaṇas*, pp. 371–72. It is not clear whether the authors of the Brāhmaṇas actually understood the content of the Vedic hymns. However, as Gonda points out, it was not the purpose of the Brāhmaṇic authors to explain the hymns but "to establish a connexion with the wisdom of the *ṛṣis* and to corroborate their own views" (ibid., p. 369).

117. See Gonda, "Etymologies in the Ancient Indian Brāhmaṇas," p. 78.

118. ŚB 6.1.1.13. There appears between the creation of the *brahman* and this event a brief myth that utilizes the motif of the cosmic egg to describe

the creation (SB 6.1.1.9–12). Although in the Brāhmaṇas this motif often appears independent of the Prajāpati mythology (see, Kuiper, "Cosmogony and Conception: A Query," pp. 100–101, who cites several such occurrences in these texts), in the version presented here Prajāpati is represented as initiating the cosmogony by entering (*pra-* /*viś*) the primeval waters. Consequently, an egg (*aṇḍa*) arises, and the *brahman* and the earth are created from it. This creation is then depicted as returning to the waters: "All this joined into the waters; it then appeared as one form alone, [that of] the waters" (ŚB 6.1.1.12). The curious form that the well-known motif of the cosmic egg takes here reflects the efforts of the authors of the Agnicayana creation myth to assimilate a variety of cosmogonic motifs to the Prajāpati mythology.

119. ŚB 6.1.1.13.

120. O'Flaherty, *The Rig Veda*, p. 39, n. 7.

121. ŚB 6.1.1.13.

122. ŚB 6.1.1.15. From the modern viewpoint such etymologies appear to be entirely unfounded. However, as Jan Gonda has noted, these linguistic analyses were "for the Vedic thinkers an important means of penetrating into the truth and reality lying behind the phenomena" (Gonda, "Etymologies in the Ancient Indian Brāhmaṇas," p. 66).

123. ŚB 6.1.2.1.

124. These are the three spheres of heavens, atmosphere and earth found in traditional Vedic cosmography, plus the ubiquitous regions. The association of the moon with the quarters is perhaps attributable to the relatively undefined location of the moon in the traditional Vedic cosmographies; see, e.g., Keith, *Religion and Philosophy*, pp. 122–23.

125. ŚB 6.1.2.1.

126. ŚB 6.1.2.2.

127. ŚB 6.1.2.3.

128. ŚB 6.1.2.4.

129. ŚB 6.1.2.6–9.

130. ŚB 6.1.2.6–9. See, Macdonell, *Vedic Mythology*, p. 130.

131. See, e.g., Keith *Religion and Philosophy*, pp. 221–22.

132. ŚB 6.1.2.11.

133. The authors complete their narrative by establishing that this particular myth of Prajāpati's creation represents the culmination of all Vedic cosmogonic speculation: "Now in which of many ways he created, so that was how he created. But Prajāpati indeed emitted this all, and this is whatever there is" (ŚB 6.1.2.11). However, as a reflection of the "integrative" nature of this text, in the section (*adhyāya*) immediately following the presentation of the creation myth, another creation myth appears, which recounts parts of the narrative that proceeds it (ŚB 6.1.3.1–20). The purpose of the second creation narrative seems to be to establish a frame

for the identification of Rudra as an "all-god"; identifying him with the many deities that form the Rudra-Śiva complex in later Hinduism (see Gonda, *Viṣṇuism and Śivaism*, pp. 18–33). That Rudra, whose "character lent itself admirably to splitting up into partial manifestations as well as to assimilation of divine or demonic powers of cognate nature, were they Aryan or non-Aryan" (ibid., p. 5), is featured in this second creation narrative again attests to the synthetic nature of the Agnicayana ritual.

134. ŚB 7.1.2.7.
135. ŚB 10.4.5.2.
136. See, e.g., ŚB 6.2.1.23; 6.2.2.9; 7.1.1.37; 7.4.1.15; 8.3.4.11–18.
137. See, ŚB 8.7.4.12; 8.7.4.19; 9.1.2.33–40; 10.6.1.2–11.
138. ŚB 6.1.2.16.
139. The building of the fire altar is replete with sexual symbolism; see, e.g., ŚB 6.2.2.27; 6.3.3.21; 6.4.1.7; 6.5.3.1–5; 6.6.1.24; 6.7.2.7; 7.2.1.6; 7.3.1.28; 7.4.1.1, and Chapter 3, "The Fire Altar (Agnicayana) as Man and Cosmos," passim.
140. ŚB 10.1.1.10.
141. It is, of course, impossible to ascertain the precise historic relationship between the Agnicayana and the Prajāpati mythology that precedes it in the Śatapatha Brāhmaṇa. Eggeling long ago observed that the rite seems to have been adapted to the myth (Eggeling, *The Śatapatha Brāhmaṇa*, pt. 4, p. xiii); however, in character with the spirit of these texts, the Brāhmaṇas do not present the sort of single unequivocal version of the Prajāpati myth that would preclude the possibility of an adaption of the myth to the rite.

3. The Fire Altar (Agnicayana) as Man and Cosmos

1. Heesterman, "Veda and Dharma," p. 87.
2. ŚB 10.1.3.1. Cf. ŚB 2.3.3.7, which describes the sun as the point of bifurcation between the mortal realm (the earth) and the immortal realm (the heavens).
3. ŚB 3.6.2.16.
4. Keith, *Religion and Philosophy*, p. 459; cf. Lévi, *La Doctrine du Sacrifice*, p. 133.
5. ŚB 11.7.1.3. Cf. CU 3.16, which represents the years of the sacrificer's life as the sacrificial offering.
6. ŚB 10.2.6.8.
7. ŚB 1.8.1.31.
8. ŚB 1.7.2.1.
9. Staal, "Ritual Syntax," p. 122.
10. ŚB 11.7.1.2–3.

11. Regarding the relationship of the sacrificer to the sacrificial stake, see, TS 6.3.4.1; to the offering area, see ŚB 1.2.5.14, 10.2.1.2, and TS 5.2.5.1; and to the sacrificial spoons, see Eggeling, *The Śatapatha Brāhmaṇa*, pt. 1, p. 67, n. 2.

12. ŚB 1.3.2.1; 3.5.3.1.

13. In the Brāhmaṇas such metaphysical connections were called *bandhu*, "association, connection," a term that is grammatically almost indistinguishable from *bandha*, "binding." Although the metaphysical *bandhu* defies a single definition (see, especially, Gonda, "*Bandhu*- in the Brāhmaṇas," pp. 1–7), its application in the Brāhmaṇas represents the ritualists' attempts to seek out the invisible, or "mysterious" (*parokṣa*) connections between what at first seem to be disconnected entities.

14. ŚB 13.2.2.1.

15. Cf. ŚB 11.7.1.1, which describes how the sacrificer who sacrifices (that is, binds) cattle near his home causes a "binding of cattle *to* his home."

16. Hubert and Mauss, *Sacrifice*, p. 32.

17. ŚB 3.8.1.10.

18. Hubert and Mauss, *Sacrifice*, p. 25.

19. See, e.g., ŚB 4.3.4.14; 3.7.3.1; AB 2.6. Cf. the story of how men and cows exchanged skins in ŚB 3.1.2.13–17 and JB 2.182 (discussed by Wendy D. O'Flaherty, *Tales of Sex and Violence*, pp. 40–42). According to this story cows originally had the skin that man now has and man the skin of cows. The cows, unable to bear the elements and the insects, offered to exchange skins with man. To induce man to accept this exchange the cows offered themselves as food.

20. ŚB 3.7.3.6.

21. ŚB 3.7.4.5.

22. In view of this human chain that connects the sacrificer to the victim it is not surprising that this passage describes the sacrificer as touching the victim in an "imperceptible" (*parokṣa*) manner (ŚB 3.8.1.10). The term *parokṣa*, however, seems also to be employed here to indicate the existence of a metaphysical bond with the sacrificer; that is, although not being held physically or in a manner that is physically visible, the animal victim is yet held metaphysically, in an imperceptible manner.

23. Lévi, *La Doctrine du Sacrifice*, p. 127.

24. ŚB 4.3.4.6; 1.9.3.1.

25. ŚB 4.5.1.16.

26. See, e.g., ŚB 13.4.1.6; 13.4.2.13; 2.2.3.28.

27. Heesterman, "Reflections on the Significance of the Dakṣiṇā," p. 243.

28. Cf. Sylvain Lévi's observation that one of the essential components of the Vedic rites "is the sacrificer's indispensible conviction that, by a curi-

ous deviation of causality, he will gather the fruits of the rites performed by the priests in his service" (Lévi, *La Doctrine du Sacrifice*, p. 113).

29. Hubert and Mauss, *Sacrifice*, p. 29.

30. ŚB 1.3.1.26.

31. ŚB 9.5.2.2–15. The text distinguishes between "building [the altar] for one self" (*cinute*) and "building [the altar] for another" (*cinoti*), through the use of the middle and the active voices. Although in later Sanskrit this distinction was lost, at one time the middle voice, or *ātmanepada*, which literally means "word for oneself," denoted actions undertaken by the subject for his own benefit, whereas the active voice, or *parasmaipada*, which means "word for another," denoted actions undertaken for others. See further Speijer, *Sanskrit Syntax*, pp. 235–38.

32. ŚB 9.5.2.13. The term *ātman*, which appears here and throughout the Agnicayana section, denotes "one's own self" or "one's being," in the sense of that which represents the totality of a person's existence (both mental and physical) and should not be confused with the subtle *ātman* that in later Hindu thought primarily refers to a "life essence" or "soul." In his edition of the Śatapatha Brāhmaṇa, Eggeling vacillates in his translation of *ātman*, employing both *body* and *self*. Unless otherwise noted, for the sake of consistency and for its wider connotations, *ātman* is translated as "self" throughout this study.

33. ŚB 9.5.2.16.

34. ŚB 9.5.2.16.

35. ŚB 9.5.2.16.

36. In general, scholars have agreed that the Agnicayana is not a part of the early Vedic cult, as it is represented in the Ṛgveda. However, there is no consensus regarding whether this rite originated within the indigenous Indian culture or was brought into India by a second (i.e., after the establishment of the Ṛgvedic religion) wave of Aryan migrations. Hyla Stuntz Converse's article "The Agnicayana Rite: Indigenous Origin?" is the seminal article arguing for the Agnicayana's indigenous origin. This article provoked a sharp response in C. G. Kashikar's "Agnicayana: Extension of Vedic Aryan Rituals," in which the author refutes, point by point, Converse's argument. However, few scholars have taken Kashikar's position. More balanced views of the origin of this rite, in light of the textual, archeological, and cultural evidence are seen in Parpola, "The Pre-Vedic Background of the Śrauta Rituals;" Thapar, "The Archeological Background to the Agnicayana Ritual;" and Staal, *Agni* 1:73–166 passim.

37. Eggeling, *The Śatapatha Brāhmaṇa*, pt. 3, p. xxvi–xxvii.

38. See Staal, *Agni*, 1:49–54.

39. As Julius Eggeling noted: "There seems, indeed, some reason to believe that it [the Agnicayana] was elaborated with a definite object in view, viz. that of making the external rites and ceremonies of the sacrificial cult the practical devotional expression of certain dominant theories of the

time" (Eggeling, *The Śatapatha Brāhmaṇa*, pt 4. p. xiii). These theories are, of course, those that saw the rising of the cosmos, following Prajāpati's primordial creative acts, occurring in correlation to Prajāpati's own being.

40. ŚB 10.4.1.1. ff.

41. This notion is clearly represented in the well-known Brahmanic mythology of Mārtāṇḍa (the "dead embryo"), the last of Aditi's eight sons, whose "living" part is fashioned into Vivasvat, the first man and first sacrificer. See ŚB 3.1.3.2 ff.; MS 1.6.12; KāthS 11.6; TS 6.5.6.1; Hoffmann, "Mārtāṇḍa und Gayomart," pp. 85–103 passim; Dumezil, *The Destiny of a King*, pp. 1–8.

42. Hubert and Mauss, *Sacrifice*, p. 98.

43. Thite, *Sacrifice in the Brāhmaṇa Texts*, pp. 109–10, 183.

44. The building of the altar is described in *kāṇḍa* 6 through 8 of the ŚB; the Agnicayana's Soma ritual is described in *kāṇḍa* 9.

45. Staal, *Agni*, 1:16.

46. Gonda, *Vedic Literature: Saṃhitās and Brāhmaṇas*, p. 339.

47. Ibid.

48. The idea that the ritual is bound up with reality is expressed in the term *bandhu*, "connection, relationship," which occurs throughout the Brāhmaṇas. (See, especially, the many citations in Jan Gonda's "*Bandhu*-in the Brāhmaṇa-s," pp. 6–23.) Some scholars have suggested that, as a reflection of the purpose of the Brāhmaṇas, the terms *brāhmaṇa* and *bandhu* are interchangeable and that *bandhu* may have been an early designation for this class of texts. (See, Weber, *History of Indian Literature*, p. 11; cf. Winternitz, *A History of Indian Literature*, p. 175, n.2.)

49. See Gonda, "The Etymologies in the Ancient Indian Brāhmaṇas," pp. 66, 78.

50. The authors occasionally interrupt their description of the building of the fire altar to refer to an aspect of the Soma ceremony. Thus, in one instance, they turn from the fire altar to the ritual buying of the Soma, a central element in the Soma ritual (ŚB 7.3.2–6). The authors use this opportunity to extol the intimate relationship between the Soma sacrifice and the building of the fire altar, comparing it to that between the body and the vital air (*prāṇa*) or life-essence (*rasa*): "Thus he connects together the fire [altar] rite with the [Soma] rite" (ŚB 7.3.1.4).

51. See, e.g., ŚB 6.6.1.4, they declare that: "Indeed this is a rite both of [building] the fire [altar] and of the Soma sacrifice . . . first there is an approaching to the Soma sacrifice, then there is [an approaching] to the fire [altar]." Since the building of the fire altar actually precedes the Soma sacrifice in the performance of the Agnicayana, the authors' intention here is clearly to establish the hierarchical order of these two aspects of the ritual. (Accordingly, Eggeling, perhaps drawing from a commentary, interpolates at the end of this passage "for the rite of the fire is an accessory rite" [Eggeling, *The Śatapatha Brāhmaṇa*, pt. 3, p. 247].)

52. ŚB 6.2.1.1–6.2.2.40.
53. ŚB 6.2.1.15.
54. ŚB 6.2.1.36. The text laconically states: "But some in this manner, as it were" (taddha eke iti). Eggeling notes that according to Sāyana "in this manner" refers to buying or otherwise obtaining the animals (Eggeling, *The Śatapatha Brāhmaṇa*, pt. 3, p. 170). In any case, the passage makes it clear that these animals are not killed within the confines of the sacrifice; they are thus called "[animals] without [sacrificial] oblations" (*anāprita*).
55. ŚB 6.2.1.37.
56. ŚB 6.2.1.38–39.
57. ŚB 6.2.1.39.
58. ŚB 6.2.1.39.
59. ŚB 6.2.2.15.
60. See Staal, *Agni*, 1:49, regarding the prototypical form of the *paśubandha*.
61. See ŚB 6.2.1.39. In the Śatapatha Brāhmaṇa the sacrifice of all five animals apparently remains a tenable option; see ŚB 7.5.2.9–10. It is worth noting that in a recent performance of the Agnicayana, which has been documented by Frits Staal, clay models are employed in place of the five animals (Staal, *Agni*, 1:306–309).
62. In the hierarchy of the Vedic ritual system, the Paśubandha precedes (in complexity and importance) the Soma rituals. However, as Staal has pointed out, "each later ritual presupposes the former and incorporates one or more occurrences of one or more of the former rituals" (Staal, "Ritual Syntax," p. 125).
63. See, e.g., ŚB 3.7.3.1. ff. According to Keith, in the Agniṣṭoma, which is the paradigm for all Soma rituals, animal sacrifices occur prior to the day of the Soma pressing, on the day of the pressing, and after the final bath (Keith, *Religion and Philosophy*, p. 327).
64. ŚB 6.2.2.38; cf. 6.2.2.40.
65. ŚB 6.2.2.39.
66. For a summary of the procedures in the classical *dīkṣā*, see Gonda, *Change and Continuity in Indian Religion*, pp. 350–77.
67. ŚB 6.2.2.38.
68. ŚB 6.2.2.40.
69. See, e.g., ŚB 4.5.1.16.
70. ŚB 6.2.2.39.
71. See van Gennep, *The Rites of Passage*, pp. 10–11, and 65–115 passim.
72. Hubert and Mauss, *Sacrifice*, p. 21.
73. ŚB 6.2.2.39.
74. See ŚB 9.3.4.10.
75. ŚB 6.3.3.21–6.5.2.22. The actual fashioning of the pan is described in ŚB 6.5.2.7–12. On the possible indigenous origins of the techniques used

in making the fire pan, see Converse, "The Agnicayana Rite: Indigenous Origin?" pp. 85–86.

76. The fire altar is added to the same ritual enclosure that is used for all the Vedic *śrauta* rites. On the relationship of the fire altar to the other ritual fireplaces, see, Staal, *Agni*, 1:44–55.

77. ŚB 6.5.3.4–5.

78. ŚB 6.6.2.16; 6.7.2.7.

79. ŚB 7.5.1.30 ff.

80. ŚB 6.7.1.16–19.

81. ŚB 6.3.3.26.

82. ŚB 6.4.1.6.

83. ŚB 3.2.1.6–7. Cf. ŚB 3.2.1.11, 3.3.3.12; AB 1.3.

84. ŚB 12.5.2.13; cf. 12.5.2.7. In other contexts, the deceased is wrapped in the skin of a cow; see, ṚV 10.16.7; JB 1.49.

85. The Vedic texts often refer to the two coverings of the womb, the amnion and chorion (*jarāyu* and *ulba*). See, e.g., ŚB 6.6.2.15; 3.2.1.11; TS 6.5.6.3; CU 3.19.2.

86. ŚB 6.4.1.7.

87. ŚB 6.5.1.3.

88. See Chapter 2. The identification of the *brahman* with water is made in ŚB 6.1.1.10.

89. ŚB 6.5.3.1.

90. ŚB 6.5.2.21.

91. ŚB 5.2.1.10.

92. Although such a state of primordial androgyny is not made explicit in the Agnicayana's creation myth, this notion is clearly represented in the interpretation of the Prajāpati myth found in the Bṛhadāraṇyaka Upaniṣad (the Upaniṣad appended to the Śatapatha Brāhmaṇa), in BĀU 1.4.3. Cf. the separation of the *virāg* (female principle) from the Puruṣa in ṚV 10.90.5.

93. BĀU 1.4.3.

94. TS 5.6.8.

95. ŚB 6.6.2.8.

96. ŚB 6.6.2.15.

97. ŚB 6.7.1.1–28.

98. See Heesterman, *The Ancient Indian Royal Consecration*, p. 28, regarding the year as the full term of pregnancy (cf. Eggeling, *The Śatapatha Brāhmaṇa*, pt. 4, pp. xii ff.).

99. ŚB 10.4.3.1.

100. See ŚB 10.5.1.4; cf. 10.2.6.4.

101. ŚB 2.3.3.7; cf. 10.5.1.4.

102. ŚB 10.5.2.3.

103. ŚB 6.7.2.7.

104. ŚB 7.1.1.15–19.
105. ŚB 7.1.1.37.
106. ŚB 7.2.1.6. Eggeling, *The Śatapatha Brāhmaṇa*, pt. 3, p. 320, ignores in his translation the implications of the adjective *bhūta*, "real, actual, existing," which modifies *retas*, "semen," here.
107. See, e.g. ŚB 1.1.1.4–6, which describes the vows undertaken at the beginning of the sacrifice as an entering into the world of the gods from the world of men. Then, at the end of the sacrifice when he divests himself of his vows, the sacrificer states that "I am that one who I really am," which apparently refers to a return to his normal state of existence in the realm of men. Jan Gonda, "Adhvara and Adhvaryu," passim, has argued that, based on etymological considerations, one of the terms for "sacrificial ceremony," *adhvara*, refers to the idea of the sacrifice as a journey, especially one leading to the realm of the gods.
108. See Lévi, *La Doctrine du Sacrifice*, pp. 88–89; and Smith, "Resemblance, Hierarchy, and Ritualism," p. 151. Cf. ŚB 2.3.4.7: "Dangerous (*varaṇa*) are the ways between heaven and earth; upon them [the sacrificer] now stands."
109. See, e.g., ŚB 5.1.1.5–10, which discusses how, by offering the Vājapeya, men ascend to the upper regions. However, the passage continues to state that one should not offer the Vājapeya because "one wins everything . . . he leaves nothing remaining here," apparently implying that it is impossible to return from the upper regions. The authors then state that, as long as the sacrificer has wise priests assisting him, the Vājapeya should be performed, apparently since these priests will be able to guide him back to this world.
110. ŚB 4.2.5.10; cf. 2.3.3.15–16. Smith, "Resemblance, Hierarchy, and Ritualism," p. 150, has discussed the related image of the sacrifice as a chariot.
111. ŚB 7.2.1.19.
112. ŚB 7.2.2.9–12; 7.2.2.14–21. The preference here for north and east (two furrows are plowed from south to north and two from west to east; one furrow is plowed from north to south and one east to west) reflects the Vedic notion that the north and the east represent the realm of the gods and the realm of men (these are often interchanged, see, e.g., ŚB 3.1.1.7; 3.6.4.12; 1.9.3.13; 1.2.5.17; 9.3.4.13), whereas the south is the realm of the fathers, or deceased ancestors (ŚB 1.2.5.17; 9.3.4.11). The region of the fathers is avoided during the sacrifice, "for the sacrificer would quickly go to that world [of the dead]" (ŚB 1.2.5.17; cf. 9.3.4.11).
113. ŚB 7.2.4.1.ff.
114. ŚB 7.2.4.14 ff.
115. ŚB 7.2.4.14–19.
116. ŚB 7.4.1.1.
117. ŚB 7.4.1.1.

118. ŚB 7.4.1.7.
119. ŚB 7.4.1.7–11.
120. ŚB 7.4.1.15.
121. ŚB 7.4.1.24.
122. ŚB 7.4.1.36. As Eggeling notes the offering spoons are the length of an arm, with the size and shape of hands (Eggeling, *The Śatapatha Brāhmaṇa*, pt. 3, p. 373, n. 2).
123. ŚB 7.4.2.22.
124. See, e.g., TS 5.6.8.
125. ŚB 7.5.1.1–38.
126. ŚB 7.5.1.35.
127. ŚB 7.5.2.12.
128. ŚB 8.1.1.1 ff.
129. ŚB 6.1.1. ff,; see Chapter 2.
130. ŚB 8.1.4.1.
131. See, Eggeling, *The Śatapatha Brāhmaṇa*, pt. 4, p. 22, n. 1, and also ŚB 10.4.3.8 ff. The contemporary fire altar described by Frits Staal consists of 1005 bricks (Staal, *Agni*, 1:202).
132. The identification of each of the five levels with Prajāpati and the cosmos appear in ŚB 7.4.2.30 (level one); 8.2.1.1 ff. (level two); 8.3.1.1 ff. (level three); 8.4.1.1 ff. (level four); 8.5.1.1 ff. (level five).
133. ŚB 7.5.1.35 ff.
134. See Chapter 2.
135. ŚB 8.5.2.8–17.
136. ŚB 8.5.2.8–17. This same notion is expressed in ŚB 9.2.3.13 ff., which refers to five regions above the sun and five regions below the sun.
137. SB 8.7.3.15–17.
138. ŚB 8.4.1.1–8.4.4.12.
139. JUB 3.20–28.
140. Oertel, "The Jaiminīya or Talavakāra Upaniṣad Brāhmaṇa," p. 186.
141. JUB 3.28.4.
142. ŚB 8.6.1.23.
143. ŚB 6.1.2.36. The notion that the sacrificer might attain the heavenly world through assuming the shape of a bird is seen in PB 5.3.5: "The sacrificer, having become a bird, goes to the world of heaven" (cf. PB 5.1.10; AB 3.25).
144. Regarding the Vedic sun-bird, see, e.g., ṚV 1.163.6; 1.164.52; 7.15.4.
145. ŚB 7.5.1.37.
146. ŚB 6.1.2.36.
147. ŚB 6.7.2.8.
148. ŚB 6.1.2.12 ff.
149. ŚB 6.1.2.12.

150. ŚB 6.1.1.1–4.
151. ŚB 6.1.2.11.
152. ŚB 6.1.2.14–15.
153. See, e.g., ŚB 6.5.3.11; 6.6.2.7; 7.5.2.9; 8.1.3.6; 10.1.4.2–7.
154. Heesterman, "Reflections on the Significance of the Dakṣiṇā," p. 245.
155. ŚB 7.5.2.8.
156. This is described in some detail in ŚB 7.5.2.8–37.
157. Smith, "Resemblance, Hierarchy and Ritualism," p. 118.
158. See ŚB 11.2.1.1; ŚB 2.2.4.8; JUB 3.11.
159. JUB 3.14.8.
160. The identification of the sacrificer with an embryo is, for the most part expressed during the initiation (*dīkṣā*) rituals; see ŚB 2.3.1.3; 3.1.3.28; 3.2.1.6; 3.3.3.12; AB 1.3.
161. ŚB 3.1.3.28.
162. AB 1.3.
163. ŚB 3.2.1.6.
164. See Kashikar, "The Idea of Ultimate Reality and Meaning According to the Kalpa Sūtras," p. 176;
165. ŚB 4.3.4.6; cf., 1.9.1.16; 1.9.1.3; 1.8.3.11; 4.6.9.12.
166. ŚB 1.9.1.3.
167. ŚB 1.8.3.1; 1.9.3.1; 4.3.4.6.
168. ŚB 4.3.4.6; cf. 1.9.3.1. Cf. ŚB 1.8.3.20, which describes the Adhvaryu and the Agnidhra priests as leading the sacrificer to the world of the gods.
169. ŚB 2.3.4.4.
170. ŚB 3.6.2.26.
171. ŚB 10.1.4.1; cf. 10.1.3.2.
172. See ŚB 10.1.3.5; cf. 14.1.2.24.
173. ŚB 10.1.4.1.
174. ŚB 10.2.4.5. Cf. ŚB 8.1.4.5; 8.7.4.12; 8.7.4.19; 10.1.3.4–5; 10.1.4.2–7; 10.6.4.1.
175. Heesterman, "Reflections of the Significance of the Dakṣiṇā," p. 245.

4. From Death to Rebirth

1. Eliade, *A History of Religious Ideas*, p. 445. Cf. W. D. Whitney's view, expressed nearly a century ago, of the conversation between Naciketas and Death (KāṭhU 1.1.21): "what we have to infer from it, doubtless, is the very unsettled state of opinion on the matter [of the afterlife], even among the advanced thinkers, at the time of our treatise" (Whitney, "Hindu Eschatology and the Kāṭha Upanishad," p. cviii.) Also cf. Rodhe, *Deliver Us from*

Evil, p. 113: "[in the Brāhmaṇas] the ideas of the fate that will meet man in 'yonder world' are not very fixed."

2. See Chapter 2.

3. The bipartite cosmic image is the subject of at least three Ṛgvedic hymns—ṚV 1.160; 1.185; and 6.70 (these hymns are translated by O'Flaherty, *The Rig Veda*, pp. 203–207—and is seen in several other Ṛgvedic hymns—for relevant citations, see Macdonell, *Vedic Mythology*, pp. 8–10; and Wallis, *Cosmology of the Rig Veda*, pp. 111–13). The image of a multileveled cosmos is especially apparent in the Brāhmaṇic passages that describe the journey of the deceased; see, e.g., ŚB 2.6.4.7 ff.; 10.2.6.8; 10.3.3.8; JB 1.46; 1.49–50.

4. Cf. J. C. Heesterman's observation that although the ritual texts represent "an effort of systematization . . . the ritualists were concerned with the preservation of obsolete diverging traditions . . . even at the price of contradicting the laboriously developed system" (Heesterman, "Vrātya and Sacrifice," p. 3).

5. The fire altar's five brick layers represent a pentadic cosmos (see ŚB 8.2.1.1–2; 8.3.1.1–2; ;8.4.1.1–2; 8.5.1.1–2). However, two additional layers, one of soil and one of gold chips, are placed on top of the bricks and together with the five brick levels depict a heptadic cosmos (see ŚB 8.7.4.12 ff.; 9.5.2.9). Within the five brick levels are three "naturally perforated" (*svayamātṛṇṇā*) bricks (placed on the first, third, and fifth levels) that represent the tripartite cosmos of earth, atmosphere, and heavens (see ŚB 7.4.2.1; 8.3.1.11; 8.5.4.9; cf., 9.5.1.58).

6. ŚB 1.2.2.14.

7. Cf. Steven Collins' statement that "we cannot look to the history of cosmology to find specifiable 'realms' of the living and the dead" (Collins, *Selfless Persons*, p. 45).

8. See, e.g., ŚB 13.5.4.3; and also Macdonell and Keith, *Vedic Index*, s.v. "Pārikṣita."

9. BĀU 3.3.2.

10. See, e.g., ŚB 13.5.4.3.

11. BĀU 3.2.13; see Chapter 1.

12. ŚB 6.2.2.27. The notion presented here that the initiation results in the establishment of a "world beforehand" reflects the place of the initiation within the larger ceremonial; just as the initiation precedes the ritual proper, so it results in the establishment of a "beforehand" world for the sacrificer.

13. Eggeling, *The Śatapatha Brāhmaṇa*, pt. 3, p. 181, n. 1.

14. Gonda, *Loka*, p. 139.

15. Ibid., pp. 143–44.

16. JUB 3.11.2–4.

17. Cf. the statement found in ŚB 1.1.1.4; that the sacrificer, in entering upon the ritual, "passes from the [world of] men to the [world of] the gods."

18. See ŚB 2.3.1.3; 3.1.3.28; 3.2.1.6; 3.3.3.12; AB 1.3.

19. Knipe, "*Sapiṇḍīkaraṇa*: The Hindu Rite of Entry in Heaven," pp. 112–22 passim.

20. ŚB 2.3.4.37. Cf. TS 2.5.6: "The sacrifice is razor edged, and swiftly one becomes good (*puṇya*) or is destroyed (*pra-* /*mī*)." The danger inherent to the ritual journey has been discussed by Smith, "Gods and Men in Vedic Ritualism," pp. 294 ff.

21. Staal, "Ritual Syntax," p. 125.

22. ŚB 10.2.6.8.

23. See Converse, "The Agnicayana Rite: Indigenous Origin?" p. 87; Parpola, "The Pre-Vedic Background of the Śrauta Rituals," pp. 49–50; Thapar, "The Archeological Background to the Agnicayana Ritual," pp. 15–16; Keith, *The Veda of the Black Yajus School Entitled Taittirīya Sanhitā*, p. cxxv.

24. Bloch, who excavated this site at the turn of the century, identified the mounds as pre-Mauryan funeral tumuli and, believing that they predated even the ritual texts, attempted to interpret his findings through utilizing Rgvedic evidence (Bloch, "Excavations at Lauriya," pp. 123–24). Caland, noting the similarity between Bloch's findings and the fire alter, then suggested that these mounds represented the remains of an Agnicayana altar (*De Archeoligische vondsten in de heuvels van Lauriya*, cited by Thapar, "Archeological Background to the Agnicayana," p. 15). In her reevaluation of the work of Bloch and Caland, Thapar suggests that the Lauriya mounds represent the sort of funeral tumuli that the ritual texts describe as approximating the shape of the fire altar (Thapar, "Archeological Background to the Agnicayana," pp. 15 ff.).

25. Caland, *Die Altindischen Todten- und Bestattungsgebrauche*, p. 172 ff., cited by Parpola, "Pre-Vedic Background of the Śrauta Rituals," p. 50. Caland's view has been reiterated by Asko Parpola; however, Parpola refers to this point in passing and declares his agreement with Caland without citing any particular evidence to substantiate this view (Parpola, "Pre-Vedic Background of the Śrauta Rituals," p. 50).

26. See Knipe, "*Sapiṇḍīkaraṇa*," pp. 111–24 passim.

27. See ṚV 10.15, which is devoted to the fathers, and cf. the entire series of hymns ṚV 10.14–10.18, which Horace Poleman has suggested reveals the general procedure of the Ṛgvedic funeral rites (Poleman, "The Ritualistic Continuity of Ṛgveda X.14–18," pp. 276–81).

28. ṚV 10.16.9. See also O'Flaherty, *The Rig Veda*, pp. 46–51.

29. See e.g., ŚB 1.2.5.17; 3.6.4.12; 9.3.4.11.

30. ŚB 1.1.1.7–9.

31. ŚB 1.1.1.8.

32. ŚB 1.1.1.9.
33. ŚB 1.1.1.9: sa yad eva aśitam anaśitam tad aśnīyād (literally, "one should eat that which eaten is not eaten").
34. ŚB 11.1.7.1, which continues this discussion (though it does not cite Yājñavalkya), clarifies Yājñavalkya's remarks by proposing that during this period of fasting "one should eat [only] forest [food]," apparently referring to uncultivated food sources.
35. See also ŚB 2.1.3.1–4; 2.4.2.11; 4.4.2.3; and KB 5.6, all of which express a concern with maintaining a separation between the gods and the fathers in performing specific ritual tasks and thus imply a confusion of the roles of these two classes of beings.
36. The story of Bhṛgu is told in ŚB 11.6.1.1–13 and JB 1.42–44 (for an analysis of this tale, and references to other relevant secondary sources, see O'Flaherty, *Tales of Sex and Violence*, pp. 32–37, 124).
37. ŚB 3.1.2.13–17; JB 2.18.
38. Heesterman, "The Ritualist's Problem," p. 1.
39. Ibid., pp. 5–7.
40. Ibid., p. 6.
41. J. C. Heesterman has suggested that the Agnicayana might be "interpreted as a funerary tumulus for a high ranking kinsman," though he does not follow this line of investigation (Heesterman, *The Inner Conflict of Tradition*, p. 53).
42. ŚB 13.8.1.17.
43. ŚB 13.8.1.17.
44. ŚB 13.8.2.3; cf. 7.1.1.11.
45. ŚB 13.8.2.2; cf. 7.1.1.12.
46. ŚB 13.8.2.6 and 13.8.3.1; cf. 7.2.2.6 ff. and 7.2.4.13.
47. ŚB 13.8.3.6–9.
48. See ṚV 10.18; JB 1.47.1 ff.; ŚB 13.8.4.11; and also Mitra, *Indo-Aryans*, pp. 126 ff.; *Encyclopedia of Religion and Ethics*, s.v. "Death and Disposal of the Dead (Hindu)."
49. See Hertz, *Death and the Right Hand*, p. 46, and pp. 42–43, regarding the Indian funeral rituals. (Cf. Huntington and Metcalf, *Celebrations of Death*, s.v. "secondary burial.")
50. ŚB 13.8.3.2–9.
51. ŚB 13.8.4.11–12.
52. See Smith, "Gods and Men in Vedic Ritualism," p. 292.
53. ŚB 7.4.2.22; see also 1.3.1.25; 1.7.1.2; 1.7.1.18. This theory is also seen in the process by which the Soma ascends to the otherworld and descends, in the form of rain, from the otherworld (see, Schneider, "Upaniṣad Philosophy and Early Buddhism," p. 311).
54. CU 5.10.3–6. Cf. Frauwallner, *History of Indian Philosophy*, pp. 36 ff.

55. ŚB 11.2.1.1.
56. ŚB 2.2.4.8.
57. On the nature of this journey, see Chapter 3 and cf. the discussion in ŚB 6.1.2.36 of the idea that the sacrificer is conveyed to heaven by the bird-shaped altar.
58. Smith, "Gods and Men in Vedic Ritualism," p. 297.
59. Ibid., pp. 297–98.
60. See ŚB 1.1.1.6.
61. See Chapter 3.
62. JUB 3.28.3–4.
63. CU 5.3–10; BĀU 6.2.
64. ŚB 10.1.5.1 ff.
65. ŚB 10.1.5.4.
66. ŚB 10.1.4.1.
67. ŚB 13.8.3.9.
68. ŚB 13.8.3.2–5. See also, Keith, *The Veda of the Black Yajus School*, p. cxxv.
69. ŚB 13.2.3.1; cf., ŚB 13.2.8.1.
70. ŚB 7.4.1.1.
71. CU 5.10.1 ff; BĀU 6.2.15 ff.
72. BĀU 3.2.13.
73. Keith, *Religion and Philosophy*, p. 441.
74. Knipe, "One Fire, Three Fires, Five Fires," p. 32.
75. CU 3.16–17.
76. CU 3.17.5.
77. Farquhar, *An Outline of the Religious Literature of India*, p. 27.

Bibliography

Vedic Texts

Atharva Veda, ed. Rudolph von Roth and W. D. Whitney, 3d ed. Bonn: Ferd. Dummlers Verlag, 1966.

Die Hymnen des Sāma-Veda, ed. Theodor Benfey. Darmstadt: Wissenschaftliche Buchgesellschaft, 1968.

Jaiminīya Brāhmaṇa of the Sāmaveda, ed. Raghu Vira and Lokesh Chandra. Sarasvati-vihara Series, vol. 31. Nagpur: International Academy of Indian Culture, 1954.

Jaiminīya or Talavakāra Upaniṣad Brāhmaṇa, ed. and trans. Hanns Oertel. *Journal of the American Oriental Society* 16 (1896): 79–260.

Kausītaki-Brāhmaṇa, ed. E. R. Sreekrishna Sarma. Wiesbaden: Franz Steiner Verlag, 1968.

Principal Upaniṣads, ed. and trans. S. Radhakrishnan. London: George Allen and Unwin, Ltd., 1953.

Rig-Veda Sanhitā: The Sacred Hymns of the Brahmans, ed. F. Max Muller, 6 vols. London: Trubner, 1849–74.

Śatapatha Brāhmaṇa, ed. Albrecht Weber. In *The White Yajurveda*, ed. Albrecht Weber, part 2. Berlin: Ferd. Dummler's Verlagsbuchhandlung, 1855.

The *Śatapatha Brāhmaṇa in the Kanvīya Recension*, ed. W. Caland. Punjab Sanskrit Series, no. 10. Lahore: Motilal Banarsidass, 1926.

Vājasaneyi-Saṃhitā, ed. Albrecht Weber. In *The White Yajurveda*, ed. Albrecht Weber, part 1. Berlin: Ferd. Dummler's Verlagsbuchhandlung, 1853.

Secondary Sources and Translations of Vedic Texts

Allchin, Bridgett, and Raymond Allchin. *The Rise of Civilization in India and Pakistan*. Cambridge: Cambridge University Press, 1982.

Barth, A. *Religions of India*, trans. Rev. J. Wood. Boston: Houghton, Mifflin and Co., 1882.

Bendann, E. *Death Customs: An Analytical Study of Burial Rites*. New York: Alfred A. Knopf, 1930.

Bhattacharji, Sukumari. *Literature in the Vedic Age*. Calcutta: K. P. Bagchi and Co., 1984.

Bloch, T. "Excavations at Lauriya." In *Archeological Survey of India: Annual Report, 1906–7*. Calcutta: Superintendent Government Printing, India, 1909.

Bloomfield, Maurice. *The Religion of the Veda*. New York: G. P. Putnam's Sons, 1908.

Bodewitz, H. W. *Jaiminīya Brāhmaṇa 1, 1–65*. Orientalia Rheno-Traiectina, vol. 17. Leiden: E. J. Brill, 1973.

———. "The Waters in Vedic Cosmic Classifications." *Indologica Taurinensia* 10 (1982): 45–53.

Brown, George William. "The Sources of Indian Philosophical Ideas." In *Studies in Honour of Maurice Bloomfield*, pp. 75–88. New Haven: 1920.

Brown, W. Norman. "The Creation Myth of the Rig Veda." *Journal of the American Oriental Society* 62 (1942): 85–98.

———. "The Rigvedic Equivalent for Hell." *Journal of the American Oriental Society* 61 (1941): 76–80.

———. "The Sources and Nature of *puruṣa* in the Puruṣasūkta (Rigveda 10.91) [*sic*]." *Journal of the American Oriental Society* 51 (1931): 108–18.

———. "Theories of Creation in the Rig Veda." *Journal of the American Oriental Society* 85 (1965): 23–34.

van Buitenen, J. A. B. "The Large Ātman." *History of Religions* 4 (1964): 103–14.

Burnell, A. C., ed. and trans. *The Sāmavidhānabrāhmaṇa (being the third brāhmaṇa) of the Sama Veda*. London: Trubner and Co., 1873.

Burrow, T. "Dravidian Studies VII: Further Dravidian Words in Sanskrit." *Bulletin of the School of Oriental and African Studies* 12 (1948): 365–96.

———. "Loanwords in Sanskrit." *Transactions of the Philological Society* (1946): 1–30.

———. "Some Dravidian Words in Sanskrit." *Transactions of the Philological Society* (1945): 79–120.

Caland, W. *Die Altindischen Todten- und Bestattungsgebrauche*. Verhandelingen der Koninklijke Nederlandse Akademie van Wetenschappen, Afd. Letterkunde, 1:6. Amsterdam: 1896.

———. "Over en uit het Jaiminīya Brāhmaṇa." *Verslagen en Medeleelingen der Koninklijke Akademie van Wetenschappen* 5 (1915): 1–106.

———, trans. *Pañcavimsa Brāhmaṇa: The Brāhmaṇa of Twenty-five Chapters*. Calcutta: Asiatic Society of Bengal, 1931.

Chapple, Christopher. *Karma and Creativity*, Albany, N.Y.: SUNY Press, 1986.

Colebrooke, H. T. "On the Vedas or Sacred Writings of the Hindus." *Asiatick Researches* 8 (1805): 369–476.

Collins, Steven. *Selfless Persons*. Cambridge: Cambridge University Press, 1982.

Converse, Hyla Stuntz. "The Agnicayana Rite: Indigenous Origin?" *History of Religions* 14 (1974): 81–95.

Coomaraswamy, Ananda K. "Ātmayajña: Self-Sacrifice." *Harvard Journal of Asiatic Studies* 6 (1942): 358–98.

Dandekar, R. N. *Select Writings I: Vedic Mythological Tracts*. Delhi: Ajanta Publishing, 1979.

Dasgupta, Surendranath. *A History of Indian Philosophy*, vol. 1. Cambridge: Cambridge University Press, 1922.

Deussen, Paul. *Die Philosophie der Upanishad's*. Leipzig: F. A. Brockhaus, 1899.

———. *Philosophy of the Upanishads*, trans. A. S. Geden. Edinburgh: T. & T. Clark, 1906. Reprint, New York: Dover Publications, 1966.

———, trans. *Sechzig Upanishad's des Veda*, 3d ed. Leipzig: F. A. Brockhaus, 1938.

Drury, Naama. *The Sacrificial Ritual in the Śatapatha Brāhmaṇa*. Delhi: Motilal Banarsidass, 1981.

Dubois, J. A. *Hindu Manners, Customs and Ceremonies*, trans. Henri K. Beauchamp, 3d ed. Oxford: Clarendon Press, 1906.

Dumezil, Georges. *The Destiny of a King*, trans. Alf Hiltebeitel. Chicago: University of Chicago Press, 1973.

Dumont, Louis. *Homo Hierarchicus*, trans. Mark Sainsbury. Chicago: University of Chicago Press, 1970.

Dumont, P. E. "The Special Kinds of Agnicayana." *Proceedings of the American Philosophical Society* 95 (1951).

Duperron, Anquetil. *Oupnek'hat*. Paris: n.p., 1801.

Edgerton, Franklin. "Sources of the Filosophy of the Upaniṣads." *Journal of the American Oriental Society* 36 (1916): 197–204.

———. "The Upaniṣads: What Do They Seek, and Why?" *Journal of the American Oriental Society* 49 (1929): 97–121.

Eggeling, Julius, trans. *The Śatapatha Brāhmaṇa*, 5 parts. The Sacred Books of the East, vols. 12, 26, 41, 43, and 44. Oxford: Clarendon Press, 1882–1900. Reprint, Delhi: Motilal Banarsidass, 1963.

Eliade, Mircea. *A History of Religious Ideas*, trans. Willard Trask, vol. 1. Chicago: University of Chicago Press, 1978.

———. *Myth and Reality*, trans. Willard R. Trask. New York: Harper and Row, 1963.

———. *Yoga: Immortality and Freedom*. Bollingen Series 56. Princeton: Princeton University Press, 1969.

Ewing, A. H. "The Hindu Conception of the Functions of Breath." *Journal of the American Oriental Society* 22 (1901): 249–308.

Farquhar, J. N. *An Outline of the Religious Literature of India*. The Religious Quest of India series. London: Oxford University Press, 1920.

Frauwallner, Erich. *History of Indian Philosophy*, trans. V. M. Bedekar, vol. 1. New York: Asian Humanities Press, 1974.

van Gennep, Arnold. *The Rites of Passage*, trans. Monika Vizedom and Gabrielle Caffee. Chicago: University of Chicago Press, 1960.

Gerow, Edwin. "What Is Karma (Kim Karmeti)? An Exercise in Philosophical Semantics." *Indologica Taurinensia* 10 (1982): 87–116.

Goman, Thomas and Laura, Ronald. "A Logical Treatment of Some Upanisadic Puzzles and Changing Conceptions of the Sacrifice." *Numen* 19 (1972): 52–67.

Gombrich, Richard F. "Ancient Indian Cosmology." In *Ancient Cosmologies*, ed. Carmen Blacker and Michael Loewe, pp. 110–42. London: Allen and Unwin, 1975.

Gonda, Jan. "Adhvara and Adhvaryu." *Vishveshvaranand Indological Journal* 3 (1965): 163–77.

———. "*Bandhu*- in the Brāhmaṇa-s." *Adyar Library Bulletin* 29 (1965): 1–29.

———. *Change and Continuity in Indian Religion*. Disputationes Rheno Trajectinae, vol. 9. The Hague: Mouton and Co., 1965.

———. "The Etymologies in the Ancient Indian Brāhmaṇas." *Lingua* 5 (1955): 60–85.

———. "Gifts and Giving in the Rig Veda." *Vishvesh-Varanand Indological Journal* 2 (1964): 9–30.

———. *The Haviryajñah Somāh: The Interrelations of the Vedic Solemn Sacrifices*. Verhandelingen der Koninklijke Nederlandse Akademie van Wetenschappen, Afd. Letterkunde, n.r. 113. Amsterdam: North-Holland Publishing Co., 1982.

———. *Loka: World and Heaven in the Veda*. Verhandelingen der Koninklijke Nederlandse Akademie van Wetenschappen, Afd. Letterkunde, n.r. 73. 1. Amsterdam: N. V. Noord-Hollandsche Uitgevers Maatschappij, 1966.

———. *Notes on Brahman*. Utrecht: J. L. Beyers, 1950.

———. *Notes on Names and the Name of God in Ancient India*. Verhandelingen der Koninklijke Nederlandse Akademie van

Wetenschappen, Afd. Letterkunde. Amsterdam: N. V. Noord-Hollandsche Uitgevers Maatschappij, 1970.

———. "The Popular Prajāpati." *History of Religions* 22 (1982): 129–49.

———. *Die Religionen Indiens.* Vol 1. *Veda und alterer Hinduismus.* Stuttgart: W. Kohlhammer Verlag, 1960.

———. "Triads in Vedic Ritual." *Ohio Journal of Religious Studies* 2 (1974): 5–23.

———. *Vedic Literature: Saṃhitās and Brāhmaṇas.* A History of Indian Literature, vol. 1., fasc. 1. Weisbaden: Otto Harrosowitz, 1975.

———. *Vedic Literature: The Ritual Sutras.* A History of Indian Literature, vol. 1, fasc. 2. Weisbaden: Otto Harrosowitz, 1977.

———. *Viṣṇuism and Śivaism.* London: Athlone Press, 1970.

Griswold, H. D. *The Religion of the Rgveda.* The Religious Quest of India. London: Oxford University Press, 1923.

Guntert, Hermann. *Die Arische Weltkonig und Heiland.* Halle: M. Niemeyer, 1923.

Haas, George C. O. "Recurrent and Parallel Passages in the Principal Upaniṣads and Bhagavad-gītā." Appendix to *The Thirteen Principal Upaniṣads,* trans. Robert Hume, pp. 516–62. London: Oxford University Press, 1931.

Hastings, James, ed. *Encyclopedia of Religion and Ethics.* New York: Charles Schribner's Sons, 1908.

Heesterman, J. C. *The Ancient Indian Royal Consecration.* Disputationes Rheno-Trajectinae, vol. 2. The Hague: Mouton and Co., 1957.

———. "Brahmin, Ritual and Renouncer." *Wiener Zeitschrift fur die Kunde Sud Ostrasiens* 8 (1964): 1–31.

———. *The Inner Conflict of Tradition.* Chicago: University of Chicago Press, 1985.

———. "Reflections on the Significance of the Dakṣiṇā." *Indo-Iranian Journal* 3 (1959): 241–58.

———. "The Ritualist's Problem." Paper presented at the Association of Asian Studies, San Francisco, March 25, 1983.

———. "Veda and Dharma." In *The Concept of Duty in South Asia*, ed. W. D. O'Flaherty and J. D. M. Derrett, pp. 80–95. London: S.O.A.S., 1978.

———. "Vrātya and Sacrifice." *Indo-Iranian Journal* 6 (1962): 1–37.

Hertz, Robert. *Death and the Right Hand*, trans. Rodney Needham and Claudia Needham. New York: Cohen and West, 1960.

Hoffman, Karl. "Mārtāṇḍa und Gayomart." *Munchner Studien zur Sprachenwissenschaft* 11 (1975): 85–103.

———. "Die Weltenstehung nach dem Jaiminīya Brāhmaṇa." *Munchner Studien zur Sprachenwissenschaft* 27 (1970): 59–67.

Hopkins, Edward W. "Modifications of the Karma Doctrine." *Journal of the Royal Asiatic Society* (1906): 581–93.

———. "Numerical Formulae in the Veda and Their Bearing on Vedic Criticism." *Journal of the American Oriental Society* 16 (1896): 275–81.

———. *Religions of India*. Handbooks on the History of Religions, vol 1. Boston: Ginn and Co., 1895.

Horsch, Paul. "Vorstufen der Indischen Seelenwanderungslehre." *Asiatische Studien* 25 (1971): 99–57.

Hubert, Henri, and Marcel Mauss. *Sacrifice: Its Nature and Functions*, trans. W. D. Halls. Chicago: University of Chicago Press, 1964.

Hume, Robert, trans. *The Thirteen Principal Upaniṣads*, 2d ed. London: Oxford University Press, 1931.

Huntington, Richard, and Peter Metcalf. *Celebrations of Death*. Cambridge: Cambridge University Press, 1979.

Ingalls, Daniel H. H. "Dharma and Moksa." *Philosophy East and West* 7 (1957): 41–48.

Kaelber, Walter O. "The 'Dramatic' Element in Brāhmaṇic Initiation: Symbols of Death, Danger, and Difficult Passage." *History of Religious* 17 (1978): 54–76.

———. "*Tapas*, Birth, and Spiritual Rebirth in the Veda." *History of Religions* 15 (1976): 343–85.

Karmarkar, A. P. "The Puruṣa-Sūkta (Ṛgveda X.90) and the Mystic Glorifications of the Human Victim." *Journal of the Royal Asiatic Society (Bombay Branch)* 18 (1942): 91–93.

Kashikar, C. G. "Agnicayana: Extension of Vedic Aryan Rituals." *Annals of the Bhandarkar Oriental Research Institute* 62 (1981): 121–33.

———. "The Idea of Ultimate Reality and Meaning According to the Kalpa Sutras." *Ultimate Reality and Meaning* 2 (1979): 172–87.

Keith, A. B. *The Religion and Philosophy of the Veda and Upanishads*, 2 vols. Harvard Oriental Series, vols. 31–32. Cambridge, Mass.: Harvard University Press, 1925. Reprint, Delhi: Motilal Banarsidass, 1970.

———, trans. *Rig-Veda Brāhmaṇas: The Aitareya and Kauṣītaki Brāhmaṇas of the Rigveda*. Harvard Oriental Series, vol. 25. Cambridge: Mass.: Harvard University Press, 1920.

———, trans. *The Veda of the Black Yajus School Entitled Taittirīya Sanhitā*, 2 vols. Harvard Oriental Series, vols. 18–19. Cambridge, Mass.: Harvard University Press, 1914. Reprint, Delhi: Motilal Banarsidass, 1967.

Kirfel, W. *Die Cosmographie der Inder*. Bonn: K. Schroeder, 1920.

Knipe, David. "*Sapindīkarana*: The Hindu Rite of Entry into Heaven." In *Religious Encounters with Death*. ed. F. Reynolds and E. Waugh, pp. 111–24. University Park: Pennsylvania State University Press, 1977.

———. "One Fire, Three Fires, Five Fires: Vedic Symbols in Transition." *History of Religions* 12 (1972): 28–41.

Kopf, David. *British Orientalism and the Bengal Renaissance*. Berkeley: University of California Press, 1969.

Kramrisch, Stella. "The Triple Stucture of Creation in the Ṛgveda." *History of Religions* 2 (1962–63): 140–75; 256–85.

Kuiper, F. B. J. "The Basic Concept of the Vedic Religion." *History of Religions* 15 (1975): 107–20.

———. "Cosmogony and Conception: A Query." *History of Religions* 10 (1970): 91–138.

———. "The Genesis of a Linguistic Area." *Indo-Iranian Journal* 10 (1967): 81–102.

Lanman, C. R. "Mortuary Urns." Proceedings of the American Oriental Society, Boston, May 1891. (*Journal of the American Oriental Society* 15 [1893]: xcviii–c.)

———. *A Sanskrit Reader.* Cambridge: Mass.: Harvard University Press, 1884.

Lévi, Sylvain. *La Doctrine du Sacrifice dans les Brāhmaṇas*, 2d ed. Bibliotheque de l'Ecole des Hautes Etudes Section des Sciences Religieuses, vol. 73. Paris: Presses Universitaires de France, 1966.

Lincoln, Bruce. "The Indo-European Myth of Creation." *History of Religions* 15 (1975): 121–45.

Macdonald, A. W. "A Propos de Prajāpati." *Journal Asiatique* 240 (1952): 323–28.

Macdonell, A. A. *Vedic Mythology.* Grundiss der Indo-Arischen Philologie und Altertumskunde, vol. 3. Strassburg: Karl J. Trubner, 1897.

———. *A Vedic Reader for Students.* Madras: Oxford University Press, 1917.

Macdonell, A. A., and A. B. Keith. *Vedic Index of Names and Subjects*, 2 vols. London: 1912. Reprint, Delhi: Motilal Banarsidass, 1982.

Mackie J. L. *Ethics.* Hammondsworth, England: Penguin Books, 1977.

Marshall, Peter J., ed. *The British Discovery of Hinduism in the Eighteenth Century.* Cambridge: University Press, 1970.

Mitra, Rajendralala. *Indo-Aryans: Contributions towards the Elucidation of Their Ancient and Medieval History*, vol. 2. London: Edward Stanford: 1881.

Muir, John. *Original Sanskrit Texts*, vol. 5. London: Trubner and Co., 1870.

Müller, F. Max. *Chips From a German Workshop.* Vol. 1. *Essays on the Science of Religion.* New York: Charles Scribner's Sons, 1900.

———. *A History of Ancient Sanskrit Literature.* New Delhi: Oxford & IBH Publishing Co., 1926.

———. *Lectures on the Origin and Growth of Religion*, 2d ed. London: Longman, Green, and Co., 1878.

———. *Natural Religion: The Gifford Lectures.* London: Longmans, Green & Co., 1889.

———, trans. *The Upanishads*, 2 parts. Sacred Books of the East, vols. 1 and 15. Oxford: Clarendon Press, 1879 and 1884. Reprint, New York: Dover Publications, 1962.

Murthy, R. S. Shivaganesha. "Vedic Sacrifice—A Conspectus." In *Charudeva Felicitation Volume*, pp. 116–24. Delhi: Charudeva Shastri Felicitation Committee, 1974.

Mus, Paul. *Barbudur: esquisse d'une histoire du bouddhisme fondee sur la critique archeologique des textes.* Hanoi: Impr. d'Extreme Orient, 1935.

Mylius, K. "Die Ideenwelt des Śatapatha Brāhmaṇa." *Wissenschaft Zeitschrift der Karl Marx Universitat* (Leipzig) 16 (1967): 47–55.

Narahari, H. G. *Ātman in Pre-Upanisadic Vedic Literature.* Madras: Adyar Library, 1944.

Oertal, Hanns. "Extracts from the Jaiminīya Brāhmana Parallel to Passages of the Satapatha Brāhmana and the Chāndogya Upanisad." *Journal of the American Oriental Society* 15 (1891): 233–52.

———, tr. "The Jaiminīya or Talavakāra Upaniṣad Brāhmaṇa."

O'Flaherty, Wendy Doniger. *Dreams, Illusion, and Other Realities.* Chicago: University of Chicago Press, 1984.

———. "The Ethical and Non-Ethical Implications of the Cosmogonic Myth of the Separation of Heaven and Earth in Indian Mythology." In *Cosmogony and Ethical Order*, ed. Frank Reynolds and Robin Loven, pp. 105–39. Chicago: University of Chicago Press, 1985.

———, ed. *Karma and Rebirth in Classical Indian Tradition.* Berkeley: University of California Press, 1980.

———. "Karma and Rebirth in the Vedas and Purāṇas." In *Karma and Rebirth in Classical Indian Traditions*, ed. Wendy D. O'Flaherty, pp. 3–37. Berkeley: University of California Press, 1980.

———. *The Origins of Evil in Hindu Mythology*. Berkeley: University of California Press, 1976.

———, trans. *The Rig Veda*. Hammondsworth, England: Penguin Books, 1981.

———. *Śiva: The Erotic Ascetic*. Oxford: Oxford University Press, 1981. Originally published as *Asceticism and Eroticism in the Mythology of Śiva*. Oxford: Oxford University Press, 1973.

———. *Tales of Sex and Violence: Folklore, Sacrifice, and Danger in the "Jaiminīya Brāhmaṇa"*. Chicago: University of Chicago Press, 1985.

Oldenberg, Hermann. *Buddha: Sein Leben, Seine Lehre, Seine Gemeinde*. Stuttgart: J. G. Cotta'sche, 1920.

———. *Die Lehre der Upanishaden und die Anfangen der Buddhismus*. Gottingen: Vandenhoeck and Ruprecht, 1915.

———. *Vorwissenschaftliche Wissenschaft die Weltenschaung de Brahmana-texte*. Gottingen: Vandenhoeck and Ruprecht, 1919.

Parpola, Asko. "The Pre-Vedic Background of the Śrauta Rituals." In *Agn The Vedic Ritual of the Fire Altar*, ed. Frits Staal, vol. 2, pp. –74. Berkeley: Asian Humanities Press, 1983.

———. "On the Proto-History of the Indian Languages in Light of Archeological, Linguistic and Religious Evidence: An Attempt at Integration." In *South Asian Archeology 1973*, J. E. van Lohuizen-de Leeuw and J. M. M. Ubaghs, pp. 90–100. Leiden: E. J. Brill, 1974.

Poleman, Horace. "The Ritualistic Continuity of Ṛgveda X.14–18." *Journal of the American Oriental Society* 54 (1934): 276–81.

Potter, Karl. "The Karma Theory and Its Interpretation in Some indian Philosophical Systems." In *Karma and Rebirth in Classical Indian Traditions*, W. D. O'Flaherty, pp. 241–67. Berkeley: University of California Press, 1980.

Renou, Louis. *Religions of Ancient India*. London: The Athlone Press, 1953. Reprint, New Delhi: Munshiram Manoharlal, 1972.

Rodhe, Sten. *Deliver Us from Evil: Studies on the Vedic Ideas of Salvation*. Lund: Hakan Ohlssons Boktryckeri, 1946.

von Roth, Rudolph. "On the Morality of the Veda," trans. W. D. Whitney. *Journal of the American Oriental Society* 3 (1853): 329–49.

———. *Zur Litteratur und Geschichte des Weda*. Stuttgart: A. Liesching & Co., 1846.

Said, Edward. *Orientalism*. New York: Vintage Books, 1978.

Schayer, St. "A Note on the Old Russian Variant of the Purushasūkta." *Archiv Orientalni* 7 (1935): 319–23.

Schneider, Ulrich. "Upaniṣad Philosophy and Early Buddhism." In *German Scholars on India*, vol. 1, pp. 307–32. Varanasi: Chowkhamba Sanskrit Series Office, 1973.

Schopenhauer, Arthur. *Welt als Wille und Vorstellung*. Leipzig: F. A. Brockhaus, 1819.

Sharma, Ursula. "Theodicy and the Doctrine of Karma." *Man* n.s. 8 (1973): 347–64.

Sharpe, Eric. *Comparative Religion: A History*. New York: Charles Scribner's Sons, 1975.

Shende, N. J. "The PuruṣaSūkta (RV 10.90) in the Vedic Literature." *Journal of the University of Poona* (Humanities Section) 23 (1966): 45–51.

Smith, Brian K. "Resemblance, Hierarchy and Ritualism." Ph.D. dissertation, University of Chicago, 1984.

———. "Gods and Men in Vedic Ritualism: Toward a Hierarchy of Resemblance." *History of Religions* 24 (1985): 291–307.

Speijer, J. S. *Sanskrit Syntax*. Leiden: E. J. Brill, 1886. Reprint, Delhi: Motilal Banarsidass, 1973.

Staal, Frits. *Agni: The Vedic Ritual of the Fire Altar*, 2 vols. Berkeley: Asian Humanities Press, 1983.

———. "The Ignorant Brahmin of the Agnicayana." *Annals of the Bhandarkar Research Institute* 68–69 (1977–78): 337–48.

———. "Ritual Syntax." In *Sanskrit and Indian Studies: Essays in Honor of Daniel H. H. Ingalls*, ed. M. Nagatomi et al., pp. 119–42. Dordrecht, Boston: D. Reidel Publishing Co., 1980.

———. *The Science of Ritual*. Poona: Bhandarkar Oriental Research Institute, 1982.

Suave, James L. "The Divine Victim: Aspects of Human Sacrifice in Scandanavia and Vedic India." In *Myth and Law among the Indo-Europeans*, ed. Jaan Puhvel, pp. 173–91. Berkeley: University of California Press, 1970.

Thapar, Romila. "The Archeological Background to the Agnicayana Ritual." In *Agni: The Vedic Ritual of the Fire Altar*, ed. Frits Staal, vol. 2, pp. 3–40. Berkeley: Asian Humanities Press, 1983.

Thite, Ganesh U. "Animal Sacrifices in the Brāhmaṇa-texts." *Numan* 17 (1970): 143–61.

———. *Sacrifice in the Brāhmaṇa-Texts*. Poona: Poona University Press, 1975.

Thompson, Stith. *Motif-Index of Folk Literature*, vol. 1. Bloomington: Indiana University Press, 1955.

Tsuji, Naoshiro, "On the Relation between Brāhmaṇas and Śrautasūtras." *Toyo Bunko Ronso* A 33 (1952): 183–247.

Turner, Victor. *The Ritual Process*. Chicago: Aldine Publishing Co., 1969.

Vira, Raghu. "Śākhās of the Yajurveda." *Journal of Vedic Studies* 2 (1935): 61–77.

Wallis, H. W. *Cosmology of the Rig-Veda*. London: Williams and Norgate, 1887.

Weber, Albrecht. *History of Indian Literature*, trans. J. Mann and T. Zacharie, 2d ed. London: Kegan Paul, Trench, Trubner, 1904.

Werner, Karel. "On Interpreting the Vedas." *Religion* 7 (1977): 189–200.

Whitney, W. D., trans. *The Atharva Veda*, ed. C. R. Lanman. Harvard Oriental Series, vols. 7–8. Cambridge, Mass.: Harvard University Press, 1905.

———. "Eggeling's Translation of the Śatapatha Brāhmaṇa." *American Journal of Philology* 3 (1882): 391–410.

———. "Hindu Eschatology and the Kāṭha Upanisad." Proceedings of the American Oriental Society, Boston, May 1886. (*Journal of the American Oriental Society* 13 [1853]: ciii–cviii.)

———. "On the History of the Vedic Texts." *Journal of the American Oriental Society* 4 (1854): 245–62.

———. "On the Jaiminīya or Talavakāra Brāhmaṇa." *Journal of the American Oriental Society* 5 (1883) viii–xi.

———. "On the Main Results of the later Vedic Researches in Germany." *Journal of the American Oriental Society* 3 (1853): 289–347.

———. "The Narrative Use of Imperfect and Perfect in the Brāhmaṇas." *Transactions of the American Philological Association* 23 (1892): 5–34.

———. *Oriental and Linguistic Studies*. New York: Scribner, Armstrong and Co., 1873.

Winternitz, Maurice. *A History of Indian Literature*, trans. V. S. Sarma, vol 1. Delhi: Motilal Banarsidass, 1981.

Index